CAPT. JEPP AND THE LITTLE BLACK BOOK

PRESS

Box 115, Superior, WI 54880 (715) 394-9513

First Edition

Copyright 2007, Flint Whitlock and Terry L. Barnhart

First Printing
05 06 07 08 10 9 8 7 6 5 4 3 2 1

ISBN Number 1-886028-83-4

Library of Congress Catalog Card Number: 2006936627

Published by:

Savage Press
P.O. Box 115
Superior, WI 54880

Phone: 715-394-9513

E-mail: mail@savpress.com

Web Site: www.savpress.com

CAPT. JEPP AND THE LITTLE BLACK BOOK

How Barnstormer and
Aviation Pioneer Elrey B. Jeppesen
Made the Skies Safer for Everyone

Flint Whitlock & Terry L. Barnhart

A man can criticize a pilot for flying into a mountainside in fog,
but I would rather by far die on a mountainside
than in bed. Is there a better way to die?

— Charles A. Lindbergh

There are old pilots and there are bold pilots,
but there are no old, bold pilots.

— E. Hamilton Lee

I didn't start out to chart the skies;
it's just that no one had ever done it before.

— Elrey B. Jeppesen

TABLE OF CONTENTS

FOREWORD

On May 20, 1927, when my grandfather set out on his perilous, historic flight in the *Spirit of St. Louis* from New York to Paris, he took with him the very basic essentials: 451 gallons of gasoline, twenty gallons of oil, $500 worth of French francs, five sandwiches, a flashlight, first-aid kit, passport, thermos of coffee, and his own 170 pounds clothed in a heavy leather flying suit. To save weight and thus save fuel, he even trimmed the excess paper from the edges of his maps. Except for a tiny St. Christopher's medal that a bystander to the take-off had given him, he refused a variety of talismans, fearing they might weigh him down and reduce the plane's range.

At 7:52 on that foggy morning, Charles Augustus Lindbergh lifted from the ground, the wheels of his plane not destined to touch it again for another thirty-three-and-a-half hours. A million "Godspeeds" lifted off with him.

Most of that time in the air was spent over water—the vast, trackless Atlantic Ocean. With the sun, stars, and compass his only navigational aids, Grandfather somehow managed to defy gravity and the elements and find his way to Europe—and into the history books. Once over Ireland, he changed course and headed southeast to France, following the road maps he had brought along. In the dark he managed to locate Paris and Le Bourget airfield.

What he accomplished on his lonely journey has been well told in numerous books, movies, and television documentaries. Had he not been a seasoned aviator and navigator, and superb at planning for and managing the potential risks, some other flyer undoubtedly would have been the first to fly nonstop between the two cities.

Grandfather's fabled flight inspired a whole generation to take up flying. One of those who became enchanted with flight in 1927, and would later become an aviation pioneer, was Elrey B. Jeppesen, better known simply as "Captain Jepp."

To my knowledge, my grandfather and Captain Jepp never met. Yet in the 1940s, when the world was at war, my grandfather undoubtedly used Jeppesen Airway Manual aerial navigation charts as he became a civilian test pilot for military aircraft and flew fifty missions in the South Pacific.

Erik Lindbergh waves from his Lancair Columbia 300 before retracing grandfather Charles A. Lindbergh's historic flight. Erik's successful journey began on May 2, 2002—nearly seventy-five years after Charles flew from New York to Paris.

As a commercial pilot and flight instructor myself, I am thoroughly familiar with "Jepp Charts." On May 2, 2002, I used Jeppesen navigation products when I retraced my grandfather's historic flight seventy-five years later. This time, flying a single-engine Lancair Columbia 300, I made the journey from New York to Le Bourget in seventeen hours and seven minutes.

Although my trip took only half the time of my grandfather's, I was still faced with bad weather, fatigue, and the need to manage the risks of such a long flight. I had the added stress of my arthritic joints complaining about being contained in the small cockpit. And yet it still felt like a breeze when compared to Grandfather's journey. Through my trip across the Atlantic, I gained a new appreciation for the stories I'd grown up hearing about my grandfather. The journey was as spiritual as it was physical. I had the chance to study, like a bird, the world below me and rededicate myself to one of my grandfather's greatest goals—the preservation of our planet's natural wonders. I was reconnected with the awareness that we humans, as stewards of this earth, all bear a significant responsibility to conserve the planet and its fragile environmental infrastructure.

I also gained renewed appreciation for the marvelous tools Captain Jepp devised for pilots. On a small printed page—and now on a computer display screen—we have at our fingertips all of the information needed to make a safe flight to and from most airports in the world.

I am indebted to the early aviators like Captain Jepp and Charles Lindbergh who, as airmail pilots, were subjected to the raw elements in their open-cockpit aircraft at a time when instrumentation was minimal and primitive. They found their way through blinding snowstorms, raging thunderstorms, and tricky mountain passes, risking life and limb simply to deliver letters, packages, and postcards. They forged the way for those of us who came later and today enjoy a much more comfortable and infinitely safer way to travel.

And so, each time I climb into a cockpit, I must tip my cap to Captain Jepp and all the other intrepid flyers that went before me, and give them silent thanks for a job well done. I trust you will do the same as you turn the pages of this magnificent journey through Captain Elrey B. Jeppesen's life story.

The sky is no longer the limit.

— Erik Lindbergh

INTRODUCTION

In the field of aviation and space flight, certain names stand out: Orville and Wilbur Wright, Louis Blériot, Charles A. Lindbergh, Amelia Earhart, Eddie Rickenbacker, Richard Byrd, Billy Mitchell, Wiley Post, Jimmy Doolittle, Hap Arnold, Curtis LeMay, Claire Chennault, Chuck Yeager, "Pappy" Boyington, Robert Goddard, Yuri Gagarin, Scott Carpenter, John Glenn, and Neal Armstrong.

Then there are the airplane and airline builders: William Boeing, Donald Douglas, Glen Cunningham, Glenn Curtiss, Glenn Martin, John Northrop, Howard Hughes, "Pat" Patterson, Igor Sikorsky, and Juan Trippe. The list goes on.

One name is conspicuous by its absence, but deserves to be listed among aviation's "greats": Elrey Borge Jeppesen, otherwise known as "Captain Jepp."

When Captain Jepp was being inducted into the National Aviation Hall of Fame in 1990, John Glenn, the World War II Marine Corps fighter pilot and one of America's original Mercury Seven astronauts, stood at the podium and said, "If it hadn't been for Jepp, I wouldn't be here." Truth be told, if it hadn't been for Jepp, a lot of people wouldn't be here.

This is the story of Elrey Jeppesen, one of the world's aerial pioneers, a man whose name is legendary among pilots and those in the aviation field but who is virtually unknown among the general public. This book, hopefully, will change that situation, for without Captain Jepp's pioneering contributions to the field of aviation, the world would be a far different place.

Born in 1907, Captain Jepp became part of the "second generation" of pilots—fliers who came along too late to make their names in wooden and canvas "crates" above the battle-scarred trenches of France's Western Front, but who still basked in the aura of the glamour that surrounded the early aviators.

Bitten by the "flying bug" at an early age, Jepp got his first taste of flying in war-surplus Jennies—those remarkable, noisy, and fatally unreliable training planes left over from the Great War—in the skies over Oregon. He went on to become a daredevil barnstormer, a flight instructor, a pilot for an aerial survey company, a courageous airmail pilot, and a captain flying Boeing 247s (and, later, DC-3s, DC-4s, DC-6s, and DC-7s) for a fledgling airline known as United.

If he had been nothing more than a superb pilot with the usual share of smash-ups, close calls, and safe landings, chances are his name would have been lost to history, a steady but anonymous aviator whose reputation would have been obscured by the high, thin clouds of time.

But Captain Jepp did something remarkable, something that has forever enshrined his name in the hall of aviation pioneers and heroes. In an effort to make the skies safer for himself, he almost inadvertently made the skies safer for everyone. He became the Father of Aerial Navigation.

A crucial part of flying is the ability to navigate. In fact, without the ability to navigate, flight would be impossible. Pilots simply must know where they are at any given moment, where they want to go, and the best and safest route to get there.

Navigation—whether by air, land, or sea—is composed of four elements: position, direction, distance, and time.

In terms of aerial navigation, pilots use four basic systems: pilotage, dead reckoning, position fixing, and homing. Pilotage—navigating by making visual reference to landmarks—and dead reckoning are today the primary navigational tools used by pilots of light recreational aircraft. In the early days of flying, *all* pilots, whether commercial, private, or military, used this method, simply because there was nothing else. As flying became more sophisticated, additional types of navigational aids were introduced—aids that were virtually invented by Captain Jepp.

Bits and pieces of Jepp's life have appeared over the years in newspapers and magazines, and several attempts at a book-length biography have been attempted but ultimately abandoned. This, then, is the first complete biography of Elrey Jeppesen, the Father of Aerial Navigation.

This is Captain Jepp's story.

1: THE EARLY DAYS

Charlie Lamborn was hopelessly lost.

Lieutenant Charles W. Lamborn, a thirty-three-year-old Army Mail Service pilot from Los Angeles, flying 404 pounds of mail through leaden skies somewhere between Bellefonte, Pennsylvania, and Cleveland, Ohio, had no idea where he was.

It was Sunday, June 8, 1919. It was supposed to have been a beautiful spring morning, but fog and low clouds had rolled in, along with high winds and torrential rains, shrouding the mountains in a thick blanket of gray.

Nevertheless, evidently believing that the fog was low and localized, Lamborn lifted off from the grassy runway at Bellefonte Airfield (nine miles northeast of State College, home of Pennsylvania State University) in his open-cockpit DeHaviland biplane Number 82 at 10:20 in the morning, pulled out his hand-held compass, and headed northwest on a bearing of 315 degrees, on the Bellefonte-to-Cleveland leg of the New York-to-Chicago mail route. Having served his country as a pilot in the Great War, Charlie Lamborn loved flying. Now, with the war over, since he could no longer serve his country in combat, flying the mail was the next best thing.

While he plowed his way through clouds as thick as mashed potatoes, Charlie Lamborn probably gave little thought to the airmail service's early beginnings.

The Great War was still three years into the future when the first sack of airmail in America left the ground. Postmaster General Frank Harris Hitchcock had been intrigued by the idea of sending mail by air, and in 1910 had even attempted a demonstration of the possibility of transferring mail from ship to shore using a float plane, but bad weather and mechanical problems ended the experiment. Hitchcock was not easily dissuaded and soon sought another way to show the practicality of using airplanes to transport the mail.

On September 23, 1911, ten thousand spectators covered Squantum Airfield at Garden City Estates, Long Island, New York, to witness an international aviation meet. Hitchcock used the occasion to demonstrate his concept of airmail and when meet organizers asked for a pilot to volunteer, Earl Lewis Ovington of Newton Highlands, Massachusetts, stepped forward.

Ovington was well known in aviation and scientific circles. A former engineering assistant to Thomas A. Edison, he had learned to fly in France in 1906, then returned to the U.S., where he won a number of prizes at air meets.

Although Hitchcock wanted to go along on this historic first airmail flight, he discovered to his dismay that Ovington's plane, a spindly Blériot with an open fuselage dubbed "Dragonfly," had but one cockpit. Hiding his disappointment, the Postmaster General handed the pilot a sack containing 640 letters and 1,280 postcards, each postmarked "Aeroplane Station No. 1—Garden City Estates, N.Y." Ovington then rolled down the grass runway, took off, and headed for Mineola, three miles away. From an altitude of 500 feet, Ovington dropped the bag to postal officials at a pre-arranged target. Upon impact with the ground, however, the bag ruptured and mail flew everywhere. Quickly gathered up by bystanders, the letters and cards were sent on their way by regular means.

So pleased was Hitchcock with the success of the operation that he soon authorized Ovington to carry mail from New York to San Francisco by way of Chicago. The engine of Ovington's plane was insufficient for the demands of such a trip, however, and so the plans were scrapped.

In 1912, a year before he retired as Postmaster General, Hitchcock authorized thirty-one more experimental airmail flights in sixteen states that would take place over the next four years. The airmail system had been born. [1]

In 1917, Congress appropriated $100,000 for the Post Office Department to continue airmail service, and in February 1918 America's fledgling airlines were allowed to bid for contracts to carry the mail. But because the companies had few planes, it was decided that the U.S. Army, with hundreds of trained pilots and plenty of war-surplus aircraft at its disposal, would carry the mail until the private air carriers were ready.

The U.S. government saw the airmail service as a win-win proposition; not only would mail service be speeded up, but inexperienced army pilots would gain valuable flight time.

On May 15, 1918, the Post Office inaugurated the world's first regularly scheduled airmail service. With great pomp and fanfare, including a brass band on hand for the occasion, a war-surplus Curtiss JN-4 "Jenny" biplane would make the inaugural flight from Washington, D.C. to Philadelphia.

In charge of the day's operations was army Captain Benjamin Lipsner, who was in an impatient mood. He was upset because the plane that was to be used was late arriving in the nation's capital and was keeping such dignitaries as President Woodrow Wilson, Postmaster General Albert S. Burleson, Assistant Secretary of the Navy Franklin Delano Roosevelt, inventor Alexander Graham Bell, Postmaster of Japan K. Kambara, and explorer Admiral Robert E. Peary, waiting.

The Jenny, with Lieutenant George Leroy Boyle at the controls, finally arrived, and four sacks holding 140 pounds of mail—including letters with the new twenty-four-cent airmail stamp accidentally printed upside-down—were loaded into its canvas fuselage. It was then found that the plane's fuel tank was nearly empty, so a further delay ensued while it was filled. At last, the prop was spun and Boyle took off to the cheers of the hat-waving crowd and the strains of a John Phillip Sousa march.

Unfortunately, with the state of aerial navigation being what it was in those days, Boyle headed south for Maryland instead of north to

Philadelphia. Totally lost, Boyle landed in a farmer's field where he broke his propeller. The chagrined pilot then transferred his cargo of letters to a mail truck; the airmail was ultimately delivered to Philadelphia by train: Not an auspicious beginning for the U.S. Air Mail Service. [2]

A year after that embarrassing start, aviation and aerial navigation were still in their primitive stages, and Charlie Lamborn was still struggling with his worrisome situation over Pennsylvania. Hoping to find clear air in a gap in the central Appalachian Mountains between Bellefonte and Milesburg, Lamborn pulled back on the control stick, trying to get above the clouds. But the overcast refused to thin. Lamborn kept craning his neck out of the open cockpit, first one side then the other, wiping the mist from his goggles in a vain attempt to spot the highway below him that ran from Bellefonte to Wingate, then to Runville—the highway he planned to follow. Having made this run a few times before, he knew that not far beyond the gap was Snowshoe Mountain, over which he would need to climb.

But he had no idea where he was, nor how far he might be from Snowshoe Mountain.

Since climbing had brought no better visibility, he decided to head for the deck and, hopefully, a break in the clouds. At 10:40 a.m., just twenty minutes after his take-off, he broke out of the cloudbank at an altitude of 400 feet over the hamlet of Dicks Run, only to see a fence and bushes directly in front of him. In a panic, Lamborn yanked back on the stick, but it was too late. The DeHaviland's fixed landing gear snagged the obstacles and flipped the plane, which crushed the fragile airframe and Lamborn's body, and spewed letters all over the landscape.

The residents of Dicks Run had heard the craft's engine inside the thick blanket of fog and, followed by the noise of a crash, dashed over in hopes of aiding the pilot. It was a futile hope; Lamborn's body was as badly smashed as his plane. He had suffered two broken ankles, a broken collarbone, and a crushed chest. He died without regaining consciousness on the way to the hospital.

A day or two later, Air Mail Supervisor Charles Stanton visited the site, conducted an investigation, examined the wreckage, and interviewed four witnesses. In his official report he wrote that there had been "open ground within two hundred yards of the wreck at an angle of about thirty degrees to the right wherein a landing could have been effected without a more serious accident than tripping over bushes or fences."

Stanton also noted that the DeHaviland's switches were on, which indicated that Lamborn "was not expecting to land, or to crash, since it is always customary to throw off both switches in making a forced landing in bad ground...in order to lessen the danger of fire in case of a crash."

Charlie Lamborn was the first airmail pilot to die flying the treacherous Bellefonte-to-Cleveland route—an area that quickly earned the sobriquet "the Hell Stretch." He would not be the last. Hundreds of mail planes crashed before private companies took over the service, and forty-three airmen lost their lives—a fate the pilots referred to as "going West." [3]

Six years later, on the night of Thursday, October 1, 1925, thirty-two-year-old Charles H. Ames, a native of Michigan, was flying the New York-to-Cleveland route in a DeHaviland similar to Lamborn's.

Ames was a very experienced pilot, having joined the Army Air Corps in 1917. He became a flight instructor and logged more than 700 flight hours before becoming an Air Mail Service pilot in December 1920. Since then he had flown nearly 133,000 miles and spent 1,334 hours in the air. Although he had had some close calls and a few forced landings during his nearly five-year career with the Air Mail Service, he was cool and fearless in the air.

Taking off from Hadley Field in New Brunswick, New Jersey, at 9:40 p.m., Ames was approaching Bellefonte two hours later. An impenetrable fog had enveloped the area. The last sound of his engine was heard about twenty miles east of Bellefonte, in the Nittany Mountains, and then there was sudden silence. When he didn't arrive at his destination and did not telephone—as was required of pilots who were forced to make emergency landings—a search party was sent out the next day to look for him.

Flying the mail was almost as hazardous as aerial combat in World War I. This DH-4 mail plane pilot crashed into Grant Park in downtown Chicago, June 16, 1919.
(Courtesy Smithsonian National Air and Space Museum)

The search was a major effort. Twelve aircraft, operated by airmail pilots from as far away as Wyoming, overflew the heavily wooded area while another thousand searchers on foot, plus 300 National Guardsmen, some on horseback, tramped through the thick vegetation that covered the rugged terrain. A reward of $1,000 was offered to whomever found Ames.

It was not until October 11 that the wreckage—and Ames's lifeless body still strapped inside the cockpit—was discovered wedged in a stand of trees that had ripped the wings off the fuselage. An investigation concluded that Ames had probably become lost and disoriented in the dark and fog, and was unaware of the mountains looming around him. [4]

Although lucrative for the carriers (after all, an airline engaged solely in the transport of mail did not have to invest money in large planes, waiting rooms, in-flight stewards, ticket agents, etc.), flying the mail was becoming nearly as hazardous an occupation as engaging Baron Manfred von Richthofen's "Flying Circus" had been over the trenches of the Western Front during the Great War.

Thinking (and with some justification) that ex-Army Air Corps pilots and former "barnstormers" were a wild and undisciplined bunch, "used to too much freedom in the army," the Post Office Department issued to its aviators a manual titled *Rules for Government Pilots.*

According to the Smithsonian's National Postal Museum, "Pilots were warned not to use their airmail airplane for performing stunts, or push them through 'any unnecessary strain.' They were told to 'never fly over cities unless you have a safe altitude,' and to always carry maps 'unless you are absolutely sure of the country to be covered.' Of course that last rule was hard for some of the pilots to follow as the Washington headquarters were exceptionally slow in getting maps out to the field."

So many of the pilots were forced to resort to "by guess and by golly" when it came to navigation that their flying careers often ended abruptly and with tragic results.

For example, on October 30, 1919, John P. Carlton lost his life when, while on only his fifth day as an airmail pilot, he slammed his aircraft into the fog-shrouded Schuley Mountains near Long Valley, New Jersey. [5]

On March 20, 1920, while piloting a DeHaviland through fog on his way from Chicago to Cleveland, Clayton W. Stoner died when he smashed into a tree. [6]

Ten days later, while making the Bellefonte-to-Newark run, Harry C. Sherlock, a veteran World War I pilot, paid the ultimate price when his DeHaviland rammed the eighty-foot-tall Tiffany silver factory smokestack adjacent to Newark's Heller Field; Sherlock died on the way to the hospital of massive internal injuries. [7]

In aviation's early years, life-saving instruments in planes were either crude or nonexistent. When flying in heavy fog or other vision-obscuring conditions with no natural horizon for perspective, pilots became disoriented after only a few minutes. Disoriented pilots flew into the ground while still believing they were maintaining a safe altitude, or turned their planes into a steep, dangerous bank without realizing it. Before devices similar to carpenter's levels showed artificial horizons within planes, pilots hung heavy objects such as bolts on strings to let them know whether or not they were maintaining a level course.

Twenty-six-year-old John P. Woodward, flying from Salt Lake City to Cheyenne, Wyoming, on September 3, 1920, became disoriented in a blinding, early-season blizzard and drove his mail plane into a hill, killing himself instantly. [8]

Frederic A. Robinson was carrying the mail from Hazelhurst Field, New York, to Bellefonte on September 27, 1920, and was navigating by following the Susquehanna River when he encountered fog and dropped his altitude, only to catch some telephone wires over the river; he died when the plane flipped and plunged into the water. [9]

The very next day, Robert Gautier, after only a month as an airmail pilot, died when his DeHaviland hit a radio mast in a rain squall near College Park, Maryland. [10]

Battling a stiff wind while following a railroad track on his way from North Platte, Nebraska, to Cheyenne on Christmas Eve, 1923, James F. "Dinty" Moore was killed when he dropped out of the clouds to an altitude of only 100 feet and unexpectedly encountered a bluff outside North Platte. [11]

Leonard B. Hyde-Pearson, a former Royal Air Force pilot and instructor, perished on March 7, 1924, when his mail plane, flying the ever-treacherous Bellefonte-to-Cleveland route, crashed into a mountaintop during a snowstorm near Grampian, Pennsylvania. Perhaps as a premonition, he had sent a poignant letter to his mother with the stipulation that it be opened only upon his death. It read, in part, "I trust your eyes may never see this. But should God desire that you do, at least know that He has called me, like many more who have given their lives for the future of this wonderful game." [12]

On his way from Chicago to Cleveland on February 12, 1926, Arthur R. Smith, one of the Air Mail Service's steadiest and most experienced pilots, lost the "game" when his Curtiss "Carrier Pigeon" aircraft

A posed photo of loading airmail packages into a Douglas M2 mail plane piloted by Fred W. Kelly, 1926. *(E. B. Jeppesen collection)*

ravaged a grove of trees near Montpelier, Ohio. [13]

On the night of October 18, 1928, while carrying half a ton of mail plus a large shipment of diamonds from New York to Cleveland, the reckless William "Wild Bill" Hopson lost his way and his life when he crashed near Polk, Pennsylvania. [14]

Elrey Borge Jeppesen, a wiry, twenty-four-year-old aerial mail carrier from Oregon, knew of all these accidents (and many more—the result of malfunctioning equipment or simple pilot error) and all of the hazards, of course, but still chose to keep on flying. To him, the numbing cold, the wind-in-your-face conditions, the constant, deafening roar of the engine, and the ever-present danger were a tonic, an elixir. He was addicted to aviation—could not think of himself doing anything other than flying. The fact that he was being paid to do something he truly loved—right in the middle of the Great Depression when millions of people were out of work—was icing on the cake.

Flying the Boeing Air Service Chicago-to-Omaha route on December 12, 1932, Jeppesen, whom everyone called "Jepp," was nearing Council Bluffs, Iowa, in the pre-dawn darkness with 287 pounds of mail stuffed into the Boeing 40-B fuselage when something went seriously wrong.

2: This Was Magic

When he was fourteen, Elrey Borge Jeppesen fell madly, deeply, hopelessly in love.

It was the summer of 1921, and the object of his deep affection was named Jenny. Actually, her full name was JN4D, and she was an old canvas-and-wood flying machine, left over from the Great War, as World War I was known. She was the most fascinating, beautiful thing he had ever seen.

One Saturday, the smitten Elrey Jeppesen had hung around Pearson Field*—an airfield near Vancouver, Washington, across the Columbia River from Portland, Oregon—all day trying, as he later said, "to get a ride for five dollars; they were charging ten and fifteen, and usually taking two passengers at a time. Mother was with me and we started walking back home. We'd walked about a quarter of a mile and I saw this airplane coming in to land. It was beginning to get dusk and I told Mother I was going to run back there and see if I could make one more try. I was able to persuade this chap to take me for a quick ride. His name was Briggs and he'd flown in World War I. He was a really dapper guy, and I remember he was smoking a cigar."

Agreeing to take the youngster for a ten-minute ride for four dollars, the pilot strapped Elrey into the Jenny's front cockpit, climbed into the rear one, revved the engine, and took off. Jepp said, "We got up there, and the sun was shining, and we'd make turns and banks and I

---

* The field, which had previously been known as Vancouver Barracks Airdrome, had its name changed to Pearson Field to honor an Army Air Service pilot, Lieutenant Alexander Pearson, Jr., of Portland, who died in 1924 when the wings of his Curtiss R-8 detached from the fuselage during an air race in Ohio. (Walker, 43-44)

could see the hills and the clouds and the colors brought on by the setting sun. This was magic. I remember how great it felt when he'd go into a bank and pull it around and you'd sit tight in the seat. The sun would shine through the canvas and you could see the ribs, the sunlight, the river below, and the mountains.

"Then, when he turned to go into the field and throttled down, he settled down in a nice glide and the wires were whistling. I thought this was really something! I'd had just a taste, but I loved flying. I could hardly believe it would be that much fun. I thoroughly enjoyed that ride. When we glided in and landed, it just seemed so natural to me. I felt like I could almost do it myself." [1]

Elrey walked—no, flew—home on winged feet that barely seemed to touch the ground, telling his parents about everything he had seen and felt on his brief initial flight.

He was hooked. From that moment on, much to his parents' chagrin and disappointment, flying was all he ever wanted to do.

Elrey's father, Jens Hansen Jeppesen, an architect, cabinet maker, and former member of the Royal Danish Life Guards (all Danish male citizens were required to serve in the military for two years), was born on October 9, 1865, in Wilbey Fyen, Denmark. Jens emigrated in February 1890 from Denmark to Estherville, a small farming community in northern Iowa with a large Scandinavian population. The town's main claim to fame is that a large meteorite fell to earth near there in 1879. In Estherville he met Petrea Marea Petersen, who was two months his junior and had come from Herelt, Denmark. The couple married in Armstrong, Iowa, on October 12, 1893. They then moved to Lake Arthur, Louisiana—a town of 1,800 residents 155 miles due west of New Orleans, in Jefferson Davis Parish—where they started a farm. [2]

Jepp recalled, "My mother was a straightforward, religious, hardworking lady. Wonderful housekeeper and a marvelous cook. She had a little adventuresome spirit in her soul, I guess, or she would have never made it over from Denmark. She came over alone on the boat."

The Jeppesen's first son, Edward, was born in 1900, followed by Elmer, who died of diphtheria in infancy; Elrey was born at Lake Arthur on January 28, 1907.

The bayou country was not kind to the young Jeppesen family. The climate was unbearably hot and humid, and fierce gulf storms wrecked their rice crop. When Elrey was nine months old, Jens and Petrea decided to pull up stakes and head to the Great Northwest.

Three-year-old Elrey Jeppesen on the porch of his O'Dell, Oregon, home with his mother and father, circa 1910. *(E. B. Jeppesen collection)*

"I'm not really sure why they picked Oregon," said Jepp, "but I think they had found Iowa a little different climate than they liked—too hot in the summer, too cold in the winter—and they had pulled out of Louisiana because of the dampness. I believe they were acquainted with a Danish family—the Thompsons—who had moved to Oregon and liked it. The Thompsons had started a dairy and a farm up there. I think they were the principal reason why my folks moved up there. They thought the climate was very similar to Denmark's—maybe a little bit better."

The rugged and beautiful nature of the Jeppesen farm in the Hood River
Valley of Oregon. *(E. B. Jeppesen collection)*

Jepp's father, Jens H. Jeppesen. *(E. B. Jeppesen collection)*

Jepp and his father with the family horse, circa 1910.
(E. B. Jeppesen collection)

The trek to Oregon was long and arduous, but the couple and their two sons finally made it, eventually using every cent of their savings to buy property in the Neal Creek Canyon area, three miles southwest of the tiny hamlet of Odell, some fifty miles north of snow-covered Mount Hood.

Jepp said, "If you look on the map at Hood River, you will see Odell is south of the town of Hood River. Dad bought a forty-acre piece of ground there. The Hood River Valley is beautiful; I've always thought it compared in many ways with parts of the Yakima Valley. Dad said when they first moved into that area with their two children, there were so many trees that when they cut the trees down, there wasn't room to raise a tent without having one or two tree stumps inside the tent."

Once the heavily forested land was cleared, Jens built a home, a barn, raised cows, and planted corn and other crops. Petrea started a dairy and sold milk and butter. Jepp said, "I just can't imagine how hard they must have worked. They cut the trees down and stacked the cord-wood on the side of the mountain and sold it and delivered it. Both my brother and my dad and, of course, mother, were just working day in and day out."

Too young to be of much help on the farm, Jepp spent his days watching the birds, which awakened in him an interest in flying. "The first thing I ever really remember is sitting halfway up in a small oak tree, about ten feet off the ground, watching my dog 'Sport' perform, and watching the birds fly, thinking how wonderful and beautiful it would be to be able to do that. I once made a parachute and jumped off the barn roof into the hay. One of the things that Mother always remembered was that when she could hear me laughing and giggling, she knew I was up on something high and about ready to jump off, and she would run like mad to catch me."

Although he would learn how to work hard, there were certain aspects of farm life that Jepp disliked. "At about age seven, or some-where in there, I had to get up early every morning to milk a couple of cows, feed the horse and slop the pigs and do a lot of work I didn't enjoy. I loved the ranch and the farm, but I'm just not a rancher or farmer at heart. It made it awful tough on Dad, I'll tell you."

Elrey would help with the planting. "When we would plant potatoes, I'd carry the potatoes and Dad would use a shovel and open the ground and I'd drop a potato in it. Then we'd change around and I would use the shovel. When we completed two long rows—and, boy, those rows looked long to me—we'd practice swordsmanship. He'd made two swords out of willow sticks and we'd duel. He had been pretty active in the military at one time and was attached to the King's Guard for awhile in Copenhagen; that's where he learned to be a swordsman. The thing that always amazed me was that when I'd make a dive at him with my 'sword'—and I thought I was pretty quick—I'd find him about three or four feet off to one side, and he'd be swatting me on the rear end with his stick. He was fast and quick, and I learned a lot from him."

One day Elrey's father told him about the Wright Brothers and their historic powered flight at Kitty Hawk, North Carolina, on December 17, 1903. Jepp said, "I kept thinking about that because I was fascinated with the birds, studying how they were flying around."

While on the farm, Elrey acquired an air rifle. "I used to shoot at the snow birds. One day I was shooting away at them and thought, 'Gee whiz, these are friends of mine. These are animals that fly.' I never killed another animal the rest of my life—with the exception of two or three prairie dogs up in Cheyenne during the airmail days."

Then hard times hit the Jeppesens. The family could not afford to raise two sons; Edward, the eldest, would have to go. The Jeppesens put him—along with the dog, the pony, and the livestock—in the care of neighbors, the Taylors, who lived down the road. "I remember when my brother left, Dad took him down in the buggy and I climbed up on the roof of the house to see the last of the buggy go over the hill, about a mile away. It was sad."

The war raging in Europe finally drew the United States into it, and in 1917 Jepp's older brother was drafted into the army shortly after he went to live with the Taylors; Edward served as an Army doughboy in the trenches of France.

Times continued to be very tough for the Jeppesens. Jepp stated, "My brother was overseas and my dad couldn't get any help on the farm. We weren't able to get the harvest in, so we lost the farm; the bank

Jepp's father (left), Jepp, brother Edward, and mother in front of their home at 8017 North Fiske Avenue, Portland, circa 1920. *(Courtesy Museum of Flight)*

foreclosed on it." It was a traumatic time for Jepp, a time that would scar him for the rest of his days.

The family moved to Portland. Jepp recalled, "We loaded up what we could salvage on an old truck that someone had brought up there and worked our way down the trail along the windy, rainy Columbia River Gorge, up the Rowena Loops, and into Portland. My dad went there to find work building ships. The only house that we were able to rent was a very poor one; it didn't even have electric lights in it. So Mother had her work cut out for her."

With his carpentry skills, Jens found work in the local shipyards and the family moved into a better home at 8017 North Fiske Avenue, but making ends meet was still a struggle.

It was important for the family's survival that young Elrey bring money into the household, and so he worked two jobs: delivering newspapers—the *Oregon Journal* in the morning and the *Evening Telegram* in the evening. By age ten or eleven, he was self-disciplined and schooled in the value of hard work. "Two years in a row," he said, "I won the award for getting the most new customers." His prize was a new suit from the Myron Frank Department Store. "It was the first suit I'd ever had. I was pretty happy about that, and so were Mother and Dad."

When Edward returned from Europe in 1919 after serving in the army of occupation for a few months following the armistice, he and Jens started a home-building business. "They were quite successful," said Jepp, "but people could talk Dad out of anything. They would ask him to put in some cabinets. Before you knew it, he was spending so much time putting in cabinets he wouldn't make much money on the house."

The family became close friends with the nationally known "fire-and-brimstone" evangelist preacher and prohibitionist Billy Sunday,* a Portland resident. "He lived about a mile away and Dad built most of the farmhouses and homes and swimming pools and tennis courts for Billy Sunday, and they became very friendly. He used to come up quite frequently and have Sunday dinner with us.

"He would ask me to go walking with him on the cow trails up in the mountains. We'd probably spend an hour or two, maybe longer; he'd say very little, but he seemed to do a lot of meditating and thinking and he enjoyed having me along."

The preacher also frequently gave young Jepp, who loved to build mechanical toys, rubber bands and old alarm clocks. "Before the Erector sets came out," Jepp recalled, "there were Mechano sets. They had electric motors that used batteries, but the batteries only lasted about a week, so I used the 'innards' of clocks for motors; you could wind them up over and over again. I would tie the main drive shaft of the clock to a pulley

---

* Sunday, who was born in 1862 and had grown up in an Ames, Iowa, orphanage, played professional baseball for the Chicago Cubs, Pittsburgh Pirates, and Philadelphia Phillies in the late 1800s before finding religion. He was one of the driving forces behind the passage of the 18th Amendment, which banned the production and sale of alcoholic beverages. He died a wealthy man in 1935 and is buried in Chicago. (www.billysunday.org)

and use it for running motor trucks and elevators and things that I made out of the Mechano set."

Jepp had a genius for mechanical things, which no doubt served him well when he decided to become an aviator. He recalled that his father had him working for two years on developing a "perpetual-motion machine." Said Jepp, "Dad told me that no one had invented anything like that and, if someone did, it would revolutionize the power structure of the world. I wound up with the usual number of windmills and water wheels, particularly water wheels on the two creeks that ran past the house, and I even hooked up a little dynamotor to it so I generated a semblance of electricity."

In those days the Jeppesens had no money to buy bicycles or tricycles or other frivolities, but Jepp invented a little motor bike of his own. "I called it a motor bike but, of course, I was the motor. I drew it all out on paper; four wheels and a lever on the left side to steer it and a lever on the right side to work back and forth like a steam engine on the rear wheel. Two big wheels in back, two little ones in front, and I rode that for several years around the house. Everybody thought it was really great," Jepp said.

Jepp's inventive mind soon turned to aviation, and he began building rubber-band airplanes and teaching himself how to fly in the dirt-floor cellar of his home. "I was probably eleven or twelve and fixed up a gadget in the basement—I guess it was the forerunner of the Link trainer. I used a broom handle for a joystick and I fixed up rubber pedals that were a bar with a bolt through the center of it. I had a clock rigged up, a gadget that would kind of turn the hexagon wheel just a little turn. It would say 'nose up;' the next one would say 'nose down,' or the 'right wing is low,' the 'left wing is low,' or the 'nose is too high,' that sort of thing. I would sit there pretending I was flying an airplane. It did give me quite a bit of coordination, apparently. None of my friends seemed to be very interested in it, but I used to do quite a bit of flying down there in the dirt basement!"

Even while in knickers at age ten, Jepp displayed an interest in aviation.
(E. B. Jeppesen collection)

At age twelve, Jepp relinquished his morning paper route but kept the afternoon one, then went to another job—delivering groceries for a store on Longmard Street, about three blocks from his house. "An older couple ran the store and I delivered the groceries," he said. "That took from about a quarter of five until well after seven o'clock."

At about age thirteen, Jepp discovered that one of his paper route customers was, with the exception of Billy Sunday, about the closest thing in Portland to a celebrity: the swashbuckling John Gilbert "Tex" Rankin. [3]

A former soldier who had chased Mexican bandit Pancho Villa around northern Mexico as part of General John J. Pershing's "Punitive Expedition" of 1916, Rankin moved to Portland in 1922 and began taking flying lessons. So hooked on flying did he become that the next year he opened his own flying school at Guilds Lake in Portland. A year later, he moved his operation across the Willamette River to Pearson Field, Vancouver. In 1926 he moved again, this time to Mock's Bottom, and then to a field at Union Avenue and Columbia Street.

Hundreds of aspiring aviators, inspired by the exciting new developments in aviation, especially Charles A. Lindbergh's solo crossing of the Atlantic in 1927, flocked to Rankin's School of Flight; the once-quiet skies above Portland buzzed continually with the raucous sound of the piston-driven engines. Within a year, Rankin and his instructors had taught more than 250 students how to fly. Rankin also published a series of instructional "how-to-fly" booklets; over sixty flying schools nationwide adopted his booklets, known as *The Rankin System of Flying Instruction*.

When he and his staff weren't teaching new pilots how to fly, Tex Rankin's "Flying Circus" kept the cash flowing by barnstorming—giving rides and doing aerial stunts and aerobatics over cities and towns throughout the West. (In 1928, Rankin made the first non-stop solo flight from Canada to Mexico and, that same year, entered the National Air Race in an aircraft with the number "13" painted on its fuselage and a black cat passenger brought along for good luck. He didn't win but the good-natured Rankin was a favorite with Portlanders.) [4]

Tex Rankin and an early female pilot, Ann Bohrer, circa 1927.
(E. B. Jeppesen collection)

Tex Rankin was on Jepp's newspaper route, and the young delivery boy made sure that Rankin was his last delivery of the day, hoping to find the aviator at home. Jepp noted, "I'd take it around to the back door and perhaps catch him sitting in the kitchen. But I always had to get back to the grocery store by five o'clock so I could make deliveries.

"I realized who Tex was the first time I read in the newspaper about him—probably when I was around twelve or thirteen years of age. Tex was one grand guy, a wonderful person. He was friendly, smiled all the time, helped everyone to fly, and knew how to readily adapt to the needs of the old and the young, the boys and the girls. Tex was a pretty steady hand."

As he dreamed about a career in aviation, Jepp found other jobs. One summer he went to work for a company that manufactured apple graters. "I was pretty mechanically inclined and liked the work. Whenever they would run into some knotty problems, they would have that 'kid' come up and take a look at it. Within a period of four or five months, I became the chap that checked the grater out last. In other words, I ran it through its paces to make sure that everything was working okay"—a position that today would be known as the "quality-control inspector."

Young Elrey also worked in the office building across from the Federal Reserve Bank in downtown Portland, cleaning the elevator and mopping the lobby floor. "I had to get up pretty early and ride the streetcar down," Jepp recalled. "My job was to polish up the elevator. Then I'd polish the doors on the different floors to earn a little extra money." Then, because Jepp also worked at the Federal Reserve Bank, he would walk over to the post office and get the mail for the bank.

"I would go to the post office, get the bags of mail, and wheel them over to the bank, take them upstairs, unload, sort, run them through the envelope opener, organize it all, and then deliver the mail." He eventually was promoted to help in one of the teller cages.

But banking seemed to Jepp like a boring, dead-end, ground-bound career. His heart was set on flying. Talking with an attractive young secretary who worked at the bank—her name was Miss Cooley—Jepp said, "You see those beautiful white clouds way up there, Miss Cooley? Well, I'm going to go up and fly with them, and I'm going to quit this job."

One day he went to see a young man named Jack Wyatt Parshall to talk about taking flying lessons. Jepp said, "Jack Parshall was the sales manager and part owner of Bell Aircraft Company and Bush's Flying School at Pearson Field, and their chief pilot. He also ran the Dean Hotel at Fifth and Main in downtown Portland. I went down to the hotel and met him and his wife, Blanche, and their two children. I introduced myself and told him I'd seen him around the field. We talked for about two or three hours and got everything lined up for a flying course."

There was only one problem, and it was a big one—Jepp did not have enough money for lessons. "So I just said goodbye and left and said I hoped to see him over on the field, and I'd see what I could do about scraping up some cash."

So impressed was Parshall with Jepp's determination to become a pilot that he reportedly told Blanche, "I'm going to see that that kid learns to fly if I have to pay for it myself."

It was 1926. Jepp was still going to school, working various jobs, and hanging out at the airfield during his free time. He became determined to get a job—any kind of job—in the fledgling aviation industry. His several part-time jobs and his obsession with flying were hurting his grades at Theodore Roosevelt High School. Whenever he heard the sound of an aircraft engine, he would turn and gaze out the classroom window and be transported into the sky. [5]

Jepp's friend and mentor, Jack Parshall, shown as an airline pilot in the 1930s.
(E. B. Jeppesen collection)

The Roosevelt High School (Portland, Ore.) track team, circa 1926. Jepp is in the front row, fifth from left. *(Courtesy Museum of Flight)*

No doubt Jepp's dream was fueled to a large extent by the intense interest in aviation that was then sweeping the country.

After the Great War ended in 1918, the United States came down with a bad case of "flying fever." Companies and government suddenly discovered that airplanes made doing business more productive. Speed became paramount. Not only had the widespread use of telephones made voice communication a reality, but airplanes made it possible to send mail, people, and low-weight products across the country in a fraction of the time that it took cars, trucks, and trains to make the same journey.

Ever since Orville Wright's twelve-second, 120-foot powered flight a few feet above the dunes of Kitty Hawk in 1903, the idea of flying across the Atlantic had become a challenge and a goal for stalwart aviators. Such a flight was, to many, nothing more than a Jules Verne science-fiction novel, as preposterous as flying to the moon. To others, attempting such a trip was suicide, plain and simple. And yet, with each passing year, aircraft got a little bit better, aircraft engines got a little more reliable, pilots got a little more experienced and, suddenly, the far-fetched notion of winged flight across the ocean transcended fantasy and entered the realm of possibility. [6]

In 1919, the journey was accomplished. On May 8, 1919, a U.S. Navy flying boat, NC-4, with Navy Lieutenant Commander Albert Cushing Read at the controls, and with a crew of six aboard, became the first aircraft to cross the Atlantic—a trip that took nineteen days. (Originally, two other flying boats, the NC-1 and NC-3, had taken off with the NC-4 from Long Island, New York, but bad weather forced them to ditch in the sea, where their crews were rescued.) After delays for repairs in the Azores, Read and NC-4 landed in Lisbon, Portugal, on May 27, to a hero's welcome.★ [7]

The next month, two British fliers, Captain John Alcock and Lieutenant Arthur Whitten Brown, both aviators during the Great War, made the first non-stop trans-Atlantic flight. Taking off in a Vickers Vimy IV twin-engined bomber from Newfoundland on June 14, 1919, the pair crossed the Atlantic and landed in Ireland after a nineteen-hour flight. The intrepid airmen, who were both knighted, shared the 10,000 pound prize that London's *Daily Mail* newspaper had offered in May 1913 for the first non-stop flight across the Atlantic. [8]

Two weeks after Alcock's and Brown's historic flight, a lighter-than-air dirigible, the British-built R-34, flew the ocean from east to west. Copied from a captured German Zeppelin, the R-34, under the command of Major George Scott, left Britain on July 2, 1919, and arrived in Mineola, Long Island (the same place where Earl Lewis Ovington had

---

★ Read's NC-4 is preserved in the Naval Aviation Museum, Pensacola, Florida.

dropped the sack of mail in 1911), 108 hours later. Because the American ground crew had no experience in handling the landing of a dirigible, one of R-34's officers, Major E. M. Pritchard, jumped by parachute from the airship to direct the landing party. A week later, the R-34 made the return trip to Britain in seventy-five hours. [9]

Suddenly, helium- and hydrogen-filled airships were all the rage and were hailed as the future of long-distance air travel. After the Great War ended, the Treaty of Versailles dictated that Germany's development of dirigibles must be curtailed—a blow which nearly put the Zeppelin Company out of business. Dr. Hugo Eckener, Zeppelin's crafty president, made the U.S. Government, which was not a signatory to the treaty, an offer it couldn't refuse: The company would build a giant (658 feet long), technologically advanced dirigible for the United States, giving America a quantum leap in dirigible technology. Over the howls of the Europeans, the U.S. awarded Zeppelin a contract. The airship began its Atlantic crossing on October 13, 1924, reaching Lakehurst, New Jersey, two days later. The dirigible was named the *ZR-3 Los Angeles* and put into U.S. Navy service, where it served until 1940. [10]

A fierce competition had begun five years earlier, in 1919, when Raymond Orteig, a wealthy, French-born American hotelier, that he would give $25,000 to the first aviator or aviators to fly an airplane nonstop between New York and Paris. A number of famous and unknown aviators declared themselves in the hunt for the prize money, and the race heated up.

Despite the fact that nearly one hundred persons had crossed the Atlantic by air since 1919, either as pilots, crew, or passengers, it was Charles A. Lindbergh's exploits that fired the public's imagination as none of the previous flights, as spectacular and important as they were, had done.

Lindbergh, a former barnstormer and an Air Mail Service pilot on leave from the Chicago-St. Louis route, was the first to complete the trip. Flying a mono-wing, one-engine plane that he had had custom built with borrowed money and his entire $2,000 savings account, "Lucky" Lindbergh accomplished the feat with a flight that began on May 20, 1927, at Long Island's Roosevelt Field and ended thirty-three-and-a half-hours later at Le Bourget in Paris. His arrival, in the dark, was greeted by a throng of 150,000 frenzied Parisians, and the news of his safe landing was flashed around the world, making him the world's first superstar, the likes of which has never been eclipsed. [11]

By the time of Lindbergh's Atlantic crossing, aviation was already well established in the U.S. and overseas. In fact, Europe's aviation industry was considerably more advanced than America's.

The first regularly scheduled U.S. passenger airline, if one can call it that, was the St. Petersberg-Tampa "Airboat Line," a single flying boat, carrying a single passenger, and piloted by Tony Jannus. The airline's first flight traversed the eighteen miles between the two Florida cities on New Year's Day, 1914. Shortly after flying its 1,200th passenger in April of that year, the airline went out of business. [12]

It was left to the Europeans, with an abundance of trained pilots and war-surplus aircraft lined up at aerodromes in France, England, and Germany, to take the lead in passenger air travel. In early 1919, the Germans, defeated but unbowed, flew daily between Berlin and Weimar. Not long thereafter the French began international flights, flying between Paris and Brussels. In the summer of 1919 the British inaugurated service between London and Paris.

Many of the aircraft making these runs were slow, lumbering ex-military bombers converted to carry small numbers of passengers. For most of the airlines, the enterprise was a money-losing business. Erratic schedules, weather delays, and faulty equipment that often required harrowing emergency landings played havoc with the fledgling airlines' bottom lines. French airlines, at least, were kept aloft by handsome government subsidies.

By the early 1920s, though, routes in the skies above and between Britain and Europe were full of passenger airliners—many of them luxuriously appointed—all determined to make a go of this new mode of travel.

Other parts of the world also became accustomed to the sight and sound of the aeroplane. Passengers in increasing numbers were being hauled across the wilds of the Middle East, India, Africa, Southeast Asia, Dutch East Indies, and Australia. [13]

The United States, however, lagged far behind these other nations. Although America was the land that had produced the Wright brothers, Lucky Lindy, and the first scheduled airline, railroads were still the preferred mode of medium- and long-distance travel. A number of aerial accidents received sensationalized coverage in the press (such as a crash off the coast of Florida where the survivors were reportedly devoured by sharks), scaring off potential passengers.

As the European experience had shown, according to author Oliver E. Allen, "an airline could not exist for long without government support, but no subsidies were forthcoming from Washington. Most Americans remained skeptical about air travel; trains, while not as fast as planes, were much safer. European governments had supported commercial aviation for reasons of national prestige, but in American politics 'subsidy' was a dirty word." One way around this problem of perception was to improve an already existing government service—in this case, the carrying of the mail. By adding airplanes to the familiar modes of goods-hauling (vehicle and railroad), the public soon became aware of the advantages of air travel and, by the late 1920s, commercial aviation in the U.S. would catch up with the Europeans and then surpass them. [14]

Once airmail service was initiated in 1917, there was no stopping it, although the Post Office Department was worried that the penny-pinching administration of incoming President Warren G. Harding in 1921 would cut off funds for airmail. To forestall this, the Post Office decided to demonstrate its ability to carry the mail swiftly from one coast to the other. Like an airborne Pony Express, a team of pilots stationed at airfields across the country carried the mail in relays from San Francisco to New York in thirty-three hours and twenty minutes. The flight convinced the Harding administration that carrying mail by air was faster and more efficient than by truck or train, and the government began seeking ways to improve the service even further.

One major improvement was the installation of a chain of lighted beacons across the country to aid in night navigation. High-powered revolving beacons were first installed between Chicago and Cheyenne, with lighted emergency landing fields located every twenty-five to thirty miles along the way. Author Oliver Allen writes, "By the middle of 1924 the lighted airway had been completed all the way from New York to San Francisco....The beacon system was a highly significant achivement, for nothing else like it existed anywhere."★ [15]

Unidentified primitive airport (believed to be Laramie, Wyoming) photographed in the late 1920s. One of the U.S. Air Mail lighting beacons that put out the equivalent of five million candle-power is visible. *(E. B. Jeppesen collection)*

★ The forerunner to the beacon system began in 1919 when two Army pilots, Lts. Donald L. Bruner and Harold Harris, began experimenting with bonfires as an aid in nighttime navigation. They soon added flashing markers, rotating beacons, and floodlit airfields. In February 1921, Jack Knight, an airmail pilot, flew all night from Chicago to North Platte, Nebraska, guiding himself by the light of fires lit by postal employees, farmers, and the public. In 1923 the U.S. Post Office began installing a network of acetylene lamps spaced three miles apart and 500-watt revolving searchlights mounted atop fifty-one-foot-tall towers at permanent airfields. By 1933, 1,500 beacons marking 18,000 miles of airway had been emplaced. On clear nights the lights were visible for 100 miles. The beacons were discontinued in 1973. (Heppenheimer, 10; www.centennialofflight/gov.essay/Government_Role/navigation; avstop.com/Stories/inspection)

Giving the fledgling airlines a considerable boost was the passage in 1925 of the Kelly Act, which authorized the Post Office Department to award contracts not only for the transcontinental shipment of mail via a coast-to-coast trunk line, but also to carriers hauling mail to and from the trunk along numerous feeder lines. It suddenly seemed that anyone who owned at least one airplane was applying to the Post Office Department for a contract to carry the mail.

Up to that point airplanes had no radios and no way to make voice communication with either the ground or with other planes in the air. There were also very few rules. There was no uniform system for the training or licensing of pilots, no safety inspection requirements for airplanes, no air-traffic control, no established method of navigation, no governmental agency overseeing the field of aviation. Like the "Jazz Age" itself, with its "flappers" and short skirts and bathtub gin and speakeasies, aviation was wild and wide-open.

Radio itself was in its infancy, the first commercial station, KDKA in Pittsburgh, having been on the air only since November 1920. The United States Bureau of Standards began experimenting with two-way radio technology in December 1926; five months later a ground-to-air radiotelephone system with a range of fifty miles was introduced. Shortly thereafter, a transmitter at Bellefonte, Pennsylvania, was able to communicate with an airmail plane 150 miles away. [16]

In June 1927, shortly after Lindbergh's stunning achievement, Jepp decided that "If I was going to get anywhere in the aviation business, I'd better get a move on."

Jepp had finished two-and-a-half years of high school and, in spite of his being a gifted athlete in several sports (baseball, tennis, and track),

Hangars at Pearson Field, Vancouver, Washington, 1926.
(Courtesy Clark County Historical Museum)

his grades were mediocre and there was talk of his teachers wanting to hold him back. Much to the consternation of his parents, he decided to drop out of school and pursue his dream of flying. [17]

He dropped out of high school, quit his job at the bank, and went over to Pearson Field to ask Jack Parshall for a full-time job. Parshall hired the enthusiastic youngster on the spot.

If Jepp had had a job description, it would have been "menial laborer." His chores were sweeping out the hangar, washing planes, cleaning up the puddles of oil on the ground, wiping down the planes' engines, keeping the tools neatly organized, acting as night watchman, and doing whatever thankless tasks the pilots and mechanics told him to do—and he loved every minute of it.

Jepp moved out of his family's home and went to live in the air-field's T-hangar, which was, as the name implies, built in the shape of a "T," just large enough to accommodate the wings and fuselage of a biplane. "I lived in a corner of the hangar," he said. "It was not a room; it was just at the tail end of the airplane. I had a cot over there, and a bench. I had electricity and a little electric flat-type heater, and that was about it."

Pearson Field also had a couple of other slightly larger hangars. One was being used by the National Guard and the other by Pacific Air Transport, owned by Vern C. Gorst. "P.A.T. had just started flying up and down the coast then—1926, I believe it was," Jepp said. "The hangar was a rather small one that would just hold one airplane and the tools and machinery. It had an office and a bedroom."

A few weeks later, after eating another cold sandwich his mother had made for him, Jepp had an idea. There was a small shack by the entrance to the airfield that wasn't being used for anything; the rumor was the owner was going to tear it down. Jepp talked the owner into renting it to him so he could convert it into a hamburger stand. Painting the shack a bright white, and borrowing an old, unused kerosene stove from home, Jepp went into business. He soon was supplementing his meager laborer's income with the money he was raking in from the hamburger stand, which was open between eleven and two. With few places near the airfield for pilots, mechanics, passengers, and visitors to eat, business quickly boomed. Jepp asked a grocer to help run the stand; he eventually gave the business to him—on the condition that Jepp could have a free hamburger anytime he wanted. [18]

When he wasn't doing his airplane and hangar chores, or selling burgers, Jepp was hanging out with the pilots and mechanics of Rankin Flying Service, absorbing their stories and advice, listening intently to every word, getting a feel for what real flying was all about. Before long Jepp knew every part of an airplane and what its function was, knew how to navigate in sunshine and showers, knew the flight and handling characteristics of every plane that flew into, out of, or was hangared at Pearson Field.

At last, on the basis of his dedication, devotion, and plain willing-ness to work hard—not to mention his "straight-arrow" image (he did not smoke, drink coffee or alcohol, kept himself neat and clean, and almost always wore a tie)—Jepp was rewarded. He was going to be given flying lessons! Exactly who paid for the lessons isn't clear, but Jack Parshall cannot be ruled out as a suspect.

"I didn't get hour-long lessons like the regular students got," Jepp said. "I only got about twenty minutes at a time."

Jepp made the most of his short lessons. After going over the the-ory of flight and the operation of the controls in a brief ground school, instructor Basil Russell, in a dual-control Jenny, showed Jepp how to take off, fly straight and level, and land. It was immediately clear that Jepp had a knowledge and knack for flying well beyond his years, and soon Russell was showing the youngster how to turn, do barrel rolls, spins, loops, wingovers, vertical banks, and other advanced aerobatic maneuvers. The veteran pilot then let Jepp duplicate his moves—something Jepp did with impressive skill and fearlessness.

Jepp didn't always follow his mentor's directions. He recalled that on one instructional flight, with Russell in the front cockpit of the two-place biplane, "He unfastened his seatbelt and turned around to look back at me and hollered, 'God dammit, when I tell you to keep that nose on the horizon, keep it there and don't let it be wandering around!' I guess I'd gotten just a little lackadaisical along there somewhere."★

Basil Russell, like many of the early pilots, was a hard drinker and hell-raiser when on the ground. Jepp recalled, "Whenever he won a flying contest, he would get his silver trophy and you would see him going down the middle of the street with two guys holding him up. He'd had his share of 'happy cider.'

"Fliers back then were pretty well accepted by the townspeople of Portland. I don't think anyone thought they were idiots, because they all gave a pretty good account of themselves in interviews and speeches. I'm sure everybody thought of them as daredevils, but they got along pretty well socially. They were always being invited to the mayor's office and, when the governor came to town, you would see him out there with Tex Rankin, or Tex would be taking him somewhere. Tex was invited everywhere and anywhere. He was always seen either in his flying suit or in a tuxedo, bobbing around town."

★ On January 19, 1930, Russell died near Oceanside, California, in a Ford 5-AT-C Tri-Motor while piloting a group of executives returning to Los Angeles from the race track at Agua Caliente, Mexico. Killed along with Russell were John L. "Jack" Maddux—a close friend of Charles Lindbergh—head of TAT-Maddux Air Lines, a West Coast carrier that began service in 1926; Elizabeth Squibb, granddaughter of drug magnate E. B. Squibb; and twelve others. A fog had settled into the area along the California coast north of Oceanside and south of San Clemente. Russell evidently decided to make an emergency landing in an open bean field on the coastal plain but misjudged the aircraft's height in the poor weather conditions and the airplane's left wing struck the ground. The Tri-Motor then slammed to earth, slid 200 feet and burst into flames. There were no survivors. (maverik.rootsweb.com/mcuz/JackMdx02; members.aol.com/jaydeebee1/crash30s)

A group from Bush's Flying School and Tex Rankin's Flying Service gathered around a Waco-10 with Curtiss OX-5 engine at Vancouver, Washington, 1927: A. Elrey Jeppesen, B. Tex Rankin, C. Basil Russell, D. Jack Parshall. *(E. B. Jeppesen collection)*

Within an incredibly short period of time—after just two hours and ten minutes of instruction, to be exact—Jepp had progressed far enough to solo in an Eaglerock with a Curtiss OX-5 engine.★ He pulled it off without a hitch.

★ The Eaglerocks were manufactured by the Alexander Aircraft Company at 3385 South Broadway in Englewood, Colorado, a Denver suburb. Two Alexander brothers, J. Don and Don M., began their company not as an airplane manufactory but as a silent-movie film studio. In 1925, J. Don suddenly decided that the company should branch out and build airplanes; the first Eaglerock flew in September of that year. In December 1926, aviator Charles A. Lindbergh approached Alexander to see if they would build for him an aircraft that could fly from New York to Paris. The company was unable to promise they could produce the plane within the two-month time frame Lindbergh specified, and so the contract went to a San Diego company named Ryan.

With the company outgrowing its Englewood location in 1928, it was decided to move the film studio and aircraft factory sixty miles south to Colorado Springs. Tragedy struck on April 20, 1928, when highly flammable chemicals, oil, paints, and fabrics exploded and the facility burned down; eleven workers lost their lives. The disaster did not shut the company down; it went on to produce nearly 1,000 biplanes over the next few years before a series of crashes, including that of the stock market, finished the aircraft company off in 1932. The film company, which eventually made television commercials, closed in 1957. (deVries, passim)

Alexander Eaglerock with radial engine.
(Courtesy Smithsonian National Air and Space Museum)

Jepp's second pilot's license (signed by Orville Wright). Note the misspelling of Jepp's middle and last names. *(E. B. Jeppesen collection)*

Jepp's first airplane, a 1916 JN4D "Jenny," number 2360, purchased for $500 in December 1927. Jepp is barely visible in the cockpit. *(E. B. Jeppesen collection)*

Not long after he had soloed, Jepp decided he had to have his own plane—quite a step for a twenty-one-year-old of modest means. Scraping together all the money he had made from his various jobs (in addition to soliciting donations from his newspaper route customers), he came up with $250—half of what he needed to purchase a war-surplus 1916 Jenny with a ninety-horsepower Curtiss engine. Jepp recalled that the crate's top speed was fifty-nine miles an hour. Fortunately, a friend, Lee Woodhouse, wanted to own the other half and contributed the remaining $250. In December 1927, Jepp and Woodhouse took delivery of the plane. Woodhouse soon pulled out of the deal but did not pull out his half of the payment, and Jepp found himself the sole owner.

"I was pretty happy owning my own airplane," he said, "and being able to fly whenever and wherever I wanted. I used to go out early in the morning, as soon as the sun came up, get myself lined up about 6,000 feet over the Columbia River, and just sit up there and make loops. I thought it was great. But I was always concerned that I didn't have any money to fix up the plane should something break."

As a pilot and Rankin employee, Jepp could carry passengers who came out to the air field, as he had once done, eager for their first flying experience. "Some weekends I could make fifty or seventy-five or eighty dollars," he said. Jepp logged about a hundred hours in the old bird then, in late February 1928, sold it to an aerial circus pilot for $500 but regretted the deal.★

"I would have never sold her had I known what the man who bought her was going to do with her," Jepp said. "For an air show they constructed a fake barn right on the field. He flew her right inside the barn door and crashed on purpose and walked away. What a ridiculous thing to do!" [19]

"Occasionally," he said, "I got an opportunity to go on one-day barnstorming trips—selling tickets, gassing the planes, that sort of thing. It was a lot of fun; I got more interested in aviation every day."

In the back of his mind, Jepp still considered returning to school at some point, getting his diploma, and going off to college to become what his folks wanted him to be—an engineer. He went so far as to fly down to the Oregon State University at Corvallis in the spring of 1928 and interview with the Dean of Men.

"I must have looked like a hippy," Jepp confessed. "I was in my puttees, leather jacket, and the rest of it—the regular flying gear we wore. I've reviewed it many times in my mind, trying to figure out what happened. The dean hardly spoke to me. I never could get a word out of him, except he finally did ask me, 'Well, how are you going to finance your way through school?'

"I told him that I had a Jenny and that I'd give flying lessons, barnstorm, and give passenger hops [rides] on Saturdays and Sundays. But it was no go. Later, I met a fellow who had graduated from Oregon State

---

★ After he sold the Jenny, he gave Woodhouse his $250 back—and even repaid his newspaper route customers for their loans.

and knew the dean. He said that the dean was a rather peculiar guy to have that kind of job in a leading college. I know that if I'd been in that position and a young man came to see me and said, 'I have an airplane,' I'd be pretty interested in getting that kid to attend my school. But that's not the way it goes." [20]

School suddenly seemed like the most stultifying thing he could think of. He decided he didn't want to do anything that would keep him on the ground.

3: A BARNSTORMER'S LIFE

After Jepp left the dean's office at Oregon State, he ran away to join the circus—the Rankin Flying Circus—and began a brief career as a barnstormer.

The dictionary defines "barnstorming" as "to tour through rural districts staging theatrical performances, usually in one-night stands; to pilot one's airplane in sightseeing flights with passengers or in exhibition stunts in an unscheduled itinerant course."

Barnstorming was a peculiarly American invention, although Britain saw her share of aerial stunt shows after the Great War. With hundreds of war-surplus aircraft—and thousands of military-trained pilots sitting idle around the country—it was only a matter of time before someone got the idea to put the pilots into the planes and travel around presenting exhibitions of flying derring-do for the local folks who were starved for entertainment.

All across the country, entrepreneurs—usually out-of-work pilots—organized aerial exhibitions called flying circuses. Pilots showed off their skills by doing outside loops, inside loops, barrel rolls, snap rolls, Immelmanns, and inverted tricks with rickety planes that were still a novelty to the vast majority of the American public. Between shows, the aviators would land and sell five-minute rides for ten or fifteen dollars.

The public, however, soon grew bored with the usual menu of aerial acrobatics. To feed the ever-growing appetite for something different, new and riskier tricks were devised. There were "wing walkers"—daredevils who would stand atop the upper wing of the biplanes as they zoomed past the grandstands at speeds up to 100 miles an hour. There were men who transferred in mid-air from the wing of one plane to the wing of another; men who leaped from a speeding car onto a rope ladder dangled by a passing plane; men who hung like gymnasts from the landing gear; men who jumped from planes with a new-fangled contraption called a "parachute;" men who purposely crashed their flimsy craft into break-away buildings; men who made dangerous "dead-stick" landings to the screams of the crowd. After the public tired of seeing men perform these stunts, women did them. There was even an all-Negro flying circus, and fliers who incorporated cats and dogs into their acts.

Aerial stuntman transfers from one plane to another while upside-down.
(Courtesy Smithsonian National Air and Space Museum)

An early barnstormer prepares to take off from an unidentifed horse-race track.
(Courtesy Museum of Flight)

There were dozens of flying circuses during the Roaring Twenties, operations sporting names such as the Gates Flying Circus, Doug Davis Flying Circus, Cliff Rose Death Angels, Jimmy Angel's Flying Circus, 13 Black Cats, Mabel Cody Flying Circus (she a niece of Buffalo Bill Cody), and the Flying Aces. [1]

Barnstorming was all great fun. And a lot of daredevils got killed or seriously injured in their efforts to entertain a public who, like the restless crowd at a Roman gladiatorial contest or chariot race, was always clamoring for more exciting and dangerous stunts.

By the late 1920s, however, interest in barnstorming had peaked and was beginning to wane; there were only so many things that airplanes and human bodies could do. Plus, as Paul O'Neil writes in *Barnstormers and Speed Kings,* "By the middle of the decade, the first wave of barnstormers, the military-trained fliers, had been well thinned out. The capable pilots had become fixed-base operators or had regular jobs testing aircraft or flying the mail. The bad or unlucky ones had been killed, and the indifferent ones had drifted out of the game. Barnstormers by 1925 were largely young men whose zeal for flying had been ignited by the postwar gypsy fliers. Haphazardly trained, unseasoned by experience and uneducated in the capabilities of their aircraft or the basics of flight, many were a real threat to the lives of their trusting passengers and the spectators who watched."

A further blow landed in 1926 with the passage of the Air Commerce Act. Stricter licensing of pilots, the inspection and registration of aircraft, and tighter regulations governing what stunts could be performed and how they could be performed spelled doom for many of the flying circuses and entrepreneurs who had neither the money nor the desire to meet the new standards. [2]

Barnstorming on the West Coast, and especially in Oregon and Washington, was still going strong, however, thanks to Tex Rankin and a handful of others. And young Elrey Jeppesen was about to join the ranks of the daredevils. On July 16, 1928, he joined the Rankin School of Flying and, by default, the Rankin Flying Circus. [3]

An Oregon aviator and instructor named Joseph R. Foltz, who owned an Eaglerock and had been impressed by Jepp's aerial abilities, invited Jepp to fly the craft up to the company's barnstorming show in Yakima, Washington. "Why, I don't know," Jepp said. "There were a lot of the old boys around there, old pilots, with a great deal more flying experience than I had. Perhaps he wanted a young, sober, serious-minded chap, and I guess I filled the bill.

"I took a mechanic, a roustabout guy by the name of O.G. Barnham, with me," said Jepp, "and Mrs. Foltz★ went along; Mr. Foltz

---

★ Edith Foltz would soon be one of the leading woman pilots of the day and a trophy-winning air racer. In World War II she would ferry fighters and bombers from factories in the U.S. to air bases in England. (deVries, 67; Walker, 41)

joined us in Yakima. I was selling tickets, gassing the airplanes, carrying water, cranking the props, all that sort of thing."

Jepp also flew passengers who lined up to take rides for ten dollars apiece. "I think nearly ninety percent of the people that went up for a ride in the airplane enjoyed it and would do it again, and probably did later on. They seemed to be quite happy and felt it a joyous experience. I know that several of them that I took up in Yakima learned to fly. It was really an exciting time."

Jepp discovered that flying in an open-cockpit aircraft could be an aphrodisiac—and a trysting spot. On occasion a young fellow would approach Jepp and tell him he wanted to take his girlfriend up "for a little fun," so Jepp would cram the fellow and his girl into one of the cockpits. Jepp said, "He would motion to me that he wanted a little 'activity,' so I'd hold up my hand with five fingers and flash it a couple of times to indicate ten dollars. He'd fish around and hand me ten dollars across the wind and I'd either give them a loop or maybe one turn spin, something like that."

When the weather cooperated and the crowds came out to see the flying daredevils, the day's "take" could be substantial. "At the end of the day," Jepp said, "we'd go back to the hotel and go up to the room and pull the money out of our shirt pockets or pants pockets and everywhere else and dump it on the bedspread, smooth it out, and count it. There'd be hundreds of dollars there."

Jepp was also recruited to perform stunts with the Circus, such as being the second-string wing walker. "My wing-walking career was rather short," he confessed. "I didn't do very much of it and it usually would take place when the parachute jumper or wing walker was late getting out to a one o'clock or five o'clock performance. So, to hold the crowd, I'd jump in the plane and somebody'd take me up and I'd crawl out and climb around on the wings a little and wave to the crowd. That was about all. I was not a professional wing walker by any means."

The regular wing walker was the group's chief mechanic, O.G. Barnham. Barnham was a heavy drinker and wasn't always the most reliable. Jepp recalled that everyone in the group was responsible for seeing to it that Barnham was out of jail and that he would see the local

Elrey "Jepp" Jeppesen in his barnstorming flying togs, Yakima Valley, Washington, circa 1928. *(E. B. Jeppesen collection)*

Catholic priest before the afternoon jump. Jepp said, "The priest would have him at the field sober enough to jump at five o'clock."

"My folks didn't think wing walking was the smartest thing to do, but I explained to them that if you stayed close to all those wires, you couldn't fall off. I was not an aerial acrobat, although I got to where I could hang onto the landing gear and a few little things like that, but I was not head-standing on the top or any of those fancy things. I was more interested in being in the cockpit doing the flying."

To stir up interest in the flying circus, Jepp said that a few days before an event someone from the group would fly or drive to the next town where the aerial circus team would be performing, stick up posters, hang banners across the streets, hand out photos and press releases to the local newspaper office, and sometimes even fly over the town trailing a banner or and dropping leaflets.

Jepp (left) with the wing-walking mechanic O.G. Barnham, all dressed up and ready for an air show, 1928. *(E. B. Jeppesen collection)*

Jepp said the best way to determine if a town would be a prime market for an air show was to make a low-level pass down the main street, just above building and telephone-pole level. "If not many people bothered to look up," he said, "that usually meant some other barnstormers had been there recently."

As the youngest and most baby-faced of the Rankin bunch, Jepp was sometimes picked on by some of the older fliers. He recalled that during a barnstorming trip to Pasco, a pilot by the name of Case began giving him a hard time. "Along about nine or ten o'clock up in the hotel room, Case and a bunch of others had been drinking pretty heavy; there was cigar smoke all over the place, and they were playing cards and romping around. I wasn't the most popular guy with some of those old fellows because I didn't play poker and I didn't drink and I didn't bring any girls around. I just didn't fit in with the World War I gang." His youthful appearance didn't help.

"I remember Case got pretty well oiled and grabbed me and said, 'God dammit, let's make a man out of this kid. I'm gonna pour some whiskey down his throat.' I hadn't even had a cup of coffee in those days. Jack Parshall, who was on that trip, grabbed Case and threw him over in the corner and said, 'You leave Jepp alone—he's getting along just fine.'"

During one stint, the Rankin Flying Circus was holed up in Yakima for ten days, waiting for the weather to break. Jepp recalled, "It was raining and snowing and we began to run up a pretty hefty hotel bill. It looked like the weather was going to turn good for Saturday and Sunday, so we called Tex and told him to bring his Ryan Brougham up—the same kind of plane Lindbergh used to cross the Atlantic. We thought that it would add a little more attraction. Tex came up and gave rides until we had enough to pay the hotel bill.

"We had three planes working that Saturday. I had the Eaglerock and it all worked out fine except that I flew from about eight o'clock in the morning to something like nine at night. I was absolutely bushed; I remember the mechanic and another helper had me by the arms and they were walking me down the hall in the hotel. They were helping me get a shower and get stretched out on the bed because I was just totally exhausted. Two ladies walked by and one of them said, 'There goes another drunken aviator.' If I'd had any strength left, I would have contradicted that a little bit."

The early aircraft were very unreliable and mishaps sometimes occurred during the air shows. In the summer of 1928 a Rankin pilot named Cecil Rawl had his OX-5 engine quit in mid-air. Jepp said, "He went into a sod field and broke the airplane up a little. We had just paid most of the bills at the hotel, and our gasoline bills, and we all had to pitch in and help him fix up his plane and get it back in flying condition; it caused some money problems."

Jepp had his own share of close calls. While flying an OX-5 Travelaire—which belonged to W. C. Bush, president of Bush Flying Service, Inc. and one of the owners of the Bell Aircraft Company of Vancouver, Washington—over the Columbia River one day, half of the eight cylinders suddenly quit. "I was over the Bridge of the Gods in the Columbia River Gorge on my way to Goldendale with a passenger," Jepp said. "I was about 7,000 feet when a bank of cylinders quit. There was no place to land down there, except down in the very swift-running current. I coaxed the airplane until I got right over the center of the Hood River."

Then the rest of the engine quit. "I knew I was going to have to set her down. I probably did one of the best jobs of flying I've ever done in my life. I was able to sideslip between a house and a big oak tree, over a fence, and was heading for a baseball field at the high school where a game was being played. Going in, I scraped the top of the trees. All the players scattered except the pitcher. He stood there on the mound, looking up at me heading straight for him. That was exactly where I was going to have to go. So when I kicked out of the slip, I just decided that if he didn't move, he would be in deep trouble, and if I didn't go in that direction, *I'd* be in deep trouble. I kept thinking he ought to move, but he didn't. I was coming in on an angle and the wings apparently went right over him. I never did know what happened to him—but I didn't hit him. It was absolutely dead stick."

Jepp said that the mechanics put in some new points and springs in the Burlington magneto and he proceeded on to Condon, Oregon, for an air show, which turned out to be a little gold mine. "I had to take off downhill and land uphill along a narrow road. That took quite a bit of precision flying. We made a lot of money that day."

Jepp had another close call while on a barnstorming tour near Prosser, in the Yakima Valley. "I took off around eight o'clock in the morning just south of Prosser. I only got up to 200 or 300 feet when the engine quit. So I went straight ahead and landed in a little back yard behind a house. I made a ground loop to the right, spun around, and was facing the back of the house, about thirty or forty feet away. The lady of the house was out there, washing clothes with a tub and one of those corrugated washboards. I can still see her with her hands down in the suds and looking at me with her mouth wide open. I must have been kind of a strange sight." [4]

Map of Jepp's travels while on the barnstorming circuit, 1926-1927.

Jepp would, on occasion, freelance for other flying circuses or assemble a small contingent of fliers himself to hit the county fairs, where stunt flying was always welcome and brought in huge crowds. "In 1928," he recalled, "I put a little group together of about three or four ships and planned a kind of flying circus up through Walla Walla and Baker, Oregon; Ontario and Weiser, Idaho; LaGrande, and Pasco, Wenatchee, Pendleton, Sunnyside, Yakima, and various places like that. Sometimes we'd go down to Silverton and Corvallis. It appeared to me that I was doing most of the organizing and directing of the group."

After this barnstorming tour ended, Jepp was flying back to Portland, exhausted. He landed on the new Swan-Allen Airport, to which Tex Rankin had moved his operation from Pearson Field. Jepp crawled out of the cockpit and saw Tex standing at the fence. "He hollered at me, so I went over and visited with him. He asked me if I would like to become an instructor for his flight school. In view of the fact that I was getting a little tired of bumming around on the barnstorming circuit, I accepted the job and stayed on for several months."

Jepp taught scores of people how to fly during his brief tenure as a flight instructor for Rankin. One of the most memorable pupils turned out to be a woman.

One day Tex Rankin pulled Jepp aside and pointed out a tall teenaged woman wearing a pair of high boots in the company's waiting room. Her name was Dorothy Hester of Portland. She was seventeen.

"She's been making parachute jumps to earn tickets to pay for flying lessons," Rankin told him. "You may as well take her up because she has plenty of tickets but she'll never learn to fly."

Jepp got her strapped into the Jenny he used for instruction and took off. "The first time I took her up with those heavy boots," he said, "she jammed down on the controls and made such a flat turn it almost threw me out of the cockpit. I made her take off the boots and get the feel of the airplane. God, what a gal. She could fly a plane upside down better than she could right side up." [5]

Dorothy Hester also went on to make a name for herself. During the summer of 1931, she barnstormed with a flying circus across thirty-eight states, became the first woman to fly special aerobatic maneuvers at the National Air Races, and at Omaha in May 1931 set a world record of fifty-six inverted snap rolls in an OX-5-powered plane and then set another record for performing sixty-nine consecutive outside loops. [6] On a copy of a publicity photo she sent to Jepp, she inscribed, "To my grouchy, indestructible instructor." [7]

1928 saw the field of aerial navigation take a major step forward. In October of that year the Aeronautics Branch of the Bureau of Standards developed a low-frequency radio navigation beacon system known as the Four Course Radio Range. On their cockpit-mounted radio receivers the pilots would hear transmitted Morse Code signals (dot-dash for "A" and dash-dot for "N"). If the pilot heard a steady tone, he knew he was flying on course ("on the beam"); if he heard either of the two Morse Code letters, he knew he was off course and needed to correct his direction. The system, as crude as it was, enabled pilots for the first time to navigate in any type of weather. [8]

In October 1928, the Rankin Flying Service was not doing well financially. Jepp's oldest son Jim said his father once told him that the number of flight students dropped off significantly in the autumn of 1928. "They had to lay off people because they just didn't have enough students." [9]

Because he was the youngest and lowest-ranking on the totem pole of instructors, Jepp perhaps saw the hand-writing on the wall and left Rankin Flying Service to seek his fortune elsewhere. "Mr. Rankin was very understanding about it," he said, "and wrote a nice letter of recommendation for me." [10]

Rankin's letter said, in part, "Although a young man, Mr. Jeppesen is an exceptionally good flight instructor and has been employed as such by the Rankin School of Flying for the past six months. Mr. Jeppesen leaves our employ on his own accord and we take pleasure in recommending him to anyone in need of a good transport pilot or flight instructor." [11]

Jepp said goodbye to his friends and his folks and headed south to San Francisco, where he got a job as a flight instructor for Summit Aircraft Company at Mills Field, then went to work briefly for West Coast Air Transport. "I stayed there three or four months," said Jepp, "and then I bought a Monocoupe—I think it was Pacific Finance Corporation that helped me buy it."

The Monocoupe, a small, sporty, closed-cockpit, high-wing aircraft manufactured by the W. L. Velie Company, a buggy and automaker in Moline, Illinois, was advertised as "the ultimate plane for the private flyer." Its flashy styling and speed (nearly 100 miles per hour with a fifty-five-horsepower engine) made it the sexiest aerial hot rod of its day. In 1928, at the National Air Races in Los Angeles, a Velie Monocoupe scored its first victory in close-course racing.

Jepp entered an aerobatic contest near San Francisco to show off what he and his plane could do. He won a trophy. "I made the most snaprolls from 2,000 feet down to about 200 feet in front of the grandstand. The little Monocoupe was a great airplane, and you could actually make precision snaprolls with it.

"Then I barnstormed down to southern California and across through Arizona and New Mexico to El Paso, Texas, and into Dallas. I had a lot of fun barnstorming but I couldn't make money with the Monocoupe. I don't know exactly why I bought it, except to have an airplane to buzz around the country in." [12]

Jepp arrived in Dallas on a warm November afternoon, the wheels of his Monocoupe barking on the runway at Love Field in front of a hangar with a huge "Fairchild Aerial Surveys" sign painted on it.

Certainly the Fairchild name was familiar to him, for it was one of the most storied new firms in aviation.

During World War I, the inventive Sherman "Shelly" Mills Fairchild, son of George Winthrop Fairchild (a New York Congressman and one of the founders of IBM), fascinated by flight and photography, developed an aerial camera better than anything that then existed. Although the Army temporarily lost interest in the camera when the war ended, Fairchild moved ahead and began the Fairchild Aerial Camera Corporation in 1920. (The maverick general Billy Mitchell used Fairchild's cameras in 1921 to document his tests to prove the bomber was superior to the battleship.)

In 1923 and 1924, Fairchild's company also created a giant photo-mosaic of Manhattan, taken from 16,000 feet, that showed every house, building, street, tree, and alleyway—and demonstrated the value of aerial mapping. This startling image helped to launch Fairchild Aerial Surveys, Inc., as the leading company in the business. [13]

Aerial surveys had come into their own after World War I. Author Roger Bilstein notes, "Aviation did usher in a new and refreshing view of the world for the geographer and geologist that could not be matched by anything else. For the landscape gardener, the architect, and the city planner, aerial views presented an unobstructed, comprehensive perspective that allowed a project to be properly visualized in relation to its actual surroundings." [14]

Fairchild's company was suddenly deluged with orders from various businesses in the western hemisphere, each wanting to document their holdings from the air, aid in planning, be used as evidence in legal proceedings, and explore new territory for future development. [15]

Shelly Fairchild realized that the biplanes of the day were inadequate for aerial mapping and thus set out to create an airplane manufacturing company in Farmingdale, New York, with a subsidiary in Canada, that could build his own high-wing aircraft complete with heated, enclosed cabins specifically for that purpose. The company was a roaring success. Actress Gloria Swanson christened his first model, the FC-1, and, following his historic trans-Atlantic flight, a Fairchild was used to accompany Charles Lindbergh and his *Spirit of St. Louis* on a goodwill tour around the country. The wealthy Fairchild also started snapping up aviation-related companies, such as the Caminez Engine Company, and launched an industrial conglomerate.

In January 1928 a Fairchild FC-2 made the first non-stop flight between New York and Miami. In June and July of that year, Fairchild was again in the news when Charles Collyer and John H. Mears flew a FC-2W-1 model, dubbed *The Spirit of New York*, around the world in twenty-three days and fifteen hours, setting a new record. (The duration would have been shorter except for the fact that the plane flew over land masses but was carried aboard ships when crossing the oceans.)

And, just in case anyone doubted the ruggedness of the Fairchild product, an FC-2W-2 was one of three planes Admiral Richard E. Byrd took on his famous 1928 expedition to the South Pole. The plane, named *The Stars and Stripes*, was used to rescue the crew of a Fokker Super Universal that had become stranded. The Fairchild was left behind when the expedition departed but was recovered and flown out, none the worse for wear, when the second expedition returned later. [16]

Jepp (right) and his friend Tony McKay with Jepp's Monocoupe, Dallas, Texas, 1928.
(E. B. Jeppesen collection)

Jepp may have dismissed any thoughts of joining such a prestigious firm while he taxied in front of the Fairchild hangar at Love Field and cut his engine. He was climbing out of the Monocoupe when he saw a handsome young Texan with his big hat tilted back and his hands on his hips. "He was a kid about my age—his name was Tony McKay. He looked me over a bit and said, 'Hey, partner, you sure look tired and hungry. You come with me.'

"Tony McKay was a mechanic for Fairchild. We became good friends, and I stayed with him for four or five months—I rented a room in the same home where he lived. I was flat broke at the time, so he got me a job instructing at Bill Long's flying school that was right next to the Fairchild hangar. Bill Long was 'Mr. Aviation' in Texas, particularly in Dallas.★ Texas was the home of the Signal Corps and the old army aviation gang, and there were lots of pilots around, so getting a job wasn't the easiest thing in the world, but I seemed to make out pretty well."

Jepp recalled that Tony McKay had a girlfriend, "a little school teacher that he was sparkin' somewhere ten or fifteen miles out in the country. He always wanted me to fly him over there above the schoolhouse about the time that school let out and do some snaprolls and loops. This one time I pulled the airplane up in a pretty tight loop. Tony was chewing tobacco and he swallowed the whole plug; I thought he was going to choke to death."

Despite his best efforts, Jepp didn't earn enough money instructing to allow him to keep making the payments on his Monocoupe. "While I was instructing for Bill Long in the Jennys, I was still trying to make a few passenger flights with my Monocoupe, but it just got to be too much. So one day Tony and I took the airplane apart and put it in a boxcar and I shipped it back to San Francisco by rail. Somewhat of a sad day. I never heard anything further from the bank, so I presume that that satisfied my obligations."

Fortunately, Jepp's flying abilities caught the eye of Fairchild's chief pilot, who offered him a job. "One day he asked me if I would like to

---

★ Major Willim F. "Bill" Long was a Great War veteran, ex-barnstormer, millionaire, star polo player, founder of three airlines, and owner of the Dallas Aviation School, which he started in the 1920s. (*Dallas Morning News*, 10/29/00)

fly one of their photographic ships, just go up for a ride. So I did, and it flew pretty well. One thing led to another and finally they asked me if I would ferry an airplane to New Orleans with their photographer, whose name was Oakes, and wait for a photographic pilot to come down from New York." But Oakes refused to fly with "that kid," meaning Jepp, and took another flight to New Orleans.

Jepp didn't care; he flew to New Orleans by himself in a Fairchild with a triangular fuselage and a J-4 engine. He said, "One of my arrangements with Fairchild was that they would allow me to take their airplane—a Liberty DH—and fly it for thirty minutes every day while I waited for the photographic pilot to arrive. Of course, Oakes would go out there with me to watch me fly and after a couple of days he decided I could fly pretty well. So he said, 'Tell you what we'll do. We'll go up and I'll show you how to do some photographic flying and break you in on this thing.' So he set up the camera and the rest of the equipment and we went up to practice awhile.

"We flew one of the jobs—I suppose we did twenty-five or thirty strips about fifteen miles wide. I flew back and forth as Oakes directed and I began to learn how to do it. He taught me how to keep a straight line, how to figure the twenty and thirty and forty percent overlap, how to listen for the click of the cameras so I would hold it steady about that time—all that stuff.

"One day we went out and flew the whole job. From 12,000 feet, we mapped everything from the Delta up to New Orleans and west for about fifty miles. Did it all in one day. We sent the film to Fairchild. Word came back saying, 'Excellent job. Perfect. Proceed to the next one.' So now I was a photographic pilot!"

Almost by default Jepp also became a second lieutenant in the

---

* The flight was the brainchild of Air Corps Commanding General Mason Patrick, and was designed to improve U.S. relations with Latin America. President Calvin Coolidge endorsed the idea and, on December 21, 1926, five Loening OA-1 amphibious observation planes left San Antonio, Texas, for the four-month, 22,000-mile trip to twenty-three countries. Tragedy struck over Buenos Aires, however, when two of the planes collided in mid-air, killing their crews. Three of the pilots on the flight would become generals during World War II: Ira Eaker, Muir Fairchild, and Ennis Whitehead. When the flight ended on May 2, 1927, in Washington D.C., it was hailed as one of the greatest feats of aviation; three weeks later Charles Lindbergh's solo crossing of the Atlantic relegated it to the back burner of aviation history. (www.nasm.si.edu/research/aero/aircraft/loening)

Photograph of New Orleans and Mississippi River taken in July 1929 from 1,500 feet, while Jepp was flying for Fairchild Aerial Survey, Inc. (Jepp drew the arrow to mark where striking transit workers pushed streetcars into the river.)
(E. B. Jeppesen collection)

Army Air Corps. One day, an army captain by the name of L. D. Weddington who, in 1926, had taken part in the historic Air Corps' Pan-American Goodwill Flight★ with a group of other military aviators, saw the Liberty DH being flown around Dallas by someone who was obviously proficient, made some inquiries, and found out it was Jepp.

"Weddington contacted me and wanted to know if I'd like to be in the Air Corps. Then he took me down and showed me all the airplanes which the Army Air Corps Reserve pilots flew. I said, 'You mean that I can come down here and fly these airplanes on Saturdays and Sundays?' That looked pretty good to me!"

Capt. L. D. Weddington. *(E. B. Jeppesen collection)*

It took no further incentives for Jepp to sign up. "I joined on a reserve basis," he said, "and got my commission. I remember that Weddington had this Sergeant Reynolds in a room with all the papers; he said to the sergeant, 'Now you sit down here and fill out all these papers and make sure Jepp gets a real good passing grade.' I never did a thing except sign my name. That's the way it worked." [17]

But military flying would not be a part of Jepp's career until many years into the future. Something else was beckoning on the horizon.

4: MEXICAN INTERLUDE

Fairchild Aerial Surveys soon found a special niche for Jepp's piloting skills: Mexico. America's southern neighbor had contracted with the company to do aerial mapping of the coast and parts of the interior—something that had not been done before.

In 1924, Tampico, on the gulf coast about 250 miles south of the tip of Texas, had become the site of Mexico's first major oil discovery. Suddenly a frenzy of oil-drilling activity took over that portion of the Gulf Coast, and rigs and derricks began sprouting like palm trees. Oil companies were searching everywhere for new fields, and aerial surveys became the way to explore the unmapped territory. [1]

Fairchild assigned Jepp their own specially designed plane—a Fairchild FC-2 with a Pratt & Whitney Wasp engine and wings that could be folded back—and sent him down to Tampico with an aerial photographer, an Englishman named Sidney Bonnick. The identification of the plane was "BADW." Jepp remembered the letters with a mnemonic device— "Bonnick Always Drinks Whiskey." [2]

Jepp recalled, "Bonnick and I lived in a house in Tampico, across the Pánuco River at the Huasteco Oil Company. We worked out of there for about eight months, photographing the land, photographing for oil. We had a swimming pool and a Chinese cook we called Santiago, who was also the houseboy who kept the place clean."

"Sometimes Santiago'd tell us he was going to go into Tampico and buy some chickens or pheasants for dinner. Well, when we'd leave for the day he would open the screen doors to the porch and coax some wild chickens or pheasants onto the porch and then he'd kill them. That's what we'd have for dinner, and they were delicious. We knew he

Jepp perched on the wing of his Fairchild FC-2 in Mexico while employed by
Fairchild Aerial Surveys, Inc., 1929. *(E. B. Jeppesen collection)*

Hangars at Tampico airport, about 1929. *(E. B. Jeppesen collection)*

hadn't gone into Tampico. We'd kid him about that and he'd get that little grin like the Chinese do so well, and he'd give you a little twinkle
from his eyes. We had a lot of fun with him. We took good care of him,
paid him well, and he took real good care of us. But he must have
thought we were a strange breed." [2]

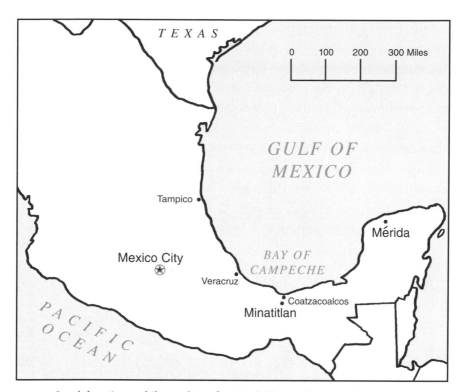

Jepp's locations while working for Fairchild Aerial Surveys in Mexico.

Jepp was issued a Mexican pilot's license, number 33, and was given an assignment to photograph a large swath of the Gulf coast. "My first assignnment was to fly a twenty-mile-wide strip down the east coast from Brownsville through Tampico, Veracruz, and on down to British Honduras," he said. [3]

Elrey Jeppesen was one of the first pilots to rely on his cockpit instruments. Of course, back then, most aircraft had limited instrumentation—usually just an altimeter, airspeed indicator, and a bank-and-turn indicator—if they had any at all.

"Not even a compass or a radio," Jepp said. "I got to be quite proficient at instrument flying. My photographer, Mr. Bonnick, did write a statement to the effect that I usually practiced instrument flying on the return flight from a photographic mission. As a matter of fact, I think on three or four occasions I flew instruments from Mexico City to Tampico. We flew into clouds, and I made a dead reckoning on Tampico and estimated the time and so forth, and let down; we were pretty close. But it required careful precision instrument flying with only the minimum instruments." It would be a skill that would serve him well later on.

After being in Tampico for a few months, Jepp and Bonnick received orders to relocate to an oil-refinery town called Minatitlan, 135 miles southeast of Veracruz, in another part of Mexico's growing petrochemical region. "We wanted to take Santiago with us, but he wouldn't go down there. 'Too wild,' he said. 'Too many Indians.' He wanted to live long enough to go back to China one day."

Minatitlan, Mexico, circa 1929. *(E. B. Jeppesen collection)*

The conditions around Minatitlan in 1930 were rather primitive—and dangerous. The Mexican Revolution had recently ended and, "There was a Royal Dutch Shell refinery about twenty miles up the Coatzacoalcos River," Jepp said. "They had no airport, so they grubbed out a strip there for us to land on and put up an old hangar to keep the rain off the airplane. But they wouldn't let us go down there until the Mexican government had sent a company of soldiers down to secure the landing strip. There was a lot of Indian and hardline, left-over revolutionary activity going on. It took them over six weeks to get there from Mexico City. When they arrived, the soldiers had their wives and kids, dogs, goats, and chickens with them—and the soldiers were bare-footed! One second lieutenant was in charge of the whole shebang. He was the only one with shoes!"

On occasion, the British military, which had bases in the Caribbean, would sail over to Mexico and march their men down to Minatitlan to cool revolutionary ardor. Jepp said, "I can still see the captain of the British gunboat marching up the middle of this old town with dust five inches thick, with six marines alongside. They were all in step with their guns over their shoulders and dust flying everywhere. The captain would very quietly explain to the mayor that if anything happened to the refinery, there would be no town the next day."

The refinery workers built a T-hangar for the Fairchild aircraft but Jepp constantly worried that the soldiers were going to set the plane on fire. "When I put my plane away in the hangar, the Mexicans would get into the back of the hangar in the shade and build their fires and cook their tortillas, and I could never break them of that. The airplane I was flying was cloth-covered and if it ever caught fire it would be gone in nothing flat. I never won that battle; as soon as I would leave, they'd crawl right back into the hangar and start their fires." [4]

There was also an ongoing fear of bandits. Talmadge E. "Tal" Miller, a former B-25 pilot during World War II who would become one of Jepp's closest friends in the 1970s, recalled Jepp telling him that the Fairchild had folding wings that doubled as a security device. "The reason they made it with folding wings," said Miller, "was because the bandits would try to steal everything. Jepp could fold the wings and push it back into the bush when they were done flying for the day and hide it from the bandits." [5]

The thirty-foot-long FC-2, with its forty-four-foot wingspan, was technologically advanced for its day. It had an enclosed, heated cabin, and two men could fold the wings, supported by V-shaped struts, in about two minutes. Unfolding them and returning them to flight configuration took about the same amount of time. Large Yale padlocks hung down in clear view so the pilot knew the wings were locked in place. [6]

Jepp's and Bonnick's first assignment at Minatitlan was to fly a strip five miles inland and three miles out over the ocean. "The maps I had just showed rivers running into the ocean," Jepp said, "and the towns on the borders, and unknown territory on the Isthmus of Tehuantepec. We were told that if we found a river, we were to fly a twenty-mile strip up the river, turn around, and come back. That's what we did."

With each passing day, Bonnick became more and more impressed with the twenty-two-year-old pilot's flying ability. Jepp modestly noted, "Bonnick said I was the best pilot he had ever flown with. He said that the day we flew into a blind canyon and I turned the plane over on its back and looped out of the place. It was kind of a half-assed loop. But he said he'd go anywhere with me."

Jepp and Bonnick had quarters at the refinery, but the conditions were less than luxurious. "We kept all the screens on the windows in our house buttoned down tight to keep out the bugs," Jepp recalled. "But in the morning someone would come in and sweep out all the scorpions and spiders and everything.

"The place was dangerous. One morning we heard a commotion at about four or five in the morning, looked out a window, and saw two Chinamen out there with their throats slit."

Navigation at that time was a hit-or-miss proposition. The duo had been directed to fly to Mexico City, but as they got closer they found the capitol was heavily blanketed in fog, or "socked in," and they could not find the airport. Using a questionable compass and the primitive maps they had, Jepp and Bonnick decided to head for Acapulco on the West Coast and lie around on the beach until the clouds cleared. "I did not know if we were going to end up in Japan or North America," he chuckled. "We finally spotted the coast and it all worked out fine."

Early instrumentation was as primitive as the maps. "The altimeters weren't very accurate in those days, if they worked at all," Jepp said. "Our altimeter was just broken down into one-hundred-foot

Jepp, on the left, and and his Fairchild photographer, Sidney Bonnick.
(E. B. Jeppesen collection)

increments. At some point we got this big Kolsman altimeter that was about eight inches across and was super sensitive. I went down to the blacksmith shop and cut up an old inner tube into big rubber bands and strapped it to the floor in the plane next to my right leg. It worked pretty well."

Knowing one's altitude was vital on many of the jobs. "On occasion," Jepp recalled, "the oil company would send a geologist and a sketch artist up with us. We were to fly 100 or 200 feet above the jungle so they could see where to lay a pipeline—whether there were any hills, rivers, or whatnot in there. Bonnick would shoot some obliques out the window. It was fun and I got paid $400 a month."

On one mission Jepp and Bonnick were taking photos over the dense jungle of the Yucatan Peninsula at 18,000 feet when Jepp saw little puffs of white smoke appearing below him; he didn't think much about it until it came time to land.

"We were making a big turn about five miles from this airstrip and coming in for a landing when a bullet came right up through the bottom of the cockpit and took the corner off our altimeter! Indians had been down there all day long shooting at my plane! At 18,000 feet they couldn't hit us, but when we were coming in for a landing they could!" The next day Jepp had a welder add a couple sheets of boiler plate to armor the bottom of the fuselage.

Jepp became frustrated with trying to conduct business in Mexico. "Everything that was happening down there in Old Mexico seemed to be under the table and dishonest and pretty crooked," he said. "I wasn't getting anything done. I couldn't get my airplane pushed in, or gassed, or get any service very fast. It was always slow—it would take me an hour just to get the plane gassed. I had to do all the mechanical work myself—the greasing of the rocker arms, the oil changes, and taking apart and cleaning the carburetor."

"Finally, one day Bonnick, who was forty-two years old, worldly, and one of the world's great photographers, put his arm around me and said, 'Jepp, you come with me. I'm going to teach you the ways of the world.' Well, in a couple or three months, I was able to get most anything done. I could spot who was boss, who had to be paid off, and so forth. It was an entirely different way of life than I, coming out of a starchy little Danish family up north, had ever experienced."

Jepp took a vacation back to see his folks and dropped down to Oakland, California, where he stayed for a few days with Jack Parshall, the pilot in Portland who had been so impressed with Jepp's desire to fly.

At that time, Boeing was more than an airplane manufacturer; the company also ran its own airline, Boeing Air Transport (BAT), which had a contract with the Post Office to carry mail between Oakland/San Francisco, Reno, Salt Lake City, Cheyenne, Omaha, and Chicago. Jack Parshall was

Even in the hot and sultry climate of tropical Mexico, Jepp usually wore a tie.
(E. B. Jeppesen collection)

flying the airmail on the Boeing leg between Oakland and Reno.

Jepp said that the idea of flying the mail suddenly sounded more exciting than flying photographic runs, and he asked Parshall how to get a job with the service. Parshall said that Harold T. "Slim" Lewis, Boeing Air Transport's chief pilot, was the man who hired the pilots. Parshall told Jepp that Slim was in Reno and offered to take Jepp on a mail run in a Boeing 40-B2 to Reno. Jepp thought that was a very good idea.

Jepp climbed into the plane and Parshall took off, heading east. "I was riding on top of the mail pit," recalled Jepp, "taking in all the scenery from Oakland to Sacramento, and on up and over the Sierras. I remember Jack got over the roughest part of the mountains between Sacramento and Reno and then he pulled the spark back to make the engine backfire two or three times, trying to make me think we had engine trouble. Then he looked at me to see how I was taking it, because there was certainly no place to land. He had a big grin on his face,

Boeing 40-B2 Air Mail plane. The aircraft had a 44-foot wingspan and 525-horsepower Pratt & Whitney "Hornet" radial engine. The plane cost $24,500 new and weighed three tons fully loaded, but the maximum air speed was only 132 miles per hour. Jepp remembered that flying the open-cockpit craft was a chilling experience. "Even wearing double boots and double mittens you would freeze," he said.
(E. B. Jeppesen collection)

showing his white teeth. I can see it to this day. I just motioned for him to push the spark ahead. He got a big kick out of it; he was always full of those kinds of tricks."

Parshall and Jepp landed at Reno, where they learned that Slim was over at the Newhouse Hotel engaging in his favorite off-duty activity: a big card game.

At six feet, four inches tall, Slim Lewis was a legend among the early pilots. He had begun his aviation career in 1916 at age twenty-two and, after taking flying lessons in Curtiss Jennys, became one of the first half-dozen licensed pilots in the United States. During World War I, he was a civilian instructor and test pilot and, in 1919, Lewis was hired by the

Harold T. "Slim" Lewis, circa 1924. *(E. B. Jeppesen collection)*

U.S. Air Mail Service. On July 1, 1924, he flew the first regular night mail flight between Omaha and Cheyenne.

Many stories are told about Slim Lewis. There were the usual forced landings in cow pastures when his unreliable engines gave out. Then there was the time he rammed his plane into the kitchen of a farmhouse; another time he rammed his plane into a bull. Once, while flying the eighty miles between Scottsbluff, Nebraska, to Cheyenne in the winter, he was forced to land in fields and pastures four times because the carburetor kept icing up. Finally he gave up, lugged the mail sacks to a farmhouse, borrowed a wagon and a team of horses, and drove the last four miles to the Cheyenne airport.

Jepp and Jack Parshall entered the hotel and went up to Slim's room. "They were playing poker," Jepp recalled, "and the place was so full of smoke you couldn't see across the room. Somehow Jack spotted Slim and he went over and introduced me. I told Slim that I wanted to join Boeing and fly the mail run, and he said, 'Well, I'll tell you what I'll do. I'll give you a flight check tomorrow afternoon over in Salt Lake.' Anyone who ever went to work for the Boeing Air Transport Company had to take a flight check from Slim Lewis."

There was only one problem: Jepp didn't have a way to get to Salt Lake. Slim told him to hitch a ride in the co-pilot seat with Al DeGarmo, a pilot who would be making the run in a Ford Tri-Motor at midnight.

Jepp showed up at the airport at the appointed hour. DeGarmo, deciding to have a little sport with the young Jepp, told him to get into the right-hand seat. "Now listen, you little son-of-a-bitch," DeGarmo, whom Jepp described as being a "big, strong, rugged-looking guy—a big gorilla," growled. "Don't you touch a goddamn thing." Jepp felt himself shrinking into the leather seat and decided he wouldn't do or say anything on the trip.

Once the Tri-Motor had lumbered over the mountains, DeGarmo looked at Jepp with a big grin. "You like to fly?" he asked.

"Yes."

"Take over."

Jepp grabbed the controls. He was familiar with Tri-Motors, having flown them before; DeGarmo was suitably impressed. The older pilot landed the ship during an intermediate stop at Elko, Nevada, and taxied over to Bill Wunderlich, the airport manager. As they were exiting the aircraft, DeGarmo yelled to Wunderlich, "Hey, Bill, what do you think about our new high-school co-pilot?" Both men had a good laugh and Jepp blushed. "I wished I had grown a mustache to make me look older," he said. "We proceeded along to Salt Lake. Al DeGarmo and I later became very close and dear friends; he helped me in many ways."

Al DeGarmo, circa 1926. *(E.B. Jeppesen collection)*

Bright and early the next morning, Jepp was at the airport waiting for Slim Lewis. Slim finally showed up and talked with Jepp for a few minutes. He had a single-engine Boeing 40-B mail plane, number 270, with a dual cockpit that they would use for the flight test. Lewis climbed into the front seat while Jepp took the rear cockpit. [7]

The Boeing 40-B was only slightly larger and heavier than Jepp's old Jenny, but instead of a 90-horsepower engine, the 40-B sported a 525 h.p. Pratt & Whitney "Hornet" engine—and Jepp loved it. Of the 40-B, a former 40-B pilot said in 1957, "This model had two mail compartments and a forward cabin for two passengers....The 40-B4 is the most remembered airmail plane of the airlines era in the years 1928 through 1932. The reason the 40 is most remembered is because it was used on all the air lines in the West and flew on numerous air lines in the East and was produced in the then unheard-of quantity of 76. This was the largest production by far of a commercial model for airmail service at that time."

The 40-B had enough room in the mail compartment to hold a cubic yard of mail. The old 40-B pilot noted, "We crammed [it] down in the space. It was dangerous and against company rules to jump up and down on the mail sacks while the propeller was turning. If there was a sack of mail left over, we would...throw it on the lap of a passenger.... Very often the passenger would carry the mail on his lap all the way to the next stop, considering it an honor to do so. Those that were in on the gag would put the sack of mail on the floor and rest their feet on it." [8]

Jepp recalled, "The 40-B was a pretty big plane, about the same size as a Liberty DH. Slim got the engine going and gave me the controls. I took a look at the wind sock, taxied out, and checked as many things as I could. I wiggled the stick and he said, 'Okay,' and away we went. I made a good takeoff, went up, and did some air work. The thing flew so much better than a Liberty DH. I made some vertical banks, took a look at the wind sock from upstairs, and came in and landed. Gosh, I made a slick landing—it was even hard to tell when we touched down. As we were taxiing back in, Slim hollered over his shoulder, 'Let's go up again and go around a couple more times.' I hollered 'Okay' back at him."

Jepp made a few more turns around the airport, giving Slim an idea of what he could do without resorting to any extreme aerobatics, then descended for a landing. "The airplane was flying so well—it had a great feel to it," Jepp noted. "When I approached the fence at the end of the runway, I slipped it just like we used to do while barnstorming and set it right down on the apron in front of the hangar.

"Well, I guess Slim thought that was pretty good, because in the years to come, I could do no wrong by him. Slim would send me on some of the dangdest missions you ever heard of, and I often wondered why. One time later, when I was living in Cheyenne, they called me around ten o'clock one night and said they had a couple over at the Rock Springs airport that Slim wanted me to fly to Salt Lake that night. Well, I went out there and flew to Rock Springs and picked them up in the 40B. It wasn't the easiest thing in the world. The Rock Springs airport was down in a ravine just south of the city—a pretty tight squeeze—with mountains all around. When you were going to take off at night, the field manager would drive his car down to the very end of the runway and we'd follow him with the airplane to get a good long run so we could make a quick turn before we got to the mountains." Jepp made it into Salt Lake that night without mishap. "Everything went great," he said. "My passengers turned out to be Mr. and Mrs. Bill Boeing!"*

Many years later, while Jepp and Slim were playing golf in Palm Springs, California, he asked the chief pilot why he had chosen him to fly the president of the company on the night flight. "You knew how inexperienced I was," Jepp said to Slim. "I didn't know the route or anything."

Slim replied, "I knew one thing—you were sober. It was a clear night and you could see for miles and there wasn't much of a problem following the beacons."

Jepp said that Lewis hired him on the spot but that he would have to be on reserve status, as there were no openings at the moment. "I hung around there for about two weeks. They had only one single-engine airplane going back and forth between Chicago and Oakland. I thought, 'Well, this isn't going to amount to anything as a transportation system for some time.'" Jepp did make a few runs, but only as co-pilot, and he felt his flying skills were going to waste.

Meanwhile, Fairchild kept pressuring Jepp to come back to work for them, so he told Lewis he was returning to aerial surveys; Slim

---

* William E. Boeing was a legendary aviation pioneer. Born in Detroit on October 1, 1881, to a wealthy family, he attended Yale then moved to Washington state to enter the logging business. In Seattle in 1915, he learned to fly and bought a seaplane, but was unhappy with its design and construction and decided he could build a better one. Joining up with a friend, Navy Lieutenant Conrad Westervelt, the two built their own seaplane and, in 1916, went into the aircraft business under the name Pacific Aero Products; the name was changed to the Boeing Airplane Company the following year. During World War I, the company made trainer seaplanes and prospered. In 1921, the company's future seemed assured when it won a large contract to build pursuit planes for the army. Then, in 1927, the newly-formed Boeing Air Transport Company was awarded the Chicago-San Francisco airmail route. Two years later, Boeing teamed up with the aircraft-engine firm of Pratt and Whitney to form the United Aircraft and Transport Company, forerunner of United Airlines. (www.michiganaviation.org)

wished him luck and told him he would always have a job with Boeing Air Transport. Jepp thanked Slim and headed back to Mexico.

In October 1929, the stock market went into a tailspin and crashed, taking most of the world's economy with it. Very quickly the shock wave and ripple effect was felt around the globe as capital dried up, businesses failed, millions of people lost their jobs, banks foreclosed on property—then went out of business themselves when people rushed in, demanding their money back.

Flying over the dense, remote jungles of the Yucatan, Jepp was barely aware of the global financial calamity. He had plenty of work to keep his thoughts occupied. But the work eventually turned boring and he began thinking about flying the mail again. He contacted Slim Lewis, who invited him to come back to the States. "BAT had put on a couple more runs," Jepp said, "and they had the big Tri-Motors. Slim Lewis hired me again and I flew the very first Boeing 80 Tri-Motor with a stewardess on board. It was May 15, 1930, on the Salt Lake to Reno route." [9]

If Jepp was known for nothing else, his name would have been in the history books as being the pilot of that segment of the Oakland-Chicago flight that included the world's first stewardess, Ellen Church.

Miss Church, a pilot and registered nurse, proposed the idea to the management of Boeing Air Transport. At first she applied for a pilot's job, but the industry wasn't yet ready for such a ground-breaking experiment. BAT liked the idea of stewardesses, though, believing that the publicity surrounding such a move would be positive and immeasurable. A trial period of three months was initiated, and Miss Church was named Chief Stewardess and put in charge of hiring and training.

Only attractive, unmarried women with nursing degrees were eligible for the job and their employment was immediately controversial. Many of the pilots (other than Jepp) refused to speak to them, and the jealous wives of BAT pilots demanded that the airline fire them. But the passengers were quite happy with them and the idea soon caught on with other airlines.

The 1930 BAT *Manual for Stewardesses* outlined the duties and responsibilities of the young ladies, including the requirement that the stewardesses render "a rigid military salute" to "the captain and co-pilot as they go aboard and deplane before the passengers." [10]

Other changes, even more profound for the nation's air carriers, were taking place in 1930, and the catalyst for change was Walter Folger Brown, the Postmaster General in the new Hoover Administration. Brown was in charge of awarding airmail contracts and, as such, wielded enormous power and influence. By the simple stroke of a pen, Brown could either enrich a carrier or send it plunging into oblivion. He also quickly realized that many airlines had been abusing the airmail system and set out to rectify the problem.

The carriers were paid based on the weight of the mail being carried. It didn't take long for some unscrupulous operators to discover that a few bricks placed in a mail bag would increase the weight—and their profits. Other airlines also learned that they could send hundreds of cards and letters to themselves (each for nine cents postage) and bring in revenues of twice that amount. The questionable practices soon became widespread. [11]

Brown ran a tight ship and was appalled by these and other signs of rampant chaos and inefficiency he saw within the airline industry. For example, United Aircraft/BAT could carry New York–addressed mail from San Francisco to Chicago but was not allowed to continue on to New York; in Chicago the mail had to be off-loaded from the BAT planes and loaded into NAT (National Air Transport) aircraft for the rest of the eastward journey. The problems were akin to the early days of the nation's railroads, when it seemed that each railroad company had tracks of a different gauge, requiring the constant unloading and re-loading of freight that needed to be hauled by more than one carrier.

There was no overall control of airlines, no one—not even the Commerce Department—with the power to tell the carriers what routes they could and couldn't fly. Nor could anyone, it seemed, encourage the airlines to wean themselves off the government airmail contracts and put more emphasis on boosting their passenger business. But, given his authority as the supreme bestower of airmail contracts, as author Henry Ladd Smith points out, Brown appointed himself "czar of civil aviation" and commenced to take drastic action. [12]

The Postmaster General clamped down on the abuses in the airmail-contract system by making the carrying of the mail less profitable. He wrote a piece of legislation, which was attached as the third amendment (known as the McNary-Watres Bill after its sponsors) to the Kelly Bill, or Air Mail Act of 1925, which had inaugurated the practice of granting airmail contracts to private airlines.

As Smith puts it, "Brown realized that the Post Office Department was the agency best fitted to aid commercial aviation. The Department of Commerce was doing its best by building the lighted airways, which the air lines could not possibly have financed, but only the post office could give the payments providing the nice balance of government aid and encouragement to private enterprise. Brown envisioned a system of strongly financed, competitive, transcontinental airlines intersected by a network of feeder routes." [13]

According to the McNary-Watres Bill, airlines would no longer be paid by the pound but by the amount of space available per plane for mail. This, Brown cleverly surmised, would force the airlines to buy larger planes, and larger planes would mean more space for passengers. To ensure greater comfort and safety, the bill promised that the Post Office Department would grant larger subsidies to those airlines with planes that had more than one engine, installed two-way radio equipment, and invested in navigation aids. Airmail contracts would still be awarded to the lowest bidder—provided that the bidder was an established entity and had proven itself to be responsible, reliable, and in sound financial health. Eventually, Brown hoped, the revenue generated by passenger fares would replace to a great extent the airlines' feeding at the government trough.

Perhaps the most amazing part of the McNary-Watres bill was that it actually worked the way Brown envisioned it. McNary-Watres boosted airline passenger traffic—and gave the czar of civil aviation nearly dictatorial powers over the airlines. Not everyone was pleased, of course. Many smaller carriers complained bitterly that the bill gave the larger carriers an unfair advantage—which it did, but this was also part of Brown's overall scheme. He was concerned by the growing profusion of small carriers and felt the nation would be better served if there were several large, well-run airlines rather than scores of little "mom-and-pop" carriers going hither, thither, and yon.

To his critics Brown responded, "Helping some little fellow make good his losses for a few years [with airmail subsidies] and have him no further along than when he started—there was nothing in that; and those were the matters in my talks with them that they did not quite get my point. They seemed to think that I was trying to foster an octopus, whereas what I was trying to do was to get somebody with a big enough personnel, with management and money back of it to test this thing out and see whether it was possible to get an air transport company that could live on its own, then there would be plenty of competition."

If a large and a small carrier both bid on the same route, Brown saw them as having to negotiate, with no guarantee that the route would go to the lowest bidder. Indeed, Brown believed that the route could very well be awarded to the *highest* bidder if he and he alone felt that that carrier were the more financially stable of the two. [14]

As a consequence, during an intense period of wrangling and consolidation that lasted from May to June 1930, Brown summoned the heads of a select group of airlines to his office for what was later dubbed by reporter Fulton Lewis the "Spoils Conferences" and told them he would assist them in redrawing the national airline map—and decide who got to fly the routes.

United/BAT, which had through stock purchases of its rival NAT gained control of NAT, was the first granted the right to fly cross-country.★

★ In 1931 Boise-based Varney Air Service and Vern Gorst's Pacific Air Transport were both acquired by United.

Brown did not want one airline to have a coast-to-coast monopoly, so he awarded Transcontinental Air Transport the central route from New York to California, via St. Louis and Pittsburgh. The airline originally was a combination of air and rail transport; since TAT did not fly at night, the passengers continued on their journey by overnight Pullman cars. Brown insisted that TAT combine with Western Air Express, which had considerable night-flying experience. The merged airline was renamed Transcontinental and Western Air, or TWA.

Next, Eastern Air Transport was granted the contract for the lucrative New York-Washington route, dooming its low-cost regional rival, Ludington Air Lines. American Airways also came out of the smoke-filled room victorious, holding the contract to fly the southern transcontinental route that linked New York and Los Angeles by way of Washington, Atlanta, Dallas, and Oklahoma City.

By Brown's standards, the airline industry was now neat and tidy, just the way he had intended it to be. [15]

In late 1930 a bank in Portland was threatening to foreclose on Jepp's parents' home because his father was $900 in arrears. Jepp contacted the bank and told them that he would send them $500 immediately and the remainder in a month. "I sent it up," he said, "and Mother and Dad kept their home. In 1930, $900 was a heck of a lot of money." The fear of being destitute was a fear that never left Jepp.

Jepp flew for BAT until February 1931, then decided to quit. "I was just a mixed-up kid, I guess," said Jepp. "It was back down to Mexico for me."

But all had not gone well for Fairchild in the interim; the Depression was taking its toll on it and almost every other company. "1931 is when everything collapsed," said Jepp. "Fairchild had about $12 million in contracts and everything was canceled. They closed their Dallas office where twenty-two cartographers and photogrammetric people had been working. They shut down American Photo Supplies, their Mexico City business, and left only two people in Los Angeles. Bonnick went back to New York. I wound up in St. Paul, Minnesota."

Fairchild salvaged one remaining contract: four groups that went together—a telephone company, a power company, a highway department, and an irrigation district. Jepp said, "Fairchild sent a Chicago photographer to work with me on this project. We mapped from Duluth to St. Paul to Eau Claire, Wisconsin. When that was done, I flew the plane back to Chicago and turned it in."

Jepp talked to the company president, Sherman Fairchild, by phone. According to Jepp, "Mr. Fairchild offered that if I would come to New York, he would make sure that I got through college. He said, 'In the meantime, you can fly enough to keep your hand in. If there's a mapping job and you want to go out on it, you can. The main thing is, I want to give you the opportunity to get through college.' He also said one other thing: 'This Depression won't start to ease until somewhere in '36 or '37.' He was about right on that."

Jepp wasn't interested in going to college, however, so he thanked Mr. Fairchild and looked around for something else that could utilize his talents.★

He drove back to Cheyenne from St. Paul and there heard that a Tulsa-based airline, S.A.F.E.way, (the "S.A.F.E." stood for Southwest Air

---

★ The aerial survey company was acquired by Aero Services, a Philadelphia-based aerial-mapping firm. The rest of the Fairchild corporation weathered the Great Depression and in 1939 acquired the Clark Duramold Company; eventually Howard Hughes's famed "Spruce Goose" transport plane would utilize the company's patented method of building airframes using a composite of layers of plywood soaked with hot resin adhesive and bonded under pressure. The company also built the M-62 trainer that was used to train pilots during World War II under the PT-19 and PT-26 "Cornell" designations. Fairchild's main contribution to the post-war effort was the design and production of the C-82 "Packet" cargo plane and its successor, the C-119 "Flying Boxcar," which was later modified into a gunship for use during the Vietnam War.

In the 1950s Fairchild got into the semi-conductor business and this segment was later acquired by National Semiconductor. In 1961 Fairchild became Fairchild-Stratos Corporation and built meteoroid detection satellites and cameras used on Apollo space missions. In 1964 they bought Hiller Helicopters but sold the company back to Stanley Hiller in 1973. It also acquired Republic Aviation in 1964 and built the A-10 Thunderbolt between 1975 and 1984. In addition to taking over several other aviation-related firms, Fairchild went into partnership with SAAB-Scania to produce the SAAB 340 airliner. In 1987, Fairchild went out of the aircraft-manufacturing business but still operates in a number of aerospace-related industries. (www.centennialofflight.gov/essay/Aerospace/Fairchild/Aero25)

Fast Express), was still in business and was one of the few airlines hiring pilots. He decided to give it a shot. [16]

S.A.F.E.way had been established in April 1929 by Bob Cantrell and the outspoken oil tycoon Erle P. Halliburton. S.A.F.E.way's routes radiated spoke-like from Tulsa to Dallas, Fort Worth, Kansas City, and St. Louis, to which passengers were flown by a fleet of nine, fourteen-seater Ford Tri-Motors. But Halliburton had bigger ambitions. Although S.A.F.E.way charged some of the highest ticket prices around, it still was not breaking even, and Halliburton felt being awarded a transcontinental route and a modest airmail subsidy would help it turn a profit.

In November 1929, Halliburton made a low bid for the airmail route between New York and Los Angeles and thought S.A.F.E.way, in conjunction with its affiliate Southern Skylines, deserved to get it. Postmaster General Walter Brown thought otherwise, and the two men locked horns, Brown rejecting S.A.F.E.way's application because of a lack of night-flying experience by Halliburton's pilots.

As a result of the rebuff, the outraged Halliburton publicly announced that he was willing to blow every competing bid out of the sky. Henry Ladd Smith writes, "On November 21 [1929], Halliburton upset the apple-cart by offering to carry the mail all the way across the country. S.A.F.E.way and its affiliate, Southern Skyways, would carry, not only special airmail, but first-class mail as well, from New York to Los Angeles—and for payment that would have toppled the whole airmail rate structure. At this time airmail was still being carried at the per-pound rate." Halliburton told Brown that S.A.F.E.way would carry the mail the three thousand miles for $2.10 a pound, "whereas, he pointed out, it cost the government in 1929 $8.77 to fly a pound of mail to Los Angeles from Washington and $5.77 per pound by way of the Chicago, Omaha, and Salt Lake route."

Naturally, such behavior on his part did not stand Halliburton in good stead with Postmaster General Brown, and the two became bitter enemies. Although not invited to the May and June "Spoils Conferences" meetings in Washington, where air routes were handed out to Brown's favorites in the industry, Halliburton crashed the meetings and proceeded to loudly heckle Brown. Smith notes, "Halliburton was an utter nuisance to the Postmaster General.... By now Halliburton was upsetting all the schemes and calculations of the [Post Office] department, for his threatened underbidding had the whole industry in a turmoil. He was flitting like a banshee through the corridors of the old Post Office building. Once or twice Assistant Postmaster General [Walter Irving] Glover all but had him ejected bodily. Halliburton only continued his heckling. He made accusations of an embarassing nature. He wrote indignant letters to influential political leaders. 'I will ruin you, if it is the last act of my life,' Mr. Glover is charged with saying. 'You have tried to buck this thing all the way through, and you are not going to do it.'" But Halliburton was convinced that he would. [17]

After the McNary-Watres Act was passed a few months later, Halliburton studied every word of it and, as R.E.G. Davies points out, "could not find a trace of a reference to night flying. From then on there was no holding him. He wrote to politicians, pointing this out, threatened court action, suggested an investigation into the Post Office Department, and made it clear that he would involve the President of the United States if necessary." [18]

With knowledge of this clash of titans no doubt in the back of his mind, it took considerable courage for Jepp to approach the man who had taken on the czar of civil aviation. But approach him he did after crafting a simple, yet ingenious, plan.

According to Jepp, every out-of-work pilot seemed to know that Cantrell and Halliburton were going to be in Dallas on a given day and, of course, every pilot was doing everything he could think of to get an interview, or at least an audience, with them. "I didn't think I had much of a chance," Jepp said, but he knew one of the bellhops at the Baker Hotel, where the duo was staying, and wangled his way into checking into a room directly across the hall from theirs.

"I kept my door open by a few inches and waited for them to come in," he admitted. "I was going to force an opportunity to make my pitch to just the two of them. They came in at about twelve-thirty that night. I rapped on the door and Erle opened it. I told him who I was and what I wanted to do, so he invited me in. They were both in their pajamas.

"I made my pitch—it went well and they were very receptive. Finally, Bob Cantrell said, 'Well, why don't you fly up to Tulsa tomorrow or the next day and I'll give you a flight test up there. I think we can use you.'"

The next day Jepp flew a borrowed plane up to Tulsa while battling a stiff, fifty-mile-per-hour wind. "When I landed I had to keep the tail up in the air just to keep the plane on the ground. I saw Mr. Halliburton and Bob Cantrell over by their hangar, waving at me. They had the doors open, so I taxied right into the hangar. Larry Fritz, the S.A.F.E.way operations manager, happened to be there, too. He was awfully nice to me. He said, 'You're hired! Anyone who can fly that little mosquito in this kind of weather must know what they're doing.' So I suddenly had a job with S.A.F.E.way as co-pilot on Ford Wasp Tri-Motors.

Ford Tri-Motor photographed in 1927 at Lowry Field, near Denver. The graphics on the fuselage read "Rapid Air Lines," a small, short-lived carrier that served the Rocky Mountain Region in the 1920s. *(© Sea Bird Publishing, Inc. 2001. All rights reserved)*

William Boeing shown making the first international airmail delivery between Vancouver, British Columbia, and Seattle, Washington, March 3, 1919. The plane behind him is the Boeing Model C. *(Courtesy Boeing)*

"Unfortunately, some of my friends from Portland were upset that I did not get them jobs, too. As a matter of fact, I tried. I did arrange for them to have interviews, but they were not hired and, of course, it was my fault as far as they were concerned. I don't think they fully realized what a chore it was for me just to get the job. The job was interesting for about a day or two. After a while, though, it got a little boring."

Jepp moved from Dallas to Tulsa and was working at S.A.F.E.way★ for only a brief period when a new door opened for him. Jepp received a telegram from an official at Varney Air Service, a company headquartered in Boise, Idaho.★★ Varney needed to borrow some pilots from Boeing to fly the Portland-Seattle route; Slim Lewis replied that he had none to spare, but he knew of a kid who had been flying aerial photography jobs in Mexico and might be interested. Always looking for a new challenge, Jepp jumped at the chance.

Jepp remembered that he wasn't exactly greeted warmly by the other Varney pilots. "I got a royal welcome on the way in from Salt Lake City to Portland, riding with most of the pilots I already knew. But when they found out that I was going to be hired permanently, the whole thing kind of chilled rapidly. They were a bunch of old World War I pilots; they told their boss that they would quit if the company kept me on. They were angry about hardly making any money and then having Varney going out and hiring this kid."

Shortly thereafter, Varney merged with Boeing and Jepp found himself a co-pilot on the Boeing Tri-Motors. He also discovered he possessed a knack for flying that many of the other pilots lacked. In those days, a co-pilot was supposed to just sit in the right-hand seat, touch nothing, and do nothing except keep his eyes open and mouth shut.

"When we flew across the Great Salt Lake desert at night," Jepp said, "I noticed that many of the pilots, almost all of them, when they'd get about halfway across that desert, or maybe only a third of the way, they had nothing to orient themselves on, and pretty soon they'd have

---

★ In late 1930, S.A.F.E.way was purchased, through Brown's connivance, by American Airways for $1.4 million—about twice what Halliburton estimated his company was worth—and American Airways was awarded the southern route. Some called the deal "hush money." (Davies, 119; Smith 195-196)

★★ Shortly after the Contract Air Mail Act of 1925 (Kelly Act) became law, allowing private contractors to bid for providing airmail service, Walter T. Varney and his partner Louis Mueller were awarded the route from Pasco, Washington, to Elko, Nevada—a route which one postal official described as "starting nowhere and ending nowhere, and over impossible country getting there." From 1926 to 1929, the routes flown by Varney Air Lines continued to expand. In 1931, Varney joined with National Air Transport, Pacific Air Transport, and Boeing Air Transport to become United Air Lines. (www.historyofaircargo.com;www.timetableimages.com/ttimages/varney/historytogo.utah.gov; en.wikipedia.org/wiki/ Varney_Airlines)

Jepp in Varney pilot coveralls. *(Courtesy Museum of Flight)*

the right or left wing down, maybe as much as five or ten degrees. Sometimes they'd struggle a bit getting the plane level and squared away again.

"They weren't using what few instruments we had back then. Sometimes they'd drop to five hundred feet or so and follow the railroad tracks; that gave them something to see and follow. I became somewhat concerned when the pilot seemed to be drifting, and on several occasions I reached over and straightened the airplane, even though I was only the co-pilot and was not supposed to do anything. Well, I found that several of the pilots would let me fly the plane over the desert, because they were having trouble navigating in the dark. I was doing a darned good job at it and the word got out, and some of the older boys decided it was not just luck and wanted me to teach them how to do it.

"One time Ray Little and I were in a Boeing Tri-Motor and flying to San Francisco to get our radio licenses, the first time any of us ever had one. I think it was 1931. Coming back out of Sacramento, we had a load of pilots on board and we couldn't get over the hump from Sacramento to Reno. I took turns with some of the others on the co-pilot's side. The weather was really bad and we had to go around it. I made the statement to Ray Little that I believed that someday we would be able to fly right through bad weather—on top of it or right through it. Later, after we landed, Ray was so mad at me that he told Slim Lewis that he'd 'better keep an eye on that Jeppesen kid. He has some really strange ideas about flying airplanes in bad weather.' I almost got fired." [19]

Ray Little, circa 1926. *(E. B. Jeppesen collection)*

Russ Cunningham modeling an early radio headset, 1929. *(E. B. Jeppesen collection)*

Jepp also remembered that when the radio ranges came in, he would take Slim Lewis's airplane up and work out a procedure. "I'd go out and shoot approaches, then record the best way to do it. I would say that I devised eighty percent of the let-down procedures between Oakland and Chicago. Nobody knew anything about let-down procedures; they weren't flying instruments. The airlines didn't really get started flying instruments until 1934 or 1935, with the Boeing 247. It worried some of the old pilots because they wouldn't adapt themselves to IFR [instrument flight rules]" [20]

Jepp decided to sign up to make night mail flights. Because of the strong, unpredictable wind currents and weather extremes over the mountains, the Oakland-Salt Lake City-Cheyenne route paid the most. Jepp and the nineteen other pilots on the route made fifty dollars a week, plus seven cents a mile—fourteen cents a mile if they flew at night. And the route was dangerous. During the winter of 1930, four of the twenty pilots were killed. [21]

Jepp's second child, Richard, recalled that his father once told him that the pilots navigated "without a map by just flying from wreck to wreck. He said that countryside was just littered with airplanes that had gone down."

Flying was indeed a dangerous profession. Richard Jeppesen noted, "Those early aviators lived by the seat of their pants. This was before gyros and air-speed indicators. They could tell how fast they were going by the sound of the wind whistling through the guy-wires on the wings. Dad talked about many times having to land at—well, they called them airports, but they weren't airports. They were just open fields with barbed wire around them to keep the cows out, and they would land totally alone. They'd taxi up to a stash of fuel; they had to keep the engine running, jump out of the cockpit, and hand-crank fuel out of fifty-five gallon drums into the airplane's tank. He said if you ever lost an engine, it was so cold they'd never get it started again.

"If you didn't fly the airmail because the weather was bad or you thought it was too dangerous, they'd fire you. They'd just say, 'All right, if you're not going to fly, then I'll get somebody who will.' A lot of pilots were lost in those days because of that mentality." [22]

The fear of being fired turned pilots and mechanics into a hardy breed. On one particularly frigid night in Cheyenne, the ground crew struggled to prepare a plane to carry the mail eastward. Fire had recently destroyed the airfield's hangar, so the men were working in a canvas tent being buffeted by a blizzard. With the temperature at 36° F below zero, the crew poured sixteen gallons of boiling water into the radiator and twelve gallons of hot oil into the engine. Mechanics then turned the propeller, being careful not to slip on the icy surface and fall victim to the whirling prop. If the engine did not start after a few attempts, the rapidly cooling water and oil had to be drained, reheated, and the whole process repeated.

The pilots also needed their own heat. Some frozen pilots had to be lifted bodily from their aircraft. As author Roger Bilstein notes, "In open-cockpit biplanes, the constant exposure to cold air was one of the worst hardships, especially in winter. Even in heavy flying suits, pilots became so bitterly chilled and benumbed that judgment was impaired. Flying became a struggle of endurance and nerves....Whether for nerves or warmth, many pilots carried liquor when they flew, and most maintained their drinking habits when off duty." [23]

Jim Jeppesen said, "Navigation at that time was still pretty much performed the way the early pioneers heading west in their Conestoga wagons did it: you saw where the sun was and figured out the four points of the compass. Then you picked out some feature on the horizon—like a mountain or a hill or a grove of trees—that was in the general direction you wanted to go, and you guided your horse or oxen in that direction. Flying was much the same. You took off, figured out which way north, south, east, and west were, looked down to find a road or a set of railroad tracks heading in that direction, and aimed your aircraft toward the horizon." (Jim Jeppesen also recalled his father telling him that, out west, pilots called navigating by train tracks "hugging the U.P.," for Union Pacific. "You can't miss Laramie—just hug the U.P.")

"If you were lucky," Jim Jeppesen said, "you might have a road map from a gas station to take along in case you got lost. And, if the weather conditions became too dangerous, you could always land on a road or in an open field——after first flying over the airport and dropping the sacks of mail, of course, and waiting out the storm." [24]

Navigation errors continued to take a toll among airmail pilots. Too often pilots flying by "dead reckoning" ended up dead. Following roads, telephone lines, and railroad tracks, and circling a town to see what name was painted on the water tower worked just fine in daylight and good weather, but daylight and good weather weren't always available.

And airmail pilots were cognizant of the Post Office's motto, "Neither wind, nor rain, nor heat, nor gloom of night shall stay these appointed couriers from the swift completion of their appointed rounds." The pressure to deliver the mail was always there, like a demanding, impatient mistress.

One dark and snowy night Jepp was flying the mail into Cheyenne when his motor quit. He found a straight stretch of highway and set the plane down. Using the primitive radio set on board, he was able to raise the manager of the Cheyenne airport. Jepp was asked if he was hurt; he replied that he wasn't, but he was worried that he might freeze during the night.

"Do you know where you are?" the manager asked.

"Yes. I'm 168 miles from Cheyenne."

"How do you know?"

"Well, because a sign along the highway where I'm sitting says I'm 168 miles from Cheyenne!" [25]

One of Jepp's best friends during those early days flying for Boeing Air Transport was a fellow pilot by the name of Berger Johann "Bob" Bergesen. His son, Richard, who would later become the president of British Leyland Europe, has fond memories of having Jepp as a baby-sitter.

"When I was just a kid," said Richard Bergesen, "Jepp used to baby-sit for me before he got married. He told me that my dad was his best friend and I know my father felt the same way about him; Jepp was always kind of a second father to me." Bergesen also remembered that Jepp loved to talk while his own father "was a man of few words. I found out more about my father from Jepp than I ever did from my dad."

Bergesen's father did tell his son some stories about flying the mail in the early '30s. "This one time he told me he was flying between Cheyenne and Salt Lake when he saw a mail plane coming the other way. They were both flying low, following the railroad tracks, and my dad saw this other pilot weaving back and forth with the airplane. He thought maybe he was drunk or something was wrong with this other guy. His name was Hugh King, and he had a .45-caliber pistol that all the airmail pilots carried, and what he was doing was swooping around the telephone poles trying to shoot out the glass insulators. I love that story because it's typical of the way a lot of those guys were." [26]

Jepp's career—and his life—almost came to a sudden and tragic end on the frigid night of December 12-13, 1932. Carrying 287 pounds of mail from Chicago to Omaha, Jepp was heading west over Iowa in a Boeing 40-B when he encountered what was at first a light snowstorm.

"I was about ten miles east of Council Bluffs at an altitude of about 800 feet," he recalled. "It was two a.m. and snowing lightly, and the engine just quit. I came in over a little rising field about a mile south of McClelland, Iowa, and picked out a cornfield to land in."

The plane bounced in the corn stubble and taxied for about eighty yards before obstacles loomed up in the darkness. A newspaper account of the accident said, "The plane passed over a foot-high fence, went between two trees that tore off the wing tips, dropped down a steep bank about 15 feet high, and then nosed into the other bank on the opposite side of the road." The impact threw Jepp forward, smashing his head into the instrument panel and briefly knocking him unconscious. He didn't recall what happened next, only that, when he came to, he was fifty feet down the road and the fabric-covered plane was on fire.

His ribs hurt terribly and there was a throbbing in his head. He put a gloved hand up to his forehead and the fire illuminated the wet blood sticking to his glove; there was a gash close to his left eye and the left lens of his goggles was shattered. He couldn't see very well and panicked momentarily—"My God, twenty-three years old and blind in one eye already," he thought. With some effort he stood up and staggered back to the plane, hoping to retrieve the mail bags, but the craft was fully engulfed in flame. Within minutes the plane and its contents had been consumed, and people began arriving on the scene.

As all the mail pilots did, Jepp carried a pistol to dissuade thieves from attempting to steal the mail. Stumbling around the burning plane, he recalled hearing one of the first persons to reach the crash site, a woman, yell out to others, "Get his gun!" [27]

Jepp said, "I found out later that I was supposed to have had a load of diamonds on board—two or three million diamonds. They [the crash investigators] dug up all the ground around the crash, sifted the dirt, and only found one diamond. I don't know what happened to the rest or even if there were ever any other diamonds on board. I later heard there was a claim that they were worth six million to seven million dollars." For the next few months, postal executives kept a close watch on Jepp's bank account to make sure that he hadn't somehow escaped the burning plane with the diamonds on him. [28]

Jepp had other concerns. He was worried about the injury to his left eye. A doctor told him that the chances were good that his vision would return. Jepp hoped so; he couldn't imagine never flying again.

During the few weeks it took for his eyesight to improve, his ribs to stop hurting, and for him to be certified to return to flight status, Jepp pondered his unnerving accident. While it was true that his mishap had been because of engine failure and not the result of encountering an unexpected obstacle, he realized how very quickly a flight—and a life—could end. [29]

Although he could do nothing about engines that might just suddenly up and quit, maybe he could do something about flying's other main hazard.

5: THE LITTLE BLACK BOOK

When Jepp told his parents of his little mishap over Iowa, they were naturally quite upset and wrote back to him, advising him in no subtle terms to quit the flying business and apply to a college so he could get an engineering degree and go into something safer.

On February 28, 1933, while in Chicago, Jepp typed a letter to his parents in Oregon:

Dear Folks,

You asked in your letter if I was going to quit flying and go back to school; well I will answer that question this way. I am studying hard and long most of the time and I intend to do that as long as I can, but under no circumstances am I ever going to stop flying. I like it to [sit] well and when the time comes when I can no longer fly I might just as well start looking for the next world.

So far as I can see the most important thing in this world is to learn the art of living and that is what I have been trying to do for [some time] and I know something I will not get very much out of life if I can not fly. So much for that. [1]

— Elrey

Because he was flying the same routes week after week after he was medically cleared to fly following his crash, Jepp began to pay closer attention to features on the ground, just in case his engine quit again and he would have to set the plane down somewhere.

He checked out the flat fields up ahead, looking for obstacles such as rocks and trees and fences and buildings that he would need to avoid should he be required to make a forced landing. He looked down on straight roads that might be useful as emergency landing strips and wondered if the telephone poles that lined them would present too great a problem for his wingspan. He made mental notes of the places along his routes where he might be able to make a safe landing, and other places where he very definitely would not want to land.

He also began to memorize certain landmarks and started guiding himself by them. He knew, for example, that when approaching a certain airfield, he had to keep the grain silo to his right and the road with its line of telephone poles to his left. Or, when taking off from another field, he had to pull up enough to clear the barn and windmill and grove of trees at the end of the runway. Simple enough, but what about when the weather was bad or the visibility restricted? Exactly how far from the runway were those poles, that barn, and those trees? Just as important, how tall were they?

It was not that there were no charts that described the early airports of the day. Jepp, like many other pilots, owned a small manual printed in June 1928 titled *Airplane Landing Fields of the Pacific West*, that contained information about fields in Arizona, California, Nevada, Oregon, and Washington. He also had several road maps he had picked up for free at gas stations. The U.S. Coast and Geodetic Survey★ had published a set of aerial charts, but the maps and manual did not have the amount of detail and information he thought was necessary for the safe operation of his aircraft. He decided to gather this information himself.

In his spare time, whenever he landed at airfields, Jepp would wander over to the landmarks and begin pacing off the distances and estimating the heights. He bought a spare altimeter and, when he had more time, would climb the hills, smoke stacks, silos, and water towers with it to get an accurate measurement of their height.

★ One of the nation's oldest agencies, C&GS was established in 1807 by President Thomas Jefferson. It was then known as "Survey of the Coast." The name was changed to "Coast and Geodetic Survey" in 1878. (www.arlingtoncemetery.net/uscgs)

The well-used cover of Jepp's original "little black book," labeled "Cheyenne - Salt Lake Airway. E.B. Jeppesen." *(Courtesy Museum of Flight)*

To organize this information so that he wouldn't have to memorize everything, he also bought himself a small black ring-binder notebook for ten cents and began taking it everywhere he went. Every time he landed at a field, he jotted down notes to himself: "Arps Ranch Beacon: Just north of Chey. Reser about one mile standard Beacon. 8500' safe at nite. Can circle a radius of about 4 miles at this elevation. Increase to 9200' coming from Chey. and 9500' from the west. The above altitude will clear everything on the hill." Many of the annotations were mysterious, shorthand scribblings, the meanings of which was known only to Jepp.

Two hand-written pages inside Jepp's notebook. *(Courtesy Museum of Flight)*

He put into his little black book everything he felt was important to establish minimum safe altitudes when approaching or departing airports: the direction and length of the runways, the altitude above sea level, the slope, the location of the wind sock, and the presence of lights and obstacles. He sketched airport layouts and drew simplified profile views of the terrain. He noted the names and phone numbers of the airfield managers and the names and phone numbers of farmers who owned the land around the airfields whom he could call in advance to inquire about weather conditions. Jepp also took the time to consult engineers and surveyors—anyone he could think of who might have valuable information to include in his manual. He was very pleased with his work. [2]

Jepp was becoming obsessed with safety—his safety. "I invented something to prevent me from getting killed," he once told a reporter. [3]

A story is told that Jepp once climbed Utah's rugged Blythe Mountain, the highest peak in the Salt Lake City area, with three altimeters strapped to his back, recorded the readings, then took the data back to the University of Utah where he asked professors in the physics department to evaluate his findings. Once they gave him their evaluations, he added a 500-foot safety margin to their calculations.

As pilots do, the flyboys would occasionally meet over dinner and the "shop talk" would inevitably drift to close calls, hairy situations, and crash landings. At some point and place lost to history, Jepp pulled out his little black book full of navigational notes and showed the other pilots what he was compiling.

Probably one of the other pilots said he was flying into Salt Lake or Cheyenne or Rock Springs or Elko, and would Jepp mind copying down the information about one of those airfields on the back of a napkin? Jepp undoubtedly replied sure and reproduced his sketch, which the other pilot pocketed for future reference.

This went on for quite some time, until the fame of Jepp's little black book became the talk of pilots throughout the western routes. No matter where he went, it seemed that pilots were always asking him to provide navigational information about various airports—especially younger pilots, who relied on the wisdom of more experienced pilots to keep them alive. Ever helpful and friendly, Jepp obliged.

In 1934 it finally dawned on him that he was providing a valuable service for free. Why not charge a little something for his time and effort? After all, it was taking an increasing amount of his free time to re-sketch everything by hand for each request. Perhaps what he should do is have the book printed. It would have to be a "loose-leaf" ring binder to allow for the information to be changed and updated as necessary. He got a bank loan for $450, bought fifty binders, and had fifty copies of each page mimeographed. [4]

Jepp recalled, "The whole idea was never to start a business to make money. I just did it to make a contribution. No Harvard graduate would ever start such a business. There were only a handful of pilots and a handful of airplanes at the time."

As the requests continued to grow, Jepp would politely smile and reply he'd be glad to provide a copy of his entire little black book—for ten dollars. This seemed like a reasonable price and the pilots snapped them up. Many pilots even started collecting data that Jepp didn't already have and passing it on to him so he could add it to his growing collection of airport and route information.

Jepp said he got the information he needed from any place or person he could—city and county engineers, surveyors, farmers, airport managers. "Once, I drove all the way from Chicago to Oakland," he said, "and checked out the emergency fields and the obstructions around them, different ways to get in, how far they were from the railroad track and the highway, those kinds of things. It was sort of funny—I was developing those 'let-down' charts for my own information, but it seemed the more information I obtained, the more there was that I did not have, so I'd go out again." [5]

Jepp also recalled his first let-down charts "were for the old four-legged radio ranges. Not even the frequencies or the legs were published anywhere before; you just had to figure it out yourself. There were no minimums; every pilot had his own. There wasn't much point in charting the high points on the routes, because the Boeing 40-B couldn't reach them anyway. What you needed to know was how low you could fly through Immigration Canyon, how low you could go across Donner Summit, that sort of thing." [6]

In the early '30s, Jepp began flying newer, more powerful, and more exotic aircraft, including the Boeing 80-A and the sleek, all-metal Boeing Monomail Model 221-A. Of the 80-A, Jepp said it was his favorite. "It was a big airplane, shook and rattled all over, and you felt like you were doing something!" The Monomail 221-A, with its 575-horsepower Pratty & Whitney engine, was streamlined and eye-catching, but rough on the pilot. There was room for eight passengers in an enclosed, relatively comfortable space, but the open cockpit left the pilot exposed to the elements. [7]

Jepp in the cockpit of a Boeing 80-A Tri-Motor (circa early 1931) dubbed the "Tin Goose" and "Flying Washboard" due to its corrugated metal skin.
(E. B. Jeppesen collection)

Jepp flew the all-metal Boeing Monomail Model 221A on the Chicago-Cheyenne route in the early 1930s. When and where this photo was taken is unknown, but note piles of snow on the ground. *(E. B. Jeppesen collection)*

In the early 1930s Jepp also made the acquaintance of Harry Combs, who would one day be president of LearJet (1971-1982) and head of Combs Aviation. Combs recalled thinking that Jepp's little black book was a work of genius.

Bundled up against the elements, Jepp poses beside one of the two Boeing Monomail aircraft. *(E. B. Jeppesen collection)*

"Jepp would often fly at night," Combs said, "and he told me that he would see a beacon—the airways in those days had a flashing beacon every twenty miles to guide the pilots, provided you could see twenty miles. Sometimes you couldn't see a mile, so what the hell good was a beacon? But he would fly that route and he was always looking for a place to put the airplane down if it got to be tight—if he got pinched between two storms or something and he had to get it on the ground before he ran out of fuel and crashed. He began taking notes and locating potential emergency landing fields all along the route, which was very clever. Of course, everybody wanted his notes. Jepp's contribution to the world of aviation is immeasurable. There's absolutely no way to relate it to any other effort that anybody else has ever made. It was genius." [8]

During the course of his travels, the boyish-looking Jepp would occasionally have the opportunity to fly a celebrity. He recalled the time in 1934 when he was piloting the humorist and "cowboy philosopher" Will Rogers across the West in a ten-seat United Air Lines plane; they stopped to refuel in Des Moines, Iowa.

"I'd flown him before," said Jepp, "but this was the last time. We landed at Des Moines and I went into the terminal's chartroom. Will would never go into the terminal; he'd just go over and lean against the fence and chat with people. They always seemed to know when he was due and they'd be there to see him.

"When I came out and walked to the plane, I heard Will remark to the crowd, 'Well, I gotta go now—here comes my seventeen-year-old pilot.'" The crowd roared.★ [9]

Beloved Depression-era humorist Will Rogers with an unidentified United Air Lines stewardess. Jepp served as Rogers's pilot on several occasions.
(Courtesy Smithsonian National Air and Space Museum)

★ On August 15, 1935, Rogers, an aviation enthusiast, and Wiley Post, a one-eyed Texas pilot who in 1931 had set a record for circling the world in a plane, died in a crash of Post's Lockheed Vega near Point Barrow, Alaska. The news stunned the nation. (www.willrogers.com)

One of the most famous and dashing aviators of his day, Wiley Post twice set records for 'round-the-world flights. In June, 1931, with a navigator along, he accomplished the feat in eight days, sixteen hours. Two years later he broke his own record by making the trip in seven days, nineteen hours—this time solo.
(Courtesy Smithsonian National Air and Space Museum)

1934 was a watershed year for America's airlines. Franklin D. Roosevelt had been swept into the White House the previous March on the heels of the Hoover Administration's inept handling of the Depression economy, and had been in office for less than a year when turmoil again wracked the airline industry.

Alabama's U.S. senator, Hugo Black, while investigating federal subsidies for transoceanic surface mail carriers, also launched a probe into airmail contracts. What he found astounded and angered him, especially

Postmaster Walter Folger Brown's award of a contract to Eastern Air Transport for a bid that was three times higher than Ludington's. In the Congressional inquiry that followed, Brown, who had been replaced as Postmaster General by James A. Farley, was called to testify, and he stood up well under questioning.

Still, Senator Black was convinced that Brown had acted illegally and in collusion with the airlines. The Air Mail Act of 1934, which roared through Congress in the wake of the scandal, brought about a divorce between companies, such as Boeing, Ford, and General Motors, who were involved in both manufacturing and transportation.

In January 1934 Black persuaded Roosevelt to cancel the Post Office's contracts with the airlines and use the Army Air Corps to transport the mail. This decision proved disastrous. The inexperienced, inadequately trained army pilots, flying in open-cockpit aircraft over unfamiliar terrain in often terrible winter weather, and without proper navigational aids, soon found themselves in deadly trouble.

During the first five weeks the army flew the mail, twelve pilots died in crashes. The situation soon became known as the "Air Mail Scandal of 1934."

With the public in an uproar over the carnage, Roosevelt moved to restore the old system. The airlines, after a bidding process, would resume the job of flying the mail. But the two-month hiatus during which the airlines received no government subsidies had nearly brought the industry to its knees; United alone lost over $850,000 during the first quarter of 1934.

Postmaster General Farley declared that the airlines that had won the contracts during Brown's "Spoils Conferences" would be ineligible to submit bids under the new system. But Farley quickly realized that he could not simply eliminate the four biggest and most experienced airlines from the competition, and so allowed them to enter under new, slightly revised names. Thus it was that American Airways became American Airlines, Eastern Air Transport became Eastern Airlines, and TWA merely added "Inc." after its name. (The name was later changed to Trans World Airlines.)

In April 1934, Farley opened the bids and found that three of the "Big Four" had all submitted rock-bottom bids; United was under-bid for the Dallas-Chicago route by new players, an Oklahoma insurance man and financier named Thomas E. Braniff and his brother, Paul Revere Braniff. Their company, Braniff Airways, had begun as a minor carrier in 1928; Farley's award of the contract pushed them into the major leagues of U.S. airlines. [10]

1935 brought a new love into Jepp's life. He had always been too busy and too absorbed by aviation to pay much attention to girls, but one day, while flying a Boeing 247 from Chicago to Omaha, he pushed the stewardess call button in the cockpit to order a cup of coffee and was in for a surprise.

Jepp said, "The stewardess opened the cockpit door and came in. She said something I didn't catch and, since my co-pilot was handling the controls, I turned around to respond. Suddenly my eyes met those of the most beautiful girl I had ever seen in my life. I did have the presence of mind to take our coffee without spilling it, and in the short conversation that followed I got her name but, for the life of me, I couldn't tell you one detail about the rest of that flight. But I can sure tell you about Nadine. She was a gorgeous brunette who looked fantastic in that uniform. Women, per se, had never really been important to me before, but all of a sudden this lady became the most important thing in my life. And she still is!"

In the years to come, Jepp would always tell an abbreviated story of how they met. "I ordered coffee," he would say, "but I got Nadine." [11]

For her part, Nadine recalled that she "opened the cockpit door, expecting to see a mature, dignified captain. To my astonishment, he looked like a kid just out of high school!" But there was something about his pale-blue Danish eyes that took hold and melted her heart. [12]

Nadine Liscomb, born on September 14, 1914, was a small-town girl from the small town of Dunlap, Iowa. According to their son Jim, in the early 1930s she studied to be a registered nurse, then became a surgical nurse rather than a "floor" nurse. He said this was quite unusual at that

Nadine Audrey Jeppesen, née Liscomb, circa 1935, in her United Air Lines stewardess uniform. *(E. B. Jeppesen collection)*

Nadine in a posed United Air Lines publicity photo, Chicago, 1935.
(E. B. Jeppesen collection)

Based on this United Air Lines portrait of Jepp, Nadine's observation that he "looked like a kid just out of high school" was accurate. *(E. B. Jeppesen collection)*

time because, "according to my mom, women were not normally allowed in operating rooms, especially assisting the surgeon." [13]

After an indeterminate amount of time in this role, she saw an advertisement from United Airlines, which was seeking trained nurses to become stewardesses (stewardesses, as they were then known, were required by regulation to be registered nurses). Nadine was evidently intrigued by the idea of flying, traveling around the country, meeting and serving important, interesting people, and discovering a world of glamour, adventure, and opportunity.

She applied for stewardess training with United Air Lines and was accepted into a class in 1935 at Omaha, Nebraska. Flying with United proved to be everything she had hoped and dreamed it would be. On her flights she met many of the famous and influential people of the day—wealthy executives, sports stars, Hollywood celebrities, radio personalities, and many more. She thoroughly enjoyed the glamorous but hectic lifestyle of an airline stewardess.

Following their initial encounter, Jepp and Nadine were constantly together when their busy schedules permitted. Besides her beauty, he

Nadine's parents, Georgia and stepfather Dobby Liscomb, Dunlap, Iowa, 1936. Nadine's real father died of the plague. *(E. B. Jeppesen collection)*

Nadine after graduation from nursing school in 1934. *(E. B. Jeppesen collection)*

especially appreciated her apparent interest in his hobby—spending every free hour flying around the country to chart the various airfields. She didn't complain when they spent endless hours under a broiling sun climbing silos, windmills, tall chimneys, and rocky, treeless hills with an altimeter, the wind messing her dark hair. If she thought Jepp and his drive to log everything in a small black notebook a little odd, she kept such thoughts to herself. To him, "Neddy"—his pet name for her—was a "good sport." [14]

Nadine in jodhpurs and cowboy boots, Cheyenne, Wyoming, 1936.
(E. B. Jeppesen collection)

Another story is told about Jepp, this one apocryphal. While pilot-ing a United 247 one night over Illinois farm lands near Lee Center, he saw flames below and noticed a barn and out-buildings on fire. He swooped low and circled the farm until the noise of his engines finally woke the family. When radio personality and America's original gossip columnist Walter Winchell (who used as his trademark staccato sign-on, "Good evening, Mr. and Mrs. America and all ships at sea—let's go to press") learned of Jepp's deed, he sent the pilot an orchid which Jepp promptly gave to Neddy. [15]

One day, in a place he evidently did not log onto any of his charts, Jepp, hopelessly smitten, proposed marriage to Nadine; she accepted.

Jepp and Nadine were married in her hometown of Dunlap, Iowa, on September 24, 1936. After a short honeymoon, they moved to Cheyenne, Wyoming, to where Jepp had been transferred for the night mail flights. Because United's regulations said that stewardesses could not be married, Nadine was required to quit her flying job. About a year later, they moved to Salt Lake City and rented a room in a home at 1958 Yale Avenue, owned by a family named Snodgrass.

The Jeppesens turned the basement of the Snodgrass home into a workshop and hired a few engineering graduate students from the University of Utah to draft the navigation charts. "The students could do a lot better job at drafting than I could," confessed Jepp, "so I sketched the charts in pencil and they would ink them in. We had enough room for seven of these boys in the basement, where they worked for fifty cents an hour." [16]

Jepp recalled an amusing incident during this period: "Nadine got tired of having these kids going in and out of the house and down to the basement all hours of the day and night. There was a little old lady who lived across the street who watched all this strange activity from her win-dow, and one day called the FBI to investigate. The FBI came out and checked out everything and said it was okay.

"But of course some of the students had to have a little fun, so they got two or three old guns and put them in a box in their car, waited for the old lady to be peering out from her window, then carried the box of guns from their car and 'accidentally' dropped it on the lawn. Out

A snapshot taken of Nadine and Jepp on their wedding day, September 24, 1936, in Dunlap, Iowa. *(E. B. Jeppesen collection)*

spilled the guns. Of course she called the FBI again.

"I got to know the FBI agent pretty well and he asked what was going on at my place. I told him, 'Just kids having fun with grandma!'" [17]

Nadine wanted to be more than just a "housewife," and soon went to work for her husband, running the part-time business, taking care of the accounting and the billing, collating the many pages of charts into the binders, and traveling with Jepp on many of his flights to help compile the data that was going into his ever-growing black book. Together they continued to fly into the various fields on United's route to take measurements, lay out diagrams of airports and runways, and jot down the names and phone numbers of contacts who could, when necessary, provide meteorological information. [18]

Nadine with the Jeppesens' newborn son, Jim, June 3, 1938. *(E. B. Jeppesen collection)*

Nadine's flying activities were curtailed; she was pregnant with their first son, Jim, who arrived on June 3, 1938.

Years later, son Jim would say that his mother was the driving force behind the operation. Whenever Jepp had a problem making a decision, it was Nadine who would give it thumbs up or thumbs down. "Dad wouldn't do anything without bouncing it off Mom first," Jim said. "If she didn't give it her blessing, it wouldn't get done. She made the decisions." [19]

In 1938 Jepp faced the biggest decision of his life. Jeppesen Airway Manual, as the tiny company was called, was making just enough money to cover expenses. But the grind—flying for United and making charts in his spare time—was wearing him down. He had about $12,000 invested in the company, and was thinking of selling it. Lou Clinton, the owner of Clinton Aviation, a Denver-based Cessna and Beech dealer, fixed-base operator, and a long-time friend of Jepp, recalled that William A. "Pat" Patterson, an early president of United, rejected Jepp's offer to sell his company to the airline. "Jepp told me that Patterson came out of a board meeting where the offer was discussed and told him, 'We decided we don't want to be in the map-making business, so we're not going to buy it.' Jepp said that was the best thing that ever happened to him."★ [20]

It was indeed fortunate for Jepp and Nadine, for the "little black book" was about to go big-time.

★ Jim Jeppesen said his parents once told him that his father wanted to sell Airway Manual because Jepp was flying full time, and Nadine felt overburdened trying to run the business while caring for an infant. (Jim Jeppesen correspondence, 4/27/06)

6: THE WAR YEARS

World events began to shape the future—and the future of aviation. Aircraft had escalated from being almost a novelty of limited military value to a terrifyingly potent weapon of war.

During the Great War, the flimsy aeroplanes had been little more than aerial reconnaissance vehicles, handy for flying over enemy lines and noting troop movements and dispositions. In the game of "one-upsmanship," someone got the bright idea that the planes could be mounted with machine guns and used to shoot down the other guy's planes. Someone else thought it would be useful to drop hand grenades and small bombs from above; the Germans took that concept to the next level and developed the huge Gotha bombers that flew information and rained tons of bombs on London.

Development of the airplane's potential did not stop during the inter-war years. In October 1935, Italian dictator Benito Mussolini used his modern warplanes to strafe and bomb primitive tribesmen during his country's invasion of Ethiopia. On April 26, 1937, German Chancellor Adolf Hitler helped fellow Fascist Francisco Franco overthrow the Spanish government when he sent waves of German bombers to flatten the town of Guernica. In September 1939, Germany invaded Poland using its dreaded blitzkrieg, or "lighting war," tactics that involved the combined use of air and ground forces. Britain and France both declared war on Germany, and a new and terrible world conflict had begun. [1]

In December 1935, Douglas Aircraft, following on the success of its DC-1 and DC-2, introduced the DC-3, one of the most revolutionary aircraft of all time. It truly made flying a fast and affordable way to travel for a large segment of the population. The DC-3 was an airplane that, for the first time, enabled airlines to make money by carrying passengers rather than government airmail contracts. The craft's rounded, streamlined design was a departure from the boxy shapes of the Ford, Boeing, and Junkers tri-motors, and, besides looking like something out of Buck Rogers, greatly improved fuel consumption. The DC-3 was technologically advanced, had the latest instrumentation, a single elevator and rudder, retractable landing gear, and cowled radial engines. It was sleek, it was sharp, and it was state-of-the-art before the term was invented.

A DC-3 in United Air Lines livery—the "workhorse of the sky."
(E. B. Jeppesen collection)

American Airlines was the first airline to order the DC-3—an order of twenty, half of them being the "sleeper" version with pull-down berths—for $79,500 each. In November 1936 United Airlines purchased the craft; by the end of 1938, ninety-five percent of all commercial air passengers in the U.S. were traveling in DC-3s. [2]

Jepp was assigned to fly DC-3s and he quickly got the hang of it. But it wasn't an easy plane to fly. Another United pilot who flew the DC-3 was Ted Boerstler, who became one of Jepp's long-time friends. He said, "You really had to work it, fight it. You didn't have an automatic pilot—the only pilot was yourself. It was hands on, all the time. There's very few pilots who could stay within twenty feet of assigned altitude without watching every second, but Jepp prided himself on being able to do that. He's precision." [3]

Jepp in the cockpit of a United DC-3, late 1930s. *(E. B. Jeppesen collection)*

On the night of June 10, 1941, six months before the United States was plunged into the global conflict, Jepp had another aerial mishap, this time while at the controls of a United DC-3 from Salt Lake City to Denver.

While coming in for a landing through a light rain shower at 9:10 p.m., the landing-gear brakes on the United plane failed. In his official accident report, which demonstrated his clear thinking and ability to problem-solve in an emergency, Jepp noted,

> I applied full brake and found they were not functioning. First Officer Allen tried the brakes on his side and found they were inoperative. Full flap was immediately applied and after rolling approximately 2500 feet with little decrease in speed, the tail wheel was unlocked. The right engine was cleaned out with the hope of steering the ship up the NW runway and if possible to ground loop it...At no time during the roll was a braking action experienced; the ship at all times seemed to be "free-wheeling." We had ample time during the roll to consider all means of stopping the ship; consideration was given to lifting the landing gear, ground looping the ship by use of the engines, steering the ship up the northwest runway or letting it run into the soft ground north of the boundary lights.
>
> Our speed as we approached the boundary lights was so great that I thought it inadvisable to attempt to complete a ground loop by use of the engines. We rolled through the north boundary lights at an estimated speed of 20 to 25 mph, the plane continuing to a stop 100 feet north of the boundary lights after the right landing gear was broken by impact with a three-foot ditch. As we passed thru the boundary lights I instructed First Officer Allen to cut the switches and turn the gas off. This he immediately did. The landing gear impact was very slight and several of the passengers were not aware of the accident. [4]

After this DC-3's brakes failed upon landing at Denver in 1941, Jepp was able to
bring it to a stop with no injuries and only minor damage to the plane.
(E. B. Jeppesen collection)

Damaged propeller and landing gear after the June 10 accident.
(E. B. Jeppesen collection)

Although the board investigating the accident deemed it "avoid-able," and Jepp and the co-pilot were temporarily suspended, they were returned to full flying status four days later.

In 1941, the Jeppesens relocated permanently to Denver, bought a home at 622 Grape Street, and set up their business, known as Airway Manual, in a small storefront on East Colfax Avenue. Working for him were Nadine and a draftsman he had persuaded to move from Salt Lake City. One was not enough. "I kept getting more customers, so I hired a couple more draftsmen," Jepp said. [5]

After moving to Denver in October 1941, the Jeppesens bought this modest home at 622 Grape Street. *(Whitlock photo)*

Shortly after relocating to Denver, the Jeppesens rented business space in this building on East Colfax Avenue. In 2006, it was a hair salon. *(Whitlock photo)*

A few months later, after Japanese bombs fell on United States military facilities in Hawaii, Wake Island, the Philippines, and other bases in the Pacific, America became fully involved in World War II. The Great Depression ended almost instantly as industries geared up to meet the demands of total war. There were very few businesses in America between 1942 and 1945 that weren't partially or wholly dependent on military contracts.

Production of military aircraft was stepped up, too, to levels never before seen. During its peak, Ford's massive Willow Run factory, for example, was churning out a B-24 "Liberator" bomber every sixty-three minutes. [6]

Due to wartime necessities, the moving of troops and military goods took priority; civilian passenger traffic on planes, trains, and buses was severely curtailed. The commercial airlines found that, in order to survive, they would have to rely on government contracts.

The same was true for Jepp's business. He got lucky. One day he

In a posed publicity shot taken in the early 1940s, Jepp points out a global feature
to Nadine. *(E. B. Jeppesen collection)*

was sitting at his desk in his United Air Lines uniform, going through his
customer list (he had about 1,500 customers by that time), when in
walked an Army colonel and a major. They introduced themselves and
showed identification—they were from military intelligence.

The colonel opened his briefcase and pulled out some aerial charts.
"Let me show you what we've got," he said. "We've got eight instrument charts in the whole Air Corps." Wanting to do his part to help the
war effort, Jepp gave the colonel fifty of his manuals. Then the orders
started pouring in.

"We got a contract to do part of the Air Corps' work," Jepp said,
"Then the Navy came in and we got a Navy contract to do all their
charts. They called them 'Jeppcharts.'" [7]

A company executive recalled, "The Navy found out that Jepp had
the only information that was available, so they came to him and asked

if we could publish the HO-510—that's the Hydrographic Office publication 510, called the Naval Airway Pilot—for the Navy, and they eventually worked out a contract where they took his charts that he had already prepared, overlaid them with a Naval Airway Pilot HO-510 logo, and started publishing them. They covered the U.S., southern Canada, and Alaska." [8]

One day in the spring of 1942, a lawyer in Portland called Jepp to inform him that his parents had not paid the taxes on their home at 8017 North Fiske in Portland since 1935 and that the state was going to seize it. The lawyer suggested that Jepp pay the taxes and " 'take possession of the house in your name. You'll own it, but you can give them a life estate. In other words, they can't sell it, but they can live in it all the rest of their lives without paying anything. You'll have it then and when they leave, you can sell it.'" [9]

Jepp reassuringly wrote to his parents, "You will be able to remain in the house as long as we continue to pay the taxes," and informed them that their other son, Edward, would immediately re-shingle the roof. [10]

Jepp said, "I paid the taxes and Edward put a new roof on it and had it painted and put in a $1,100 furnace, which was a pretty good furnace in those days. And I was able to send them some money every month. Of course, Nadine did that, and I thought that was pretty nice of her, because we didn't have a lot of dough ourselves then. When Mother and Father eventually left, the house became mine and I was pleased and happy about the whole episode."

In the fall of 1942, someone in the War Department was evidently looking through old personnel records to find pilots who were, or had been, in the military, because Jepp was notified that he would be called up for active duty in the Army Air Corps.

He said, "Nadine and I had two baby boys [son Richard had just been born on June 9, 1942], about $800 in the bank, and we owed everything on the house, furniture, and other miscellaneous items. In the meantime, we were beginning to put out the manuals for the Navy. My call-up was canceled for some reason; I'm not really sure to this day what happened. So I was still flying for United and producing and delivering the charts and manuals to the military."

Realizing the Jeppcharts contained classified information, the military quickly moved Airway Manual out of its vulnerable storefront location and into Suites 529-535 of the University Building at 17th and Champa in the heart of downtown Denver.

A view of the Jeppesen office in its larger, more secure downtown location in Denver's University Building. *(Courtesy Museum of Flight)*

"There we had vaults, guards, and security," Jepp said. "I moved our operation there and in six weeks' time we built up the charts—everything—for Western Canada, and all of Alaska and the Aleutian Islands.

We processed the information on a compilation basis. For instance, on lots of the peaks in Alaska and out on the Aleutian Chain, we had as many as seven different 'official' elevations. So all I did was pick out the highest elevation and enter it with a plus-or-minus 500 feet, then added a little note down in the index, pointing out, 'Use at your own risk, because we don't have a survey on it.'

"We heard that our charts of Alaska and the Aleutian Islands were especially valuable in the country's efforts to take them back from the Japanese, who had invaded Attu and Kiska in the Aleutians in 1942. The Navy contract lasted thirteen years. A competitor, Coast and Geodedic Survey, tried to do what we were doing, but they weren't really up to speed until 1945, when the war was over." [11]

As happened with many commercial airlines pilots at that time, Jepp soon found himself flying for a government military entity known as ATC, or Air Transport Command. United Air Lines, as well as three others (American Airlines, T&WA—Transcontinental and Western Airlines, later known as Trans World Airlines—and Consairways, a subsidiary of Consolidated Aircraft), had a contract for some of its civilian pilots to fly military planes (the C-87, a modified B-24 "Liberator" bomber converted into a twenty-five-seat troop carrier) with military markings and U.S. Army Air Force serial numbers from the West Coast to Australia and New Zealand.

The Air Transport Command was most famous for flying the treacherous route over "The Hump"—the route through the Himalayas, the highest mountain range in the world—between India and China. After Burma was conquered by the Japanese in April 1942, the enemy cut the Burma Road, the only Allied supply route into China. To supply Chiang Kai-Shek's Nationalist Army that was waging guerrilla warfare against the invaders, the Air Transport Command established, in September 1943, the famous over-mountain route. This round-trip flight, from Patterson Field, Ohio, to China and back again, covered 28,000 miles and took an average of twelve days to complete. The route was so dangerous it was estimated that the Air Corps lost three crewmen for each thousand tons of cargo that reached China; over a thousand crewmen died flying The Hump.

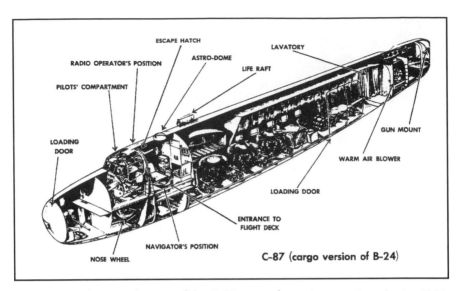

A cutaway schematic drawing of the C-87 cargo plane. *(Army Air Forces drawing, 1944)*

The C-87 crews were not especially pleased with their aircraft, either, which often developed severe problems with the engines, had major fuel-system leaks that frequently led to fires, and had unreliable cockpit accessories. The C-87 also had a propensity to ice up while flying over the mountains. Other routes were not as hazardous but, as with all flight operations, a certain amount of risk was involved. [12]

In 1943 ATC awarded a contract to United Airlines to fly trans-Pacific routes and to fly shuttles that ferried military personnel between the front lines on Pacific islands to rest-and-recuperation centers in Australia and New Zealand; Jepp was one of those civilian pilots who was chosen for these flights.

In the summer of 1943, the thirty-five-year-old Jeppesen, commissioned as an Air Corps captain, was assigned to the inter-Pacific route. He learned of the death of a fellow United pilot flying for ATC and passed on the sad news in an August 9, 1943, letter to Jack Parshall, the man who had arranged for his first flying lessons in Portland:

Hurst Laughlin, one of our mutual barn-storming pals of the good old days was killed off of New Zealand last Saturday or Sunday. He was act-ing Captain on a four engine Consolidated C-87. No details except co-pilot and navigator survived. Accident occurred on the take-off with rumor of fire on board.

The original report stated Eddie Eshelman was the acting Captain and United picked up Eddie's dad in North Platte. Charles, Eddie's broth-er, flew to Oceanside to inform May (Eddie's wife) of the accident. Three days elapsed before Jack O'Brien arrived in New Zealand and was able to confirm the actual members of the crew. Pretty tough on the Eshelman family.

I spent a little time with Joe Smith in San Francisco the other day...and it was his lot to tell Mrs. Laughlin of the tragedy. It hit Joe pretty hard and when I last saw him he was really broken up....

I have completed my navigation, engineering, and flight training on the C-87 and will make my qualifying trip to Australia sometime around the twenty-third of August.

Nadine, Jimmie and Dickie send their love. [13]

Jepp made one run to Brisbane, Australia (with a stopover in Fiji), but the War Department realized that he was much more valuable to the war effort back in Denver supervising his Airway Manual company than by flying shuttle routes over the Pacific, and he soon found himself once more "flying a desk."

On December 30, 1943, Jepp complained about his situation in a letter to a fellow United pilot in Illinois:

As you know, I have been stuck at my desk here in Denver for the past three months, running "Naval Airways Pilot" for the Navy, with a little "Airway Manual" thrown in on the side.

It is not much fun, and honestly I have never worked harder in my life. I am getting to hate the sight of my office building, along with the name, "Airway Manual." At any rate, I am scheduled back to Pacific Operations on January 1, 1944, a date I will be unable to keep [he does-n't explain why], which may mean the termination of my career with

Jepp in Army Air Corps uniform with native Fijians, 1943. *(E. B. Jeppesen collection)*

United Air Lines. They have been extremely patient and kind, but I don't think they can stand very much more from "Jepp."

To make a long story short, this all adds up to one thing. I will definitely (that is, if I fly at all) have to go back on Domestic Operations until my Navy contract [with Airway Manual] is terminated in July. [14]

Jepp later noted in an interview, "I was getting ready to go out again when the Secretary of the Navy James Forrestal pulled me off flying status and told me they wanted me to spend my time on my military charts. After about three or four months of that, I got tired of it, so I snuck back on United's domestic run and flew between Denver and San Francisco."

Not all of Jepp's work was done for the Navy and Air Corps. He said, "We started creating some charts for the infantry, which is another story in itself. I've got a great respect for the infantry company commander—what he's supposed to know and what's really supposed to be on those charts. It's an amazing thing." [15]

A Jeppesen executive remembered that the company also picked up a contract for Western Airlines, which had a ferry contract between the States and Alaska, and also began selling manuals to individual United pilots. [16]

The war in Europe ended in May 1945, but the Japanese were of no mind to surrender. Charts of the Pacific were still in great demand. In June 1945, Jepp received a letter from Rear Admiral G. B. Bryan of the Navy's Hydrographic Office, expressing the Navy's desire that Jepp spend less time flying and devote more time to supervising the output of charts. Said Bryan, "I feel free in suggesting this procedure to you in the knowledge that the Navy Department contract with you provides for a specific monthly payment to you for personal services attendant to the production of Naval Airways Pilot. Such an arrangement will be in the interest of the Navy in producing the important information which is made available through Naval Airways Pilot." [17]

Jepp fulfilled his patriotic duty and cut back on his hours with United, hoping the airline would not fire him as a result.

On September 2, 1945, following the dropping in August of two atomic bombs on Hiroshima and Nagasaki, the Japanese surrendered and World War II was over.

There was considerable worry throughout America, however, that the economic boom brought on and fueled by the war would also end. Nineteen forty-six was a bad year for the stock market and some financial experts predicted that the country would drift back into the same type of high-unemployment depression that had characterized the two decades between world wars. Jepp also worried that, with the military's need for flight charts supposedly at an end, his company was not long for this world.

"After the war," he said, "I had a meeting with my employees to decide whether to fold up or continue. They encouraged me to keep going and suggested that we change the name from 'Airway Manual' to 'Jeppesen and Company.'" [18]

Jepp also continued flying for United, but the flights sometimes were anything but routine.

In the early hours of September 5, 1946, for example, Jepp was at the controls of an airliner from San Francisco to Denver when he received a radio message indicating that a charter DC-3 flown by Trans-Luxury Air Lines from New York to San Francisco was presumed to have crashed near Elko, Nevada.

Co-pilot Bruce Painter reported, "Jepp immediately made a 360° of the Elko airport and said, 'There, above Slim's Service Station. See that orange glow where the blinker should be? It flickers like a flame. I'll bet that's the wreckage of that DC-3.' Jepp then told Company Radio to tell someone to proceed to Slim's and search the hill above."

About twenty minutes after leaving Elko, Painter said, "Company Radio called to say that a highway patrolman had gone to Slim's, looked up the hill, and could see nothing. Jepp, in the sternest voice I had ever heard him use, said, 'Tell that Patrolman to go back to Slim's and walk up the hill a hundred yards and he should be able to see something.' Later, Company Radio called to report that the patrolman had done as Jepp instructed. As he groped his way up the hill, he heard the crackling of flames before he could actually see them. A bit farther up he heard a baby's cry. An infant [two years old] had been thrown clear of the wreckage and was the lone survivor...." [19]

The Denver Post, in its September 5, 1946, edition, reported that the bodies of twenty-one passengers and crew members, many horribly burned and mangled, were strewn across the Elko hillside. The article included a photo of the two-year-old survivor, Peter Link, of Brooklyn, New York, lying in a hospital bed, in addition to pictures of his parents, who had perished in the crash. The Links' two-month-old daughter also died. They had been on their way to Oakland, California, to visit the father's mother, who was seriously ill.

The article said, "A United Airlines pilot [Jepp] unwittingly reported the crash first when he radioed the Elko field of a fire. Mortician Robley Burns was in the first party to arrive at the wreck scene. 'As we approached the flaming plane we found a woman in the brush, unconscious but alive,' Burns related. 'She died shortly afterwards. Then I told the men to be quiet. I heard a baby crying. He was bawling something awful. I went over and picked him up. He had been thrown clear of the plane and was sitting there on the hillside. His crying was loud enough to be heard over the crackle of the flames.'"★ [20]

Co-pilot Painter said that "doctors stated that this little boy could not have survived until a morning search would have found him. Jepp undoubtedly did save the boy's life." [21]

At some point in the mid-1940s, Jepp made the acquaintance of another pilot, William Corbin "Corky" Douglas, who had flown DC-4 transports for the Navy in the Pacific and was now a co-pilot with United. The two became—and would remain—the closest of friends for the rest of their lives.

★ In the early nineties, an effort to locate Peter Link, the crash survivor, was mounted for the television program, *Unsolved Mysteries*, but the search was unsuccessful.

Douglas recalled that, unlike many other United captains, Jepp allowed him to take control of the DC-3 as a learning experience, especially during landings and takeoffs. "If we were flying an interesting approach," he said, "he'd caution me about something so I wouldn't put our plane or our passengers in jeopardy, but he let me go. But he would not let me make some serious blunder so he could recover it. He'd let me stagger through some particular procedure because you have to do it and make the mistakes and find out about them to do it right. Of course, flying then was a sight more complicated than it is today. We had only the beam with the 'A' on one side and the 'N' on the other for navigation. We had no direction finders. We had to listen to the damned thing and be able to interpret it by the sound of it."

Douglas was unstinting in his praise of Jepp as a pilot. "The man was unique. Not just capable, but head and shoulders above the rest. Everyone at United knew he was the best."

Douglas remembered Jepp's sometimes oddball sense of humor. "Whenever we landed, he'd slap me on the back and say, 'Damn it, Cork, we made it again! Let's get the hell out of here before the son-of-a-bitch explodes and we're all burned to cinders!'"

Douglas also recalled Jepp had a way of calming nervous passengers. "We'd get ready to fly on some gloomy day when the weather was terrible and Jepp would go back and see the people huddled in their seats and he'd smile and say, 'Folks, don't be concerned. Everything is in order. And if you need us, we're right up there in the cockpit.'" [22]

Jeppesen and Company rode the post-war economic wave toward prosperity, but it was not always a smooth ride. Jepp said that his company's main competitor, Coast and Geodedic Survey, a U.S. government agency, "was nearly giving their charts away for about what it cost me in postage. It took me four years to get a bill through Congress to force Coast and Geodedic Survey to charge a realistic amount for their charts." [23]

After moving from downtown Denver, the company relocated to this building between two hangars at Stapleton Airport. *(E. B. Jeppesen collection)*

In 1947, the Air Force became a separate branch of the armed services, and Jeppesen and Company received new contracts from it, along with additional contracts from the Army and Navy, which ensured the survival of the company. In addition, the firm began receiving more orders from the commercial airlines, which were then undergoing a rapid expansion of routes and service.★

Also in 1947, an important contribution to air safety was made when Standard Instrument Approach Procedures were adopted. Jeppesen and Company worked closely with the Civil Aeronautics Administration (the forerunner of the Federal Aeronautics Administration, or FAA) to create the approach template design. [24]

The airline industry was indeed booming in the late forties and early fifties. New carriers, some with just a dream and a handful of planes, were starting up, and the established airlines were expanding. America was on the move as never before, and cars, trains, and buses just

★ In that same year of 1947, Jepp was deeply saddened to learn of the death of his friend, mentor, and Portland aviation pioneer Tex Rankin, who was killed when the Republic Seabee he was flying hit a power line after taking off from Klamath Falls, Oregon. (Walker, 30)

Jepp's mother, Jepp, and his two sons, Dicky and Jimmy, on the occasion of Petrea's 70th birthday, 1949. *(E. B. Jeppesen collection)*

didn't move people as fast as they now wanted to go. Jeppesen and Company's business grew like a Colorado wildfire. In fact, the company soon outgrew its downtown office space and moved out near Stapleton Airport, where it rented space between two hangars.

As his firm expanded, Jepp added more and more employees to handle the specialized tasks. Long-time Jeppesen employee Harald Prommel had been the production coordinator at the Gates Rubber Company in Denver before joining Jeppesen in the late 1940s. He

Formal United Air Lines portrait of Jepp, circa 1948. *(E. B. Jeppesen collection)*

recounted how he came to the firm: "I answered an ad in the newspaper that sounded interesting. I was interviewed by Mr. Jeppesen and was hired. His reputation was that he was probably one of the ten best guys in the left seat [pilot] in the entire country."★

Studio portrait of Nadine, 1948. *(E. B. Jeppesen collection)*

Prommel was also a pilot and had taught celestial navigation while in the service. He said, "I started working at Jeppesen before there were two sales divisions there. I think I talked the company into going into two divisions—one for natural color relief maps and one for the aviation product. Natural color relief maps fascinated me. So I became the first manager of what was called the Contract Map Division or the 'Natural Color Map Division'; the name changed from time to time."

The company contracted with the well-known relief-map artist Hal Shelton to do the paintings that would become the color maps. The relief maps were also purchased by the airlines and printed in the in-flight magazines. Prommel said, "The Jeppesen natural color relief map is like a picture of the ground. When you looked at these aeronautical charts, as opposed to the aviation maps, you didn't see a bunch of wavy lines and tell yourself that was a mountain. It looked like a mountain and it was accurate. Shelton was a tremendous artist, and he was internationally renowned." [25]

Hal Shelton recalled that he began doing work for Jepp after the two literally bumped into each other in the late 1940s. "I was going around a corner in downtown Denver and physically we bumped into each other," he laughed. "He knew a little bit about what I did and I knew a little bit about what he did. I had made a lot of aeronautical-chart types of things during the war when I was with the Air Force, and I think that's how he first became aware of my work. Anyway, this day Jepp said, 'Follow me and don't say a word.' So we went up to the sixth floor of an office building and entered a commercial art studio. There were two or three artists there trying to make a map. Jepp said he wanted passengers to enjoy their flight, and part of that was to be able to recognize the terrain they were flying over; the artists were attempting to do that."

After the two men left the building, Jepp asked Shelton what he thought about the illustrators' work. Shelton said, "They were commercial artists and were very good, but they were not equipped to do this

---

* In 1949 Jepp was honored with the Certificate of Pilot Merit in recognition of his being selected one of the top ten commercial airline pilots in the industry.

particular thing. I didn't think you could recognize the terrain from what those artists were producing."

Jepp then asked Shelton if he would produce a few sample draw-ings—strip charts—of the route between Denver and the West Coast that realistically depicted the hills, rivers, forests, mountains, highways, and cities as they would look from the air. Shelton said yes and captured the concept perfectly; Jepp was so impressed he took the drawings to Pat Patterson, the president of United, who also liked them and bought the idea of Shelton and Jeppesen producing maps that were far better than what Rand McNally was currently supplying. Soon the concept expanded beyond maps for the flying passenger, and Jeppesen, with Shelton's detailed paintings, began making wall maps for schools. Some of the maps also found their way into textbooks and encyclopedias. [26]

Drawing the maps was extraordinarily time-consuming. The April 1960 issue of *Airlift* magazine, in an article about Jeppesen and Company, noted, "A skilled artist, faced with the job of getting mountains, rivers and highways shaded exactly right, does well if he completes one square inch per hour. Original artwork on the map of California took 1,500 man-hours." [27]

An interesting sidelight to the maps: When they were printed for United, most of them bore a dot and the name "Dunlap" over Iowa, in honor of Nadine's hometown. Residents of other Iowa towns, which happened to be larger than tiny Dunlap, wondered why their places of residence were ignored. Jepp responded, "To those who would blink at Dunlap, I will simply say that if you saw what I saw in Dunlap, you'd be blinking yet. She was, and still is, a beautiful woman, and I am telling you quite simply to never underestimate the power of a woman, espe-cially if she is gorgeous and marriageable and worth living with the rest of your life.... It is a tribute to my wife and the fine people in the town that produced her." [28]

Son Jim also noted that his father had another reason for including Dunlap on the maps. "He said that if Dad ever saw a map of the United States printed other than for United Airlines, and he saw 'Dunlap'" on it, he'd know that someone had plagiarized it." [29]

Shelton said he worked for Jepp for about twenty years "until there were no more maps left to paint. I enjoyed working for him. He was

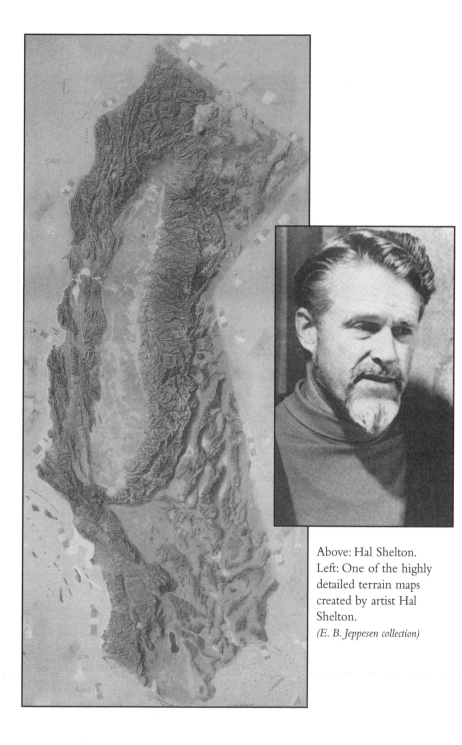

Above: Hal Shelton.
Left: One of the highly
detailed terrain maps
created by artist Hal
Shelton.
(E. B. Jeppesen collection)

loyal, he was understanding, he was great. We were very good friends. Sometimes we would have disagreements about one thing or another, about the scale of a map or how to depict a particular terrain feature, for instance, but he didn't know enough about art to know how an artist arrives at certain things." [30]

Orders for the Jeppesen manuals were coming in faster than the small staff and cramped quarters could accommodate them. Additionally, airports themselves were expanding and each new improvement necessitated a revised page in the manual. Jepp was forced to "bite the bullet" and hire additional draftsmen to keep up with the changes. The expansion of international air travel also led to the company adding hundreds of charts for foreign airports. The profits and possibilities seemed endless—and so did the headaches.

The pace was killing Jepp. Not only was he still flying a full schedule for United but, between flying assignments—his days off—he was also putting in twelve hours overseeing Jeppesen and Company. A bad back was making it difficult for him to fly. "Sometimes," his son Jim said, "his back hurt him so much that, in flight, the co-pilot would have to take over while Jepp lay down and stretched out on the cockpit floor." [31]

In 1954, Jepp's doctor told the forty-seven-year-old pilot that he was risking a heart attack if he didn't give up one of his two jobs. Jepp made the emotionally painful decision to quit his first love—flying—and concentrate on the chart business that was, if not as satisfying as flight, making him a wealthy man. In 1954, he retired from United after having logged 18,000 hours and over three million miles in his twenty-four years of service.

Leaving the airline was one of the most difficult things Jepp ever did. It was so very painful that, for three years afterwards, he took a roundabout route to his office near Stapleton, just so he wouldn't have to look at the United sign on the hangar there. [32]

In 1955, Jeppesen's contract with the Navy ended. One of the results of this severing of ties was that Jeppesen lost a critical source, not only of revenue, but also of update information necessary for the other charts.

Wayne Rosenkrans, a World War II fighter pilot who had joined the company in October 1945 as a draftsman and worked his way up to Vice President of Operations and, eventually, company president, noted, "We had our Washington office in operation at that time, so we were able to make arrangements to get the missing information from the Federal Aeronautics Administration. We asked them for it and they supplied it. We took it off the FAA teletype in Washington and then transmitted it to our office in Denver." [33]

Luckily, as soon as the Navy contract ended, Jepp picked up contracts from both the Army and the Air Force. Then more contracts came in from the airlines—Continental, Braniff, Eastern, Chicago and Southern, Northwest—nearly all the U.S. carriers.

Because of the Army contract, Jepp realized that he needed to open an office in Europe to handle the new business, and he needed someone competent to get it started. He looked around in-house and selected Harald Prommel, manager of the Color Map Division.

"We lost the Navy contract at almost the same time we got the Army Aviation contract," said Prommel, "and that contract required charts for a good part of Europe, Germany especially. In order to get the contract, the company made a commitment that we would set up a plant over there."

When Prommel arrived in Frankfurt on April 1, 1957, he had to start from scratch. "The company had gotten a lawyer and a printer," he said, "and one of the biggest printers in Germany. Beyond that, nothing. My job was to incorporate the company under German law, get space, hire and train a bi- and tri-lingual staff, and be ready to deliver on the military contract in two-and-a-half months. I had a budget, but nobody had looked for any space."

In spite of his German name, Prommel did not speak German; he had to learn in a hurry. He also discovered some differences between Americans and Germans. Because of the short time frame required to get the branch up and running, corners had to be cut, solutions devised on the fly, and good old American know-how improvised on the spot.

"When it comes to innovation to solve problems," Prommel noted, "and success through improvisation, there is nobody in the world like the American. The American can improvise in order to get ahead better than any other nationality that I have ever worked with."

One of the German office's early problems was a lack of phone service. "We didn't have telephones for about eight weeks," Prommel said. "We had to go down and line up at a public phone on one of the downtown streets, or we would call our production manager's wife at home and tell her who to call or handle what needed to be handled. Even when we got phones, it took about eight hours to set up a telephone call to the United States. Today you just pick up a phone and dial it. It wasn't that way when we were there in 1957."

German labor law also was a consideration. Prommel explained that in Germany a worker, after being on the job for six weeks, could not be fired except for extreme problems such as thievery. One day Prommel saw two of his employees fighting because one had called the other a "mechanic."

"In Germany," Prommel said, "calling someone a 'mechanic' is bad, an unforgivable insult. I hauled them into my office and said, 'I don't see anything wrong with calling a man a 'mechanic,' but this is your language, so if it's wrong, it's wrong. But let me tell you one thing—there will be no more fighting about it on company time. If, at the end of the day, you get out of the elevator and go out onto Kaiserstrasse and kill each other, it's perfectly all right with me. But you do it on your own time or I'm going to fire both your asses, and to hell with the labor court." Prommel said his status after handling this incident zoomed within headquarters—and in the eyes of his German staff.

Prommel and his team quickly began turning out the needed approach, or "let-down," charts using a combination of information from the U.S., German, airline, and Army sources. The European airlines had their own chart system in place at that time, but Prommel thought it would be better if the Army pilots used the same types of charts they were accustomed to using in the States. "The Jeppesen system was so much better in just plain, common-sense terms, so everybody started changing to the Jepp system. It was better, and people trusted it because they trusted Jeppesen."

Prommel stayed with the Frankfurt office as its director for twelve months before returning to the headquarters in Denver. [34]

In 1957, the Jeppesens hired an African-American cook and house-keeper named Ernestine Boyd, who worked for them for thirty-seven years. She has fond memories of the couple: "Mr. Jeppesen was very nice, a jokester. He always had a joke for me every day. And Mrs. Jeppesen was his very life. I hope someday to find a man that would be that close to me.

"I did most of the cookin', but Mrs. Jeppesen did some cookin' herself. She liked the way I cooked pot roasts and the way I cooked a leg of lamb."

Ernestine was one of the few people to see a giving, generous side to Jepp. Sometimes, she said, when no one was around, he would slip her money. "He'd say, 'Take this twenty dollars and go for lunch, Ernestine. You deserve it. Don't tell anybody now.' Or it might be forty dollars. I'd say, 'Oh, Mr. Jeppesen, this is two twenties,' and he'd say, 'Oh, take it. I didn't see that.' You know, that kind of stuff."

Nadine was also generous. Once, when Ernestine mentioned that she'd like to go on a cruise, Nadine asked her how much it would cost.

"Not much. About eighteen-hundred dollars," the housekeeper replied. Nadine handed her a check for a thousand dollars.

"Don't tell anybody," Nadine said. "This is just our secret." [35]

The 1950s were unexpectedly golden years for Jeppesen and Company. The firm's expansion kept pace with the growth of the world's airlines. The money flowed in and the money flowed out, for the company's operations were very labor-intensive.

Jepp's printing bill was also growing with each chart change, and he decided that, in order to save money and maximize profits, the company would need to have its own printing plant. This, in turn, meant Jeppesen and Company would need to abandon the office space it rented between two hangars at Denver's Stapleton Airport and build its own facility to accommodate the presses and additional people. So, in early 1959, the firm began construction on a $250,000, 45,000-square-foot building on a two-acre parcel of land on Smith Road, just north of Stapleton. [36]

After Jeppesen and Company moved from its rented space to its own building near Stapleton and began to do most of its printing in-house, more employees had to be hired to do the printing, collate the pages, and insert them into the binders; others were hired to send out the monthly updates to the subscribers. The postage bills alone were enormous.

"We had draftsmen who would draw every chart by hand," said Wayne Rosenkrans. "This was way before computerized drawing programs—before computers, really. Most of the employees were collators in paper assembly. Everything was done by hand, and the hand collation just drove Jepp nuts. He thought there had to be a better way. We tried various types of collating machines, but the paper we had to use to keep the weight of the book down was just too light. The machines would pick up a sheet and wave it around and it would float away and get static on it." Jepp eventually found a machine that, with a little tinkering, would do the job, and most of the collation team was let go.

The company also tried to get all the airlines to standardize their approaches to the different airports so that it wouldn't have to print different charts for each airline to use for the same airport—a task akin to herding cats. Rosenkrans remembered that he once spent two weeks in a big room in Washington with representatives from each airline as they went over their sectional charts and tried to agree on minimum altitudes.

"They would take a segment of an airway and would agree on a minimum altitude for that segment; we then took that information and published it for those airways. Prior to that time, they didn't have a standardized minimum altitude. Sometimes they would get into the dangdest arguments. Let's say Braniff was flying into Denver—their approach was aligned with coming in from the south; they couldn't care less about the guys coming in from the north or east or west, and that was true of about every approach. Northwest had their favorite approaches and they'd say, 'We don't give a damn what Braniff wants coming up from the south.' But eventually we got them to agree and it came to pass." [37]

With the company on a seemingly non-stop upward flight, it was inevitable that major changes were in the offing.

7: A Changing of the Guard

By all accounts, Jepp was a most unusual—and sometimes difficult—person to work for.

He operated the company the way he flew his first Jenny—by the seat of his pants. He had not finished high school, and, except for a correspondence course or two, had received no training in business management, had taken a one-man company and, almost in spite of himself and with his own creativity, sweat equity, and several strokes of good fortune, had jury-rigged it into an enormously successful enterprise. In many ways, he had reached what some would call his "level of incompetence."

His handling of officers and employees was equally haphazard. In the blink of an eye he could go from being kind to difficult and demanding and back again. One thing he never was was monetarily generous. By all accounts, he was tight, frugal, and, yes, cheap. He rarely, if ever, gave money away, no matter how worthy the cause or well-meaning the charity, and his refusal to pick up a check was almost legendary. "Whenever Jepp and I would go to lunch or something," Wayne Rosenkrans laughed, "he'd always slide the check over to me and say, 'Wayne, that looks a lot better on your expense account than mine.'"

Jepp had many interests and passions. Besides his business and Nadine, Jepp loved baseball—especially the New York Yankees. Rosenkrans recalled, "He remarked to me on more than one occasion: 'If I had my druthers, I would fly the airmail in the wintertime and play center field for the Yankees in the summertime.' He loved the Yankees."

Whenever the Yankees were playing in the World Series, Jepp

loosened his purse strings so that he and Nadine could take off and travel to the games. During one World Series, Wayne Rosenkrans happened to be in New York on company business and Jepp and Nadine generously invited him to attend a game with them.

Later that evening the three of them were having dinner at the expensive Waldorf Astoria when Nadine asked Wayne to dance. They stayed on the dance floor for hours. When Rosenkrans complained that his feet were getting tired, Nadine told him, "We're going to dance until Jepp picks up the check—even if we have to dance all night!"

They almost did dance all night. Finally, after a lot of fidgeting, Jepp paid the bill. [1]

Friend Tal Miller recalled a time when he, Jepp, and another pal had gone to lunch at Denver's Golden Ox restaurant: "Jepp was very tight with money. Eddie Mehlin and I decided, 'This time the bugger is going to pay,' so Eddie and I went to the bathroom when the bill came. We stayed in there for about a half hour. We watched him and he fumbled and looked for us, and he finally had to pay. It was kind of fun." [2]

Some felt Jepp's stingy streak was because he and his parents had been so poor that they almost lost their house during the Great Depression, and he was afraid that it could happen again. Only this time he had so much more at stake.

Jepp also had an odd management style. "He never delegated," said Rosenkrans. "He would 'assume.' He would let you do something your way but would reserve the right to criticize, to say, 'I didn't think it would work' if you failed. For example, he'd talk to a draftsman and voice his opinion, then walk away with, 'Do whatever you want.' So if the draftsman did it his own way and it worked out fine, okay. If it did not, Jepp was quick to remark, 'Didn't I tell you that I didn't think it would work?' He had a very peculiar management style. But he also had a very creative and inventive mind. If we encountered a problem, he always knew there must be some solution, so he would let people try and figure it out. He never said, 'Do it my way.' He just would get everybody thinking about a solution until they came up with it."

For someone who often had to make quick decisions at the controls of a plane, Jepp sometimes seemed totally indecisive at the helm of his company. He would dither, pace, and agonize over the simplest issues. Rosenkrans said, "He was accused by many, including me, of being a procrastinator. He just could not make up his mind, could not make a decision. Instead of saying, 'Yes, go with this,' he would think it over. And over. What he was doing was refining the idea in his mind and would get a better product down the line. But his decision-making in the cockpit was instantaneous. I would say to myself, 'God, if he would just do that in the business.' A lot of people said, 'Why the hell can't he make up his mind?'" [3]

One trait that made Jepp sometimes difficult to work for was his absolute, unbending commitment to accuracy, for he knew that every chart his company published could literally be a matter of life or death.

Don Sellars who, for many years was involved in the production of the charts, said, "Jepp was a positive stickler for absolute fact being on those charts. When I worked directly for him, he would question me to the point of exasperation—'Do you know this length for sure? Do you know the altitude for positive?' and we'd go through the facts once again. If there was a mistake on a chart, it was always a real, personal crisis for him—even a small mistake that didn't have any relationship to the safety of the flight. If a pilot called in and said, 'Hey, this isn't the way it actually is,' Jepp would have several people working late into the night to correct the error and get the new chart out the next day. Jepp had trained enough people in that kind of 'accuracy mentality' that the company was left in pretty good hands when he retired." [4]

Harald Prommel, former chief of production, echoed Sellars' comments. "Everybody who worked for Jepp knew that accuracy was of paramount importance. Everybody was very careful. They knew what would happen if there was an error [in the charts]." [5]

By 1960, the company was churning out an unbelievable amount of data, all of which needed to be perfect; the slightest error could have disastrous consequences. The Jeppesen workers were receiving daily reports from the government and other sources about changes affecting millions of miles of charted airways, 8,000 airports, national weather interpretation, the latest information about approach patterns, takeoff and landing procedures, radio frequencies, and radar and electronic information.

As the information poured in like an unending tsunami, it needed to be immediately read, studied, and analyzed. Then a determination as to whether or not a change to existing charts was warranted needed to be made. If change was necessary, then skilled draftsmen went to work revising and updating the obsolete charts, which then were checked, scrutinized, and subjected to five separate editing conferences before they were approved. After receiving their final blessing, the fresh charts were sent to the printing department, where printing plates were made, the required number of copies printed by the bank of high-speed presses, the sheets cut, the binder holes drilled, the sheets collated, and then put in the mail to be whisked off to the appropriate subscribers—all within two or three days. In special cases, changes could be made, printed, and mailed within twenty-four hours! It has been estimated that, some weeks, the number of drafting changes, which could run several per page, exceeded 20,000.

The Frankfurt office operated the same way, except on a slightly smaller scale. The language on the charts was in English, the world-wide standard language of aviation, but much of the data came into Frankfurt in different languages, which would need to be translated. In addition, the measurements of the Frankfurt charts had to be in knots and metric values. [6]

Jepp was a great story teller, and the following apocryphal tale sent his audience howling. In 1980, when he was in Mexico City to receive the William E. Downes Award from the Airport Operators Council International, he related the enormity of his printing challenges—and the day a fly flew in through the open window of his company's press room. "The fly landed on the ink roller, where he was promptly smashed," Jepp said. "His perfectly printed image appeared on all the following charts, and was so positioned that he appeared to be making a final approach into Reno. We got a lot of letters about that, but at least the fly told us that people were looking at our charts. And the fly must have made it to Reno okay, because I never saw him again after that." [7]

In addition to the airway manuals, the company also introduced a loose-leaf booklet titled *Radio-Air-Route Guide*, which contained current radio navigation information for all charted airways, airway traffic control procedures, and civil regulations. Like the airway chart changes, the changes to the *Radio-Air-Route Guide* were constant. It seemed that whenever an aviation need was identified, Jeppesen and Company set out to satisfy that need—a monumental task that had no end. Annual sales in 1960 topped $2.5 million. Jeppesen and Company quickly grew to become the Post Office's best Denver customer, with more than $200,000 spent per year on postage alone. [8]

At one point Jepp gave some serious thought to expanding the company's offerings and making highway road maps. It seemed like a good way to supplement the aerial-navigation chart business, for automobiles weren't as subject to the whims of government regulators and the marketplace as was the airline industry.

As luck would have it, the company managed to secure contracts with a couple of oil companies which planned to give them out free to their service-station customers, as was the custom at that time. But

America's principal map-makers, Rand McNally and H. M. Goushá, did not like the upstart company horning in on their business and told Jepp they would sue him unless he sold them forty-nine percent of the company.

Jepp stewed over this development but then realized it represented a potential gold mine. In spite of the growing success of the company, worries about liability had begun to consume him. *What if one tiny piece of information on one single chart is wrong,* he would obsess. *What if that one tiny piece of erroneous information led to a crash and people were killed? The company would be sued. I would be sued. Nadine and I could lose everything!*

For once it did not take long for Jepp to make a decision; in April 1961 he sold fifty-one percent of his compny to Goushá.

In 1961, the entire Denver headquarters staff posed for this group photo.
(E. B. Jeppesen collection)

Shortly thereafter, the Times Mirror Corporation, which was acquiring various companies all over the country, became interested in buying the Goushá road-map company. During the negotiations, Times Mirror learned that Goushá owned part of Jeppesen and wanted to include the purchase of the chart maker in the deal.

Although reluctant to lose control of his company, Jepp's mounting worries about liability finally got the upper hand. Family friend Paul Burke said that Jepp "could conceive of every kind of fatal occurrence, and one of them was the liability associated with an improperly drawn chart that might result in an accident. What would the liability be—would it wipe out the company? He couldn't insure it for enough money, so I think that finally brought about the decision to sell the remainig shares of the company to Times Mirror." [9]

The deal was done, but there was an unexpected consequence.

For whatever reason, Al Casey,* head of Times Mirror, was not enamored of Jepp and did not want him hanging on as president, and so had made Jepp sign an agreement committing him to selecting his successor within a five-year period. But Jepp's inability to make decisions—or perhaps a deep-seated reluctance to be ousted—kicked in.

Jepp pretended to go along with the plan. Six or eight people, including the improbably named Forward C. "Bud" Wiser, Jr., who in 1969 became head of TWA, interviewed for the job, but none, in Jepp's view, were good enough. [10]

In 1961, about the time of the sale of the company, the government threatened to break the monopoly Jeppesen had on the chart business by contracting with U.S. Coast and Geodetic Survey and saving the government a great deal of money in the process. [11]

Wayne Rosenkrans recalled clearly the battle with Coast and

---

* Albert Vincent Casey was the hard-driving president of the company that owned the Los Angeles Times. He turned the corporation into a media conglomerate which eventually owned numerous newspapers and broadcasting entities around the country. Casey was born in Boston in 1920 and graduated from Harvard before serving in World War II. Prior to coming to Times Mirror, he worked for Railway Express and the Southern Pacific Railroad. After eight years at the helm of Times Mirror, he went on to become CEO of American Airlines from 1974 to 1985, then served as U.S. Postmaster General for eight months in 1986. In 1991 he was selected by President George H. W. Bush to head the Resolution Trust Corporation which oversaw the disposing of financial and real estate assets left behind when many savings and loan companies failed in the 1980s. He died in July 2004 at age 84. (Congressional Record, Nov. 16, 2005)

Geodetic Survey. "The government had a competitive service in the Department of Commerce called Coast and Geodetic Survey, and they were pricing their service under an 1895 statute that was made before the airplane was invented. That statute said they had to recover the cost of printing, period, but it didn't define 'printing.' So they were just pulling a figure out of the air and putting it down."

Jeppesen and Company went to the Department of Commerce and suggested that they be realistic about their pricing so that the company could compete fairly. "They wouldn't listen to us," Rosenkrans said, "so we went to Colorado Senator Gordon Allott and Colorado Congressman Byron Rogers and told them the story. They said, 'This isn't right,' so they went to bat for us." [12]

Rogers pointed out on the floor of the House of Representatives that many of the C&GS maps were simply copies of Jeppesen charts. "It is obvious that private industry is doomed if this practice continues," he told his fellow lawmakers. [13]

Jepp found himself prowling the hallowed halls of Congress, ready to button-hole any lawmaker who would give him a few seconds to state his case. "When I caught a politician," Jepp said, "I had to get his attention, fast. I had a fifteen-second speech, a forty-five-second speech, and a three-minute one." [14]

Rosenkrans said, "During this period, Allott wanted Jepp to testify before the Senate Appropriations Committee, so we prepared this long address for the Committee. I was there and we had our attorney there. They put Jepp at the head of the table; he gets very nervous with those types of things, so I suggested that I sit beside him and in case he choked up, I could take over and read it. Well, he just got started and beads of perspiration were coming down and he choked, so I grabbed the script and read it. We get back to Allott's office and Allott told Jepp, just like a father to a son, 'Now, this is how you're going to run your business from now on.' Of course, Jepp didn't like anyone telling him what he was going to be doing." [15]

Later, after regaining his composure, Jepp told reporters, "We are not afraid of competition and will welcome any challenge predicated on quality of product and fairness of price. But we cannot contend with subsidized practices or fractional pricing legislated by the government." [16]

The night after the Senate hearing, Rosenkrans and Jepp retired to their rooms at the Washington Hilton. Rosenkrans said, "We had adjacent rooms and I'm thinking, 'This is going to be a hell of a night,' because Jepp was all upset. So we have dinner and he's still talking and talking, and we go to bed and I just get to sleep when the adjoining door to his room opens and in he came in his shorts and said, 'Now, Wayne, listen to this,' and I'd listen and said, 'All right. Let's get some sleep.' He said, 'Okay,' and ten minutes later, in he'd come again. By morning he had it all figured out—Allott didn't know what he was doing; that that was no way for a senator to act."

Allott didn't care to see Jepp after that, but Jeppesen got the statute passed. It defined the cost of the printing and increased what C&GS considered their true costs. "Of course," said Rosenkrans, "their charts went by indicia mail, so their price had to include post-office postage, and that brought their pricing up. It also included printing labor. Initially, then, their pricing and ours were pretty close."

The government subsequently dropped their plans to put Jeppesen out of business through unfair competition. Admiral H. Arnold Karo, director of C&GS, even admitted that the Jeppesen charts were more comprehensive than his agency's maps and "offered a worldwide service that the government did not." [17]

"The government wasn't much of a competitor," Rosenkrans noted. "They couldn't graphically execute as well as we could, and they didn't put their charts in the forms that pilots like. There was also another reason. When we and C&GS started, the charts were just for the U.S. Then times changed and the business became worldwide and C&GS couldn't be worldwide; they were restricted to just the U.S. There are an awful lot of pilots who operate worldwide, so they were no longer candidates for government service—of any government. We were the only commercial supplier, and we still are."* [18]

---

* On August 14, 1965, Congress passed the bill leveling the aviation-chart playing field. (*Checklist*, 3)

The early 1960s saw Jepp and Nadine move from Grape Street into an expansive ranch-style home at 37 Sedgwick Drive in the Devonshire Heights section of Englewood, a Denver suburb, and Jeppesen and Company expanding the types of products and services it offered, such as instructional courses. Don Sellars was an ex-Marine Corps aviator who joined Jeppesen in September 1963 and was put to work developing what was then called the ATR, or Airline Transport Rating Course (today a certification course known as the ATP—Air Transport Pilot Course).

Not long after he sold the company, Jepp and Nadine moved to this ranch-style home in the Denver suburb of Englewood. *(Whitlock photo)*

Sellars said, "There was almost nothing out in the market at that time to teach a person how to be a pilot, and the courses we were developing just sold like hotcakes. Everybody then was learning how to fly.

"Jepp was sure the way to teach these courses was to have a stand-up instructor lecturing to a class, but he wanted us to present really good graphics that would support the instructor. We had a huge set of over-head transparencies that supported the instructors, and those sold very well. Our primary competition in the market about the same time was an outfit called Sanderson Films, and we competed nip and tuck with them." In a few years, the two firms would become one. [19]

Despite being squeezed out of his own company in the mid-1960s, Jepp, instead of becoming bitter, never lost his pride or enthusiasm in the firm. Indeed, he continued to ballyhoo and promote the company as if he were still running it, and delighted in showing celebrities around the facility.

One of those celebrities was Arthur Godfrey who, at the time, was a huge radio and television star. It was said that Godfrey, known as "America's grandfather," was such a smooth pitchman that he could sell refrigerators to Eskimos.

On several occasions, while talking about his love of flying, Godfrey would mention Jeppesen and Company on the air and how much he relied on their aerial charts. In 1950, the celebrity had qualified for his pilot's license; the following year he trained to fly jets and extolled the virtues of American pilots fighting in the Korean War. Godfrey, said Eddie Rickenbacker, the legendary World War I aviator and president of Eastern Airlines, did more to promote aviation than any other single person since Charles Lindbergh. For many non-pilot listeners, Godfrey's glowing words about Jeppesen's navigation charts were the first time they had ever heard the name of the company mentioned.

On October 17, 1964, the red-haired, freckle-faced Godfrey, a private pilot and friend of Jepp's, was in Denver to address the Aero Club. To take advantage of this opportunity, Jepp invited Godfrey to visit the company—a visit Jepp personally guided and which was recorded by a photographer the firm hired. Jepp and Nadine were all smiles. [20]

Jepp and Nadine beam as they show radio and television personality Arthur Godfrey (right) around the company on October 17, 1964. The man in white shirt and tie is George Reeves, Manager of Distribution. *(E. B. Jeppesen collection)*

The smiles came to an abrupt end a month later when Jepp's worst nightmare came true. On the snowy night of November 15, 1964, a crash occurred that was blamed on a Jeppesen chart. Although he was personally indemnified from any liability that might arise from errors in the charts, Jepp was nonetheless devastated at the news.

Flying from Phoenix to Las Vegas, Bonanza Airlines Flight 114 suddenly ran into a blizzard on its approach to McCarren Airport. Ten miles south of the airport, with visibility at zero, the Fokker-Fairchild F-27A clipped the top of a 5,000-foot mountain; all twenty-three passengers and the flight crew of three perished.

Wrongful death claims were paid by Bonanza's insurer, Aetna Casualty and Surety Company of Connecticut, who then sued Jeppesen to recover its loss. After Jeppesen's request for a jury trial was denied because the company's lawyers had not made the request within the prescribed time frame, a bench trial was held in 1969 in the U.S. District Court of the District of Nevada. The judge found the chart maker liable for having produced a "defective" chart which the judge said led directly to the crash, while the airline was found to have been negligent in failing to discover the defect and alert its pilots. The judgment apportioned damages between the two parties—eighty percent to Jeppesen and twenty percent to Bonanza.

The case was tied up in the courts for more than a decade; twelve years would pass before Jeppesen's appeal was heard by the Ninth Circuit Court of Appeals. Although the parties to the lawsuit did not dispute the accuracy of the Las Vegas chart, the defect was found to be in the "graphic presentation" of the information. Each Jeppesen chart portrays two views of the proper approach: a "plan" view which shows the approach segment of the flight as if viewing it from above, and an "elevation," or side view, as if looking at the same scene in profile. This latter view shows a descending line depicting the minimum safe altitudes as the approach continues. Each chart thus provides information in two ways: by words and numbers, and by graphics. (See Appendix.)

The problem with the chart, according to the plaintiffs, was twofold: that the "elevation" or profile drawing did not show obstacles more than three miles from the airport, and that both the "plan" and "elevation" appeared, at first glance, to be drawn to the same scale when, in fact, the scale of the "plan" was five times that of the "elevation."

An aviation industrial psychologist called as a professional witness by Aetna testified that most of the Jeppesen approach charts are drawn in approximately the same scale for both the "plan" and "elevation"

views; that a pilot or navigator would come to take this graphic relationship for granted, and would, without reading the fine print, assume that
the scale of the two views on the Las Vegas chart was the same as on the
Jeppesen charts for other airports. It was this discrepancy, or "defect,"
which evidently caused the pilots to think they had already left the deadly mountain safely behind them when they began their approach into
McCarren when, in fact, the mountain was dead ahead.

For their part, Jeppesen's lawyers disputed the claim that the Las
Vegas chart was an anomaly, and called several experienced pilots to testify that they never made assumptions such as those apparently made by
the Bonanza crew, and did not know of any pilots who did.

The Ninth Circuit Court disagreed with Jeppesen's assertion, writing, "While the information conveyed in words and figures on the Las
Vegas approach chart was completely correct, the purpose of this chart
was to translate this information into an instantly understandable graphic representation. This is what gave the chart its usefulness; this is what
the chart contributed to the mere data amassed and promulgated by the
FAA. It was reliance on this graphic portrayal that Jeppesen invited. The
trial judge found that the Las Vegas chart 'radically departed' from the
usual presentation of graphics in the other Jeppesen charts; that the conflict between the information conveyed by words and numbers and the
information conveyed by graphics rendered the chart unreasonably dangerous and a defective product."

The court's decision cost Jeppesen and Company millions. [21]

The Bonanza case was the first, but would not be the last, lawsuit
against Jeppesen. Perhaps the surprising thing is that there had been no
similar suits during the first thirty years of the company's existence.

Another crash for which a Jeppesen chart was blamed occurred on
September 8, 1973, when a plane carrying six persons slammed into a
mountainside near Cold Bay, Alaska. The pilots were completely lost;
referring to the charts would have done them no good because the area
over which they were flying was not shown on any chart.

Tragically, all six persons on board were killed. In the lawsuits that
followed *(Brocklesby, et al. v. Jeppesen,* and *Brocklesby, et al. v. United States)*,
the Jeppesen company's lawyers—the Los Angeles firm of Mendes and

Mount—argued that the erroneous information had been supplied by the FAA and that Jeppesen should not be held liable because of a mistake by a federal agency. The District Court, however, held the Jeppesen chart at fault, even though it was basically copied from an FAA document.

In 1985, the Ninth Circuit Court, after hearing Jeppesen's appeal, held with the lower court, saying that "manipulating" (i.e., re-drawing) the FAA's data "not only shielded, but also absolved, the government from liability in Brocklesby."

Another contentious issue was the fact that the prosecutors were portraying the case as one involving "product liability"—with the charts being the "product." Jeppesen's lawyers vigorously fought the idea.

The case went all the way to the U.S. Supreme Court but, in the end, Jeppesen lost. It was a serious blow to the company and its insurance agency, which had to pay $12 million to Barbara A. Brocklesby and the other families of the deceased. (As a result of this case, however, a federal law was passed that amended the FAA Act and provided chart makers with indemnification should a similar situation arise in the future.) [22]

In spite of the accidents, Jepp's lifetime of contributions to the safe operation of the aviation industry were becoming recognized. In 1965, the National Business Aircraft Association presented him with its Meritorious Service Award which, until that time, had only been given to four others: Charles A. Lindbergh, General Jimmy Doolittle, aircraft manufacturer Donald Douglas, and Igor Sikorsky, the man who had developed the helicopter—quite an exclusive and prestigious club. [23]

But, just as Jepp was being inducted into such exalted ranks, he was simultaneously being squeezed out of his own company. Wayne Rosenkrans stated, "The five years Times Mirror had given him went by and Jepp still hadn't picked a successor. Actually, he had no intention of ever letting loose of the presidency or his company. This was another aspect of him. At that time I was his number two man, and he interviewed I don't know how many guys Times Mirror sent over, and then I would interview them. Why I interviewed them, I never knew. But I would talk with them and give them a tour through the place. There were some really great guys, really good businessmen. But I could see what Jepp was doing. He had no intention of ever letting anyone else in that office."

Tired of waiting for Jepp to select a successor, Times Mirror installed a fellow by the name of Chester "Chess" Pizac as president of Jeppesen. Rosenkrans said, "He and Jepp immediately locked horns. Pizac did not want Jepp around, and vice versa." As a way to ease the hurt feelings, Times Mirror gave Jepp the title of Chairman of the Board,

Chester Pizac was president of Jeppesen for only a short time.
(Courtesy Jeppesen)

Emeritus; Jepp has his business cards reprinted with the word "Emeritus" removed. "Jepp continued to tell everyone that he was the company's chairman, which he wasn't."

"Pizac was different," said Rosenkrans. "For example, he immediately changed his office and put a strong light right over his desk; when you went in, his desk was right under the light. You could see him, but beyond that, everything was dark. You had no idea who else might be in the room." [24]

For many long-time Jeppesen employees, seeing Jepp forced out of the company he had built and raised from scratch was sad. The man who had invented the aerial-navigation chart business found himself a man without a company.

Al Casey could abide Jepp's hanging around the company no longer. The story is told that one day, while Jepp was out of town, Times Mirror arranged to have his entire office transplanted from the Jeppesen building into a space on the fourth floor of the Stapleton Airport terminal. When Jepp returned and discovered he had been unceremoniously moved, he was very angry. Rosenkrans recalled, "But Jepp got even. He elaborately decorated his new office over at Stapleton at the expense of Times Mirror." [25]

Tal Miller had first met Jepp during the 1940s when Jepp was flying for United and Miller was working at Denver Municipal Airport. He thought the world of Jepp's innate ability to take off, fly, and land in even the worst weather. "He was just a pretty lucky pilot," Miller said.

Miller's personal relationship with Jepp began when he had an office on the third floor at Stapleton Field and Jepp had an office on the fourth. "My office was next to the Red Carpet Room," said Miller, "and he was constantly meeting celebrities like Danny Kaye and Victor Borge and other well-known people like Governor John Love, Bob Six, the president of Continental, and Ray Wilson, who started Frontier Airlines; I'd leave my door open to watch him and his guests. Finally we got acquainted. After he finished his business for the day, he'd come down to my office and we'd shoot the bull. I didn't realize what a great person he was; to me, he was just a hell of a nice old pilot. He was always trying to get me to move into the office upstairs because he didn't have much to do. He wanted somebody to talk to."

Jepp regaled Miller with stories about flying in the early days, about forced landings he had made in the 40-B and the DC-3s, and about all the famous old pilots he knew. He talked about flying the mail and about all the pilots who got killed. "That's when he started designing a way of knowing where you are and being able to land when the weather wasn't right," Miller said. [26]

It is perhaps understandable that most businesspersons, aware that they were being ushered out the door, would feel embittered, even angry, would want to yell "to hell with you," and perhaps even start a competitive enterprise. But Jepp's slow, ignominious departure from his company brought on no such hostile reactions. Instead, he continued to be an ambassador for the firm that bore his name, even if "A Times Mirror Company" shared the signage. No, to all outward appearances, Jepp continued to be the smiling, congenial face of the company, the benevolent patriarch, granting newspaper reporters as many interviews as they cared to conduct, just as long as they referred to him as the company's "chairman of the board of directors." In the December 24, 1967 edition of the *Denver Post*, for example, a business columnist referred to him in exactly that way, and that was just fine with Jepp. [27]

Even if Casey didn't appreciate what Jepp brought to the business, many of the Times Mirror people did. At one point, Times Mirror sent some people to see the Jeppesen operation first hand and Jepp was asked to address the group. Durham "Durrie" Monsma, a lawyer for Times Mirror and later executive vice-president and general counsel for Jeppesen, remembered an occasion when he saw Jepp speak to an assembled group of Times Mirror executives.

Monsma said, "They allowed people to ask questions and, you know, you're talking about pretty hardened business types who aren't easily impressed. Obviously, Jepp was held in veneration by these people and, because of the respect in which they held him, the questions tended to be of the 'softball' variety. All of those he handled with great wit and humor. When he was done, this whole room of executives from Times Mirror stood up and gave him a standing ovation. They had been absolutely transfixed while he was talking about his early days as a pilot and entrepreneur. I mean, there was no way you couldn't like the man and be extremely impressed with what he had accomplished." [28]

Jeppesen and Company's business was growing almost exponentially. In 1968, there were forty-two million loose-leaf pages in circulation in tens of thousands of Jeppesen Airway Manuals around the world, including 75,000 large charts of low-and high-altitude airways.

Such a tremendously large database needed to be updated constantly. The charts needed to be revised every twenty-eight days to account for changes in airport tower and terminal radio frequencies, air traffic control procedures, new construction around airports, old obstacles removed, and a dozen other items that could have a bearing on safety. A 1968 newspaper feature story on the company stated that an average of 25,000 changes were sent each week from Washington, D.C., to Denver for processing. "The company is one of Denver's largest air shippers," said the reporter, "and its annual postal bill is between $300,000 and $400,000." [29]

In 1968, Times Mirror acquired Sanderson Films, Inc. Don Sellars recalled that Times Mirror was worried that the Federal Trade Commission would not look kindly upon Jeppesen buying out a competitor, even though Sanderson was grossing but a fraction of Jeppesen's income. "Times Mirror owned a magazine called *Popular Mechanics*," said Sellars, "and bought Sanderson Films through *Popular Mechanics*. [30]

Like Jepp, Paul Sanderson was another of modern aviation's most

Paul Sanderson *(Courtesy Jeppesen)*

innovative and creative pioneers. In 1942, Sanderson joined the Navy and spent six years in naval aviation. Subsequently, he attended the Pittsburgh Institute of Aeronautics, after graduation becoming an instructor there. In 1950, he moved to Florida and began instructing at the Emory Riddle School of Aviation; five years later he opened his own business, the Sanderson Aviation Ground School. He worked long and hard hours, mainly because he couldn't find anyone else who could teach the subjects the way he thought they should be taught. Then it hit him: automate the teaching process as much as possible.

As Sanderson said, "I decided to duplicate myself on slides and tape." He reproduced 800 slides, four reel-to-reel audio tapes, and supplemental manuals that comprised a complete private-pilot training program. It represented the beginning of audio-visual training in general aviation. This systematic approach to ground training became an immediate success, and in 1960, his company, Sanderson Films, Inc., moved to Wichita, hometown of several small-plane manufacturers. One of his early clients was the U.S. Air Force Strategic Air Command, based in Omaha.

Sanderson continued to refine his teaching materials, changing the format of his audio-visuals to a phonograph record/filmstrip combination on the correct assumption that automatically synchronized sound and pictures would offer better training.

By 1961, Sanderson had sold his first Customized Private Pilot Course to Cessna Aircraft. The program became the forerunner of several courses tailored to specific airplane manufacturers, such as Beechcraft, Piper, Gulfstream, and others. He was also selling his more general courses to more than 2,500 flight schools across the country and becoming immensely successful. [31]

Although Jepp was lukewarm to the idea, Don Sellars saw a natural tie-in between Jeppesen and Sanderson: "We realized that there were a lot of instructors who used the Sanderson audio-visuals but used our text materials." The idea of combining the two firms began to germinate.

Sellars noted, "Jepp talked to Chuck Schneider, who was then a vice president of Times Mirror and responsible for Jeppesen and several other Times Mirror subsidiaries. Schneider did a lot of research and decided that Sanderson Films was an up-and-coming company and maybe they [times mirror] ought to look at acquiring them."*

According to Sellars, Jepp did not like the name change but, by then, he was out of the picture. "I think it was because Jeppesen had such a golden reputation in the industry and Sanderson was small and a relative upstart. A lot of our larger customers, such as United and Pan Am and Eastern, said, 'Who in the world is Sanderson?' Everybody in pilot training knew who Sanderson was, but our larger customers didn't know them then." [32]

Chester Pizac's reign at the helm of Jeppesen was short-lived. "He stayed there about a year-and-a-half," said Wayne Rosenkrans. "He was an interesting guy, but he wasn't an aviation guy. He had no idea what

---

* It would take a few years, but in 1974 the two companies would merge and become known as Jeppesen Sanderson.

we were doing. He had been with Emerson Electric in St. Louis at one time and came to Jeppesen from a defense contractor, Dynalectron, in Washington, D.C. He was a management person, but not an aviation person." [33]

Jepp and Pizac never hit it off well. Although Jepp was no longer in charge and could have just walked away and sailed off into retirement, something deep inside him refused to allow anyone else to run "his" company without his blessing. Don Sellars recalled that "it may have been just a personality conflict, or it may have been because Chess did not come from the aviation industry, but Jepp just wasn't confident that he could continue to make this company grow. Jepp, like any other pioneer, hated to see his company take a different direction than what he'd been leading it all these years. Jepp was not one to just turn the reins over easily and gently. He was too much of an entrepreneur—too much of a strong personality." [34]

Times Mirror now needed to find another president to replace Pizac. The company had never said a word to Rosenkrans about him becoming Pizac's successor but, according to Rosenkrans, "They just called me one day and told me they had terminated him and I was to check him out of the facility. I was to watch him like a hawk until he was out the front door and then they wanted me to come out to Los Angeles; I went out and that's when they made me president."

In their meeting, Al Casey asked Rosenkrans to write up his ideas of what he would do if he were head of Jeppesen. "He gave me a couple of days to do that," Rosenkrans said. "It wasn't all that exciting." But it must have been exactly what Casey was looking for, for a few days later Rosenkrans was offered the job; he took it and held it for twenty-two years. [35]

Family friend Paul Burke knew that Jepp's ouster wounded him deeply. "I don't think Jepp ever got the credit that was due him when Times Mirror was running the show," said Burke, "and he was supposedly the chairman. He was never given the kind of credit or the recognition by Times Mirror. I know that there were years that went by when he didn't even go near the plant. In any event, his accomplishments were, I think, significant and his contribution to aviation is unparalleled

Wayne Rosenkrans became company president in 1967. *(Courtesy Jeppesen)*

—or at least parallel to many others who are better-known figures in aviation." [36]

Rosenkrans said his relationship with Jepp was "mostly good. The first thing I did was tell him that I knew he hadn't been welcome under Pizac, but that he was always welcome to come out to the facility. I said, 'Just conduct yourself properly and let me know when you're here because I realize a lot of our people would like to see you again and say hello and you'd like to do the same thing.' He started coming out and he conducted himself very well." [37]

By 1968 Jeppesen and Company had become the world's largest compiler and publisher of aerial navigation aids, and Jepp was a millionaire.

Every airline in America was a Jeppesen customer, as were seventy percent of the country's non-airline pilots and the bulk of foreign airlines and pilots. Even Air Force One, the president's aircraft, used (and still uses) Jeppesen flight and navigation aids.

The firm's headquarters in Denver then employed about 200 people; there were a handful in the Washington, D.C. office, and the office in Frankfurt, Germany, which served Europe, Africa, and Asia, had about sixty employees. [38]

And Jepp, from the sidelines, continued to challenge the company that bore his name to look into the future and be on the leading edge of navigation. The past was already filled with Jeppesen innovations—the first enroute charts, airways charts, area charts, SIDs, STARs, VORs—and Jepp expected the company would continue moving forward. Don Sellars noted, "When radio range came in, which was the predecessor of VOR, he designed those charts. Then, when VOR [Very-High-Frequency Omnidirectional Radio Range] was coming in, Jepp personally designed the first VOR chart. He had a lot to say about the graphics—the color, the size and style of the type fonts, everything. They changed over the years, but they are still basically the same." [39]

Without a company to run, to spend nearly every waking minute intensely thinking about and obsessing over, to walk into a building and have hundreds of people—his people—wave and smile and say "good morning," made Jepp bored and unhappy. Busy and active all his life, he found the enforced idleness anathema. Even his two sons were gone, both out of college and off to their careers.

At least he still had Neddy. And golf. Jepp and Nadine were both hooked on the game and were members of suburban Denver's exclusive Cherry Hills Country Club, site of the 1960 U.S. Open, playing whenever their health and the weather permitted. In the winter they went to Thunderbird in Palm Springs, California, where they sometimes teamed up with Bob Hope, Lucille Ball, Arnold Palmer, and Jack Nicklaus.

Jepp and golfing legend Arnold Palmer, May 1974, at Cherry Hills Country Club.
(E. B. Jeppesen collection)

Jim Jeppesen knew that his father had been an excellent athlete in his youth and found solace in golf. "My dad had been outstanding at track and tennis and baseball in high school," said Jim. "He and my mom also loved to ski. In later years he took up golf and really loved it. I seem to recall that he once had an eight handicap, which is darned good. And his name is on a plaque at Cherry Hills for having made a hole-in-one in 1964 on the fifteenth hole with a four-iron." [40]

Family friend and former president of Frontier Airlines Paul Burke remembered that Jepp was a fierce competitor on the links. "He really enjoyed golf and it was good for his spirit, his nature, but it would just upset him dreadfully when he'd miss a putt and lose the hole. I think it was very much a competitive situation for him. He was out there to beat somebody. Nadine played very competitive golf, too." [41]

Another good friend and golfing buddy was Ray Lee, a former fighter pilot who flew in World War II, Korea, and Vietnam, then worked in the oil business. "Jepp was a very good golfer," recalled Lee. "Hit the ball a mile and straight. Good putter, too. Nadine was a very nice lady, very charming and gracious. I liked Nadine very much and so did my wife Kay." [42]

True, Jepp loved the game with a passion, but there was only so much golf that could be played in a given week. Even the best day on the course wasn't as fulfilling as running his company, of going over the smallest detail on a chart with a draftsman to make sure that absolutely every bit of it was correct, of proudly squiring visiting clients and dignitaries around the building with his name on it, like the lord of the manor. As his restlessness grew, he began thinking of ways to get back the company he had created.

In 1970, Wayne Rosenkrans got wind of a plan by Jepp to buy back the company. When the president confronted him, Jepp initially denied it but Rosenkrans said he had heard it from two different sources; Jepp then admitted it was true. When Rosenkrans told Al Casey about the plan, the Times Mirror head blew a fuse.

"Al came out with some expletives," Rosenkrans noted, "and said he would be in my office the next morning. I called my executives together and Al really laid it out to my people. He told them, 'Jepp is not about to buy the company back. We've had no conversation along those lines, nor will we ever.'" Al Casey also called Jepp and told him in no uncertain terms that he would not be able to buy the company back. [43]

The doors of the multi-million-dollar company were being barred to the man who had started it all.

8: NEW BLOOD

By 1986, Jepp was enjoying his "forced" retirement and his golden years with Nadine. Son Jim, an executive at Stearns-Roger Corporation, was living in Denver with his wife Joyce, a United Airlines flight attendant. Son Richard, a former airline pilot and now a real-estate developer, was residing in Australia with his wife Nancy.

On September 24, 1986, Jepp and Nadine celebrated their fiftieth wedding anniversary with a gala bash at Cherry Hills Country Club. They did not know it, of course, but big things were on the horizon. [1]

The Times Mirror Corporation had a policy that senior executives were required to retire when they reached the age of sixty-five.

Therefore, in 1986, with two years left to go before he reached the mandatory retirement age, Wayne Rosenkrans was told to find someone to succeed him. Times Mirror also hired an executive search firm in Chicago to begin looking for a suitable replacement. Rosenkrans reportedly interviewed dozens of outside candidates for the top spot but, like Jepp before him, did not feel any of them was right for the job.

Someone at Times Mirror finally decided that they would promote from within the company. Horst A. Bergmann, who had been the managing director of the Frankfurt office, was tapped as the crown prince of Jeppesen Sanderson; in June 1987 Bergmann and his wife Renate came to the States to begin the process of learning the business from the top.

Jepp, Nadine, and son Jim with wife Joyce at the Jeppesens' fiftieth anniversary party, September 24, 1986. *(E. B. Jeppesen collection)*

Bergmann was born near Frankfurt, Germany, in 1938. After attending business school and reaching draft age in 1956, he was conscripted into the newly created West German *Bundeswehr* (Armed Forces) and, after basic training, chose to join the German Air Force. He initially served with the 440th Fighter Interceptor Wing at an American air base in southern Germany. "I did the flight planning and scheduling at this air base and managed to get some flying time in," he said.

Bergmann then was part of the team that established a transport wing whose mission it was to fly members of the German government. Taking university courses in his spare time, he completed his Masters degree in Flight Operations and served with the German Air Force Weapon School 50 (fighter bomber and reconnaissance). He enjoyed the flight aspects of his jobs so much that he re-enlisted twice and served a total of six years on active duty.

Horst A. Bergmann and his wife Renate. Bergmann became president of Jeppesen
Sanderson in 1988. *(Courtesy Jeppesen)*

After leaving the military in 1963, he was hired by Jeppesen's
Frankfurt office. He first worked as an Enroute Compiler, where his job
was to take the information provided by various government agencies
and use it to update and create aeronautical charts for enroute navigation. This was followed by a variety of other assignments, such as manager of Enroute, manager of AIS (collecting data from government agencies), and manager of Marketing and Sales. In 1977, he was named managing director of the Frankfurt office.

In those days, Jeppesen's Denver headquarters was responsible for
the development, production, sales, and customer service for the North
America, South America, and the Pacific Basin to Thailand; the Frankfurt
office took care of Europe, Africa, China, Asia, the Soviet Union, and the
Middle East.

The first time Bergmann came to the States was in 1974, and he expressed a desire to meet Jepp. "We met at Cherry Hills Country Club," Bergmann said, "and somebody took a number of photographs which are still on the walls in Frankfurt. This was basically the first time somebody from the Frankfurt office, other than the early founding people who were not there any more, had met and talked to Captain Jepp."

After that initial meeting, Bergmann usually stopped in at the Denver headquarters whenever he came to the States for annual budget meetings with Times Mirror in Los Angeles. "I would meet with Jepp and Nadine and had some dinners and things like that, but I never saw him in the company in whatever official capacity," Bergmann said. "He did not elaborate on it, but I had a feeling that Times Mirror did not allow him to set foot inside the door."

As Bergmann was the first non-U.S. Managing Director, Times Mirror insisted on "Americanizing" him. With the help of Al Casey, by then the Postmaster General of the United States, Otis Chandler, Chairman of Times Mirror and publisher of the *Los Angeles Times*, and Bob Erburu, President and CEO of Times Mirror, he was accepted into Harvard Business School.

Upon Wayne Rosenkrans's retirement in 1988, Bergmann was selected by the parent company to become president of Jeppesen. He felt that it would be a positive thing to bring Jepp back into the company, as well as to find a new role for Paul Sanderson, who also was no longer involved in day-to-day operations.

After a while, Horst and Renate began to feel as though they were Jepp and Nadine's adopted children. "They took care of us when we moved here, helped us get settled, introduced us to their friends, and sponsored our membership at Cherry Hills. We were both very grateful to them."

Bergmann believed deeply that the future of the company was irretrievably connected to its past, and to its founder: "I felt that if you have a historical basis for a company, it's good to work from there and move toward the future. A lot of companies don't have that, but the Jeppesen company had this heritage, so why not use it effectively? The employees appreciated very much to have Jepp around. They helped the company to move forward. They helped to start thinking, 'What else can we do in order to promote him and really give him his place in the history of aviation, which he deserves?' During my initial years with the company in Germany, Jepp was basically invisible and was not recognized at all in the industry. I wanted to change that."

Thus, Horst brought Jepp and Paul Sanderson back into the company. "I had regular contact with Jepp," Bergmann said, "and we brought Paul Sanderson back in a consulting role. Jepp had no official function or consultancy role, but we would meet on a regular basis and just talk about the company. He had another little black book full of ideas, and about every month we would get together and talk about his ideas and my ideas. He was always wondering—what is new? How is the company going to move forward? He'd say, 'These charts; they look the same as when I started in 1934—you have to do something about it.' He was asking the pointed questions and helped me also as sort of a sounding board. He continued to be very interested in what we were doing, why we were doing it, and what new things could be done. Sometimes he would even call me at all hours—six in the morning on Sunday, or late at night—whenever he had an idea." [2]

Durrie Monsma remembered that Jepp went out of his way to welcome Bergmann to the company and, in turn, Bergmann repaid Jepp's kindness. "I think that Horst correctly saw that, as the founder of the company, Jepp could really be an an asset and an icon about which the company could rally. Much of what he exemplified—passion about accuracy and the entrepreneurial drive that created the company—were virtues that were necessary at this stage of the company's development." [3]

Janet Conner, Wayne Rosenkrans's administrative assistant, said, "I think that Europeans probably revere the elderly more than we do—the parentage, the heritage, and all that. So Horst had Jepp come back on a sort of part-time basis, and that's when I got to know Jepp first-hand. Horst saw the advantages of bringing him back because of the name, and he and Horst stayed connected for the rest of his life. The two of them were very close. Horst was always extremely kind to him. I could see many of Jepp's qualities that Wayne had talked about so many times. He was a fascinating person. In the early 1990s, I became manager of Corporate Communications and it became my function to escort Mr. Jeppesen around whenever he came out to the company. The people here absolutely revered him. His name was known everywhere within aviation. It certainly opened a lot of doors and we took advantage of it." [4]

In late 1977 and early 1978, the company's facilities again underwent expansion. Instead of maintaining its headquarters near Stapleton Airport, the company broke ground on a thirteen-acre site for a $5 million, 133,000-square-foot ultra-modern facility in the Inverness Business Park, south of Denver in Englewood. [5]

The Jeppesen corporate headquarters in Englewood, Colorado. *(Whitlock photo)*

Bergmann recalled that, as he talked to some of the employees, he learned that Jepp had been "a very difficult boss; he was almost impossible to please. He could be very demanding and sometimes gave people a difficult time. But they still liked to work for him. They were really very fond of him. When he showed up at our company parties and functions, they really appreciated that." [6]

One reason why people liked working for Jepp was summed up by Don Sellars: "When you went to work for Jepp, he knew your name, he knew your wife's name, he knew your kids' names. He memorized your kids' birthdays. If your wife was sick, he sent you home to take care of her. He was a hard, tough businessman, but he knew how critical it was to have loyal employees." [7]

In the 1990s the company began making great strides into the arena of computerization. Instead of opening up a Jeppesen Airway Manual and searching for the right page, all a pilot or co-pilot needed to do was press a button and a real-time display of the aircraft's position, speed, and altitude in relationship to the distance to objects on the ground appeared in multicolors on a small monitor set into the cockpit instrument panel.

The printed charts never really became obsolete. They continued to be used by pilots who did not want to invest the money to upgrade to full compterization, and they remain a back-up system to the electronic charts. But compared to the charts, the Jeppesen electronic navigation system was as sophisticated and advanced as a Boeing 747 was compared to an old Jenny or Eaglerock.

By 1987, Jepp was deep into retirement, trying to play as much golf as his health would allow (he was suffering with a bad hip and was also beginning to show the early signs of Parkinson's disease).* He hired Annette Brott, a licensed practical nurse, to come to their suburban Denver home and take care of Nadine, a heavy smoker who was ill with

---

* A chronic and progressive neurological disorder that mostly affects persons over fifty. Symptoms can include tremors or trembling, difficulty maintaining balance, rigidity or stiffness of the limbs and trunk, and general slowness of movement (also called bradykinesia). Parkinson's patients may also eventually have difficulty walking, talking, or performing other simple tasks. (www.understandingparkinsons.com)

A Jeppesen cartographer revises an electronic chart. *(Courtesy Jeppesen)*

emphysema—and him, if his Parkinson's worsened. "I really didn't know who Mr. Jeppesen was before I started working for him," she said. "He started bringing out all his memorabilia and showing me what he did. That's how I found out who he was."

When she first started, Annette thought the job would require about four hours of work a week, but it soon escalated to a full-time position. "I started going out to the house in the morning and I'd fix them breakfast and help them get ready and made sure Mrs. Jeppesen took her pills. If I had to take her to the hospital, I'd come back and do whatever he needed me to do. Most of the time it was really nothing to do with nursing. He mainly wanted me to make phone calls for him, or we'd just sit in the den and he'd talk about how he got started in the business.

"Nadine liked to be by herself. She didn't like a lot of noise or conversation. She'd watch television without the sound on. And she read a lot; she could read a book a day. She was kind of...well, she didn't like a lot of company. She did like to work puzzles, though—she loved them and was good at them. But she was just a very private person. He, on the other hand, would have the whole house full of friends every day if he could."

Jepp and Nadine once confided to Annette that they were content, that they had done with their lives what they had wanted to do. "He once said to me, 'You know, I cannot say that there's ever been anything I've not done. I've played golf all I've wanted, I've traveled wherever I've wanted to, I've seen things that most people haven't seen.' I think they felt their life was really fulfilled."

On occasion Nadine would discuss private details of her life with Annette: "This one time she said that, when she was a stewardess, United Airlines had summer and winter uniforms. She and Mr. Jeppesen were dating at that time and she asked him, 'Are we going to get married? It's almost time for me to buy a winter uniform. If we aren't going to get married soon, I'm going to buy my winter uniform and I'm not marrying you until after. I'm not wasting my money on that winter uniform.' I thought that was really cute."

Annette also was aware of the deep affection the couple had for each other. "They were really close in their own special way. He was just always hugging her, giving her little kisses and stuff. They just had a really special relationship. She wasn't the kind of person who was real lovey-dovey with other people, but she was with him."

Annette expanded her nurse role to that of housekeeper, augmenting what Ernestine Boyd did. At one point Annette decided she would give the house a good scrubbing, and moved all the furniture out of the living room. Jepp came home and, astonished, asked, "What in the hell are you doing?"

"I'm cleaning the house," Annette replied.

"That's what Ernestine's for," he said.

"That's okay—I'm cleaning it."

Nadine said, "You moved all the furniture. You'll hurt yourself." But after it was done, the Jeppesens loved it.

"I even got up on a ladder once and cleaned out the gutters," Annette said. "It gave me something to do and it helped them out. I don't think I will ever get as close to anybody again as I did with Jepp and Nadine. It was not the regular nurse-patient relationship. There were times when I'd go over there and they were sad and, by the end of the day, we were all happy and laughing." [8]

Jepp was a pack-rat and an archivist's dream; he never threw out anything. The basement of his home was an unorganized treasure trove of historic, aviation-related memorabilia. Boxes, bags, and filing cabinets were stuffed with more than a half-century's worth of correspondence, receipts, paid invoices, hundreds of old photographs, model airplanes, certificates, award plaques, scrapbooks, trophies, sporting goods, parts of old airline uniforms, aerial charts, early copies of the little black book, and other objects that defied description.

Each item in his collection, whether it be a photo of an early aviation pioneer or a receipt for some insignificant item he had purchased fifty years earlier, held meaning and memories for Jepp. He especially liked items connected with Boeing. He said, "Sometimes...my mind wanders back to the old airmail days, and I think of those great guys pushing the mail through any kind of weather. What great days. Boeing gave us a beautiful airplane. The sky was ours." [9]

On occasion Jepp would take Ted Boerstler down to his basement that was filled to the ceiling with boxes loaded with memorabilia of all sorts. "He'd show me all this stuff," Boerstler said, "and he'd say, 'Ted, What am I going to do with all this? Give me your ideas.'

"I said, 'Jepp, what you should do is try to somehow get all that stuff together and send it to some museum.'"

In the late 1980s, Boerstler and Jepp's other pals, knowing that his collection represented a valuable snapshot into the history of American aviation that must not be sold off, thrown out, or allowed to deteriorate, began pressing him to do something with it. Some urged him to donate it to the Smithsonian, others to the Air Force Academy; still others suggested that the Air Force museum at Wright-Patterson Air Force Base in

Dayton, Ohio, would be the appropriate repository. Jepp hemmed and hawed and refused to make a decision. [10]

Ray Lee said, "I recall several of us got together to help Jepp make sure that his various artifacts were kept in a good place. The Air Force Academy didn't want to take care of things. You see, when you give somebody something, it's got to be taken care of. Every museum seemed to want Jepp to give them $100,000 or so to make sure that everything was kept nicely which, of course, Jeppesen wasn't about to do. Yet, he wanted to have something done." [11]

"In the 1980s," said Tal Miller, "we had lots of conversations and debates about this situation. It took over two years to convince Jepp to do something with all his archives. A man by the name of John Andrews, who had been a submariner in World War II, was a good friend of the Jeppesens and had a great deal to do with helping me convince Jepp to donate his archives to a museum. John spent many hours with me at Sedgwick Drive trying to convince Jepp that his records and collection of aviation history must be preserved for future generations." [12]

Truth be told, Elrey B. Jeppesen was no Wright, no Lindbergh, no Wiley Post, no Jimmy Doolittle, no Amelia Earhart, no Mercury Seven astronaut, no celebrity. Outside of the tight-knit aviation community, very few even knew his name. His contributions to aviation were, and are, for the most part, hidden from the general public's view. Yet, those contributions greatly enhanced the safety of pilots and the flying public. No doubt someone, at some point, would have invented aerial navigation charts similar to what he had developed. But "Captain Jepp" was the pioneer, and a number of people around him began to realize that he and his achievements should be honored in some major way—not by a simple framed certificate or an engraved plaque, but through something consequential, something lasting.

In the 1980s, while Jepp's friends tried to convince him to do something with his archives, planning began for the construction of a new Denver airport. The then-current airport, Stapleton International, had become cramped, outmoded, and dangerous. When it first opened in October 1929, the month of the great stock market crash, Denver Municipal Airport, as it was then known, was located on the far eastern fringe of the "Mile-High City." During the ensuing decades, more and more residential areas began encroaching upon the airport, and the city was hit by more and more lawsuits from citizens complaining about aircraft noise. It was decided by city leaders and state legislators that a new, larger, "all-weather" airport, located farther from the city, with greatly expanded runways, was drastically needed.

In 1985, the Colorado General Assembly brokered a deal with neighboring Adams County that enabled the City and County of Denver to annex fifty-three square miles—an area twice the size of Manhattan Island—twenty miles east of Denver on which to build the new facility. After Adams County and Denver County voters approved the plans in 1988 and 1989, respectively, one of the nation's largest public-works projects went forward.

The architects designed the airport to be visually stunning. The distinctive main terminal, with its translucent white fabric roof symbolizing the snow-capped Rocky Mountains, is one of the most striking airport facilities anywhere. Three concourses, linked by an underground shuttle rail system to the main terminal, were constructed. However, delays and horrendous cost overruns (sixteen months behind schedule and more than three billion dollars over budget—not to mention United Airlines' notorious automated baggage-handling system that "ate" luggage) eroded public enthusiasm. Still, the airport's gala grand opening in February 1995 and its subsequent decade of outstanding operations (in 2005 over forty-three million passengers passed through DIA) have made it one of the world's ten busiest airports.

During the planning phase of DIA, someone had the bright idea of having the new airport named for Jepp. Tom Hudgens, a retired United Airlines captain, sent a letter to the *Denver Post,* which was printed in the July 23, 1988, edition:

Denver is the home of a great aviation pioneer for whom the new airport should be named. E. B. Jeppesen is the one who conceived of having charts for instrument approaches, so that pilots would be able to navigate to safe landings in instrument weather, in clouds unable to see the ground.... Today there is not an instrument-rated pilot in the world who has not used Jepp's charts and is aware of the name of E. B. Jeppesen.

Jepp has received hundreds of awards for his contributions to aviation, including induction into the Colorado Aviation Hall of Fame, the Tony Jannus National Hall of Fame, and the Daedalian Society, plus election to honorary chairman of Silver Wings.

We have airports named for military heroes, such as O'Hare in Chicago, and those that are named for political heroes, such as J. F. Kennedy in New York and Stapleton in Denver. It's high time we name an airport after a civil-aviation hero. Denver has the unique opportunity to do just that by naming its new airport in honor of one who has been a Denver-area resident for 47 years, who has contributed much to the city's economic growth, and most importantly, has contributed so greatly to the safety of air travel worldwide.

Every pilot in the world would join me in recommending that the new Denver airport be named E. B. Jeppesen Airport.

Don Sellars, Jeppesen Sanderson's director of Flight Training Design and Research at the time, recalled seeing the letter and thinking, "That guy has a great idea." [15]

Sharing that thought was Ralph Latimer, then head of the Colorado Chapter of the Silver Wings Fraternity—a group of pilots who had soloed twenty-five years earlier or more. Almost simultaneously, both the Silver Wings Fraternity and Jeppesen Sanderson hopped on the idea and began working in concert. Some initial inquiries were made but it soon became apparent that the city was going to name it Denver International Airport rather than for any person, so Sellars, Latimer, and others close to Jepp brainstormed other ways of seizing the unique opportunity. Then it came to them—what if they campaigned to get the main terminal building named after Jepp? Maybe they could even raise enough money to commission some sort of statue in his honor.

Tal Miller, pilot, neighbor, and one of Jepp's closest friends for more than twenty years, recalled, "A committee was formed to work on this, and we met at the Jeppesen Sanderson Company. We had to be very hush-hush about it because we didn't want anyone to think that the company was pushing the idea."

Miller said that the Colorado Chapter of the Silver Wings Fraternity was the driving force behind the idea. "Our committee was the tool that Silver Wings used," noted Miller. [16]

On September 15, 1988, Ralph Latimer and another group representing Jeppesen Sanderson and other interested parties met to discuss their thoughts on what their chances were of success. "I felt confident that it could be done," said Latimer, and the Jeppesen contingent gave him their blessing to spearhead the effort; they said the company would help in any way possible.

Silver Wings Fraternity Airport Committee: Back row: Don Sellars, Eddie Mehlin, Robert Williams, Walter Williams, Edward Gerhardt, Bill Madsen. Front row: Peter Luce, Ralph Latimer, Jepp, Tal Miller. *(E. B. Jeppesen collection)*

Latimer was a good choice to head the committee, for he had worked as a lobbyist for the National Association of Blue Cross Plans in Washington and knew how bureaucracies functioned and how to get things done. After making a few initial contacts, he discovered a great deal of support for the idea at city hall.

Latimer also met with Jepp on several occasions and explained to him that the committee's primary goal was to have the main terminal named for him. If that fell through, then they would attempt to have the highway that would connect Interstate 70 to the airport named Jeppesen Boulevard. "Jepp was flattered," Latimer said, "and I suppose in the depths of his heart and in the back of his mind he was hoping this would happen, but I always thought he just didn't think it would. I just don't think he thought such an honor would be bestowed upon him. As it progressed, however, he really became more optimistic." [17]

The group realized that the first order of business was to make Jepp more visible to local civic leaders and the general public and began an all-out blitz to make the name Jeppesen familiar to pilots and non-pilots alike. The efforts paid off; *Flying* magazine, one of the aviation industry's most prestigious and widely read publications, ran a six-page article about Jepp. The committee received more than 150 phone calls and letters in support of the idea to honor Jepp in some grand fashion. News releases and reprints of the article were mailed to 440 Colorado news-papers, local radio and TV stations, and the national aviation trade media. As a result, numerous other articles about Jepp appeared in a number of publications. It was now time to blitz the City and County of Denver.

"Each of the members of the committee went to the city council and to the mayor, Federico Peña," said Tal Miller. "We met several times and finally, after about two-and-a-half years, it finally happened—it was decided that the main terminal would be named after him. Suddenly, Jepp was much in demand. Everybody was ringing his doorbell and wanting him to go here and there, make this speech or that speech, and giving him all sorts of honors. He got an honorary doctor's degree from Denver University, and Coors Brewing Company named him the Industrial Man of the Year,★ and he was inducted into the National Aviation Hall of Fame." [18]

★ The actual award was the Coors American Ingenuity Award, which was presented to Jepp in March 1993. In an unexpected act of generousity, he donated the entire $15,000 prize to the University of Denver.

Jepp and Nadine and astronaut John Glenn smile for the photographer upon the occasion of Jepp's induction into the U.S. National Aviation Hall of Fame, 1990. Glenn sponsored Jepp's induction. *(E. B. Jeppesen collection)*

Close friend Corky Douglas also recalled that Jepp was a big hit on the lecture circuit: "One time he spoke to Rotary and they gave him a standing ovation. Rotary never gives anybody a standing ovation." [19]

On January 29, 1990, the day after Jepp's eighty-third birthday, the Denver City Council passed Resolution 13, honoring him. [20]

An entire year passed before the matter of what to name the terminal was officially resolved. On February 12, 1991, after Ralph Latimer meet with Mayor Peña, the mayor declared his support for the idea and, a week later, a formal resolution to that effect, Resolution 19, was passed,

Denver city councilwoman Stephanie Foote presents Jepp with a copy of Resolution 13, honoring him on the occasion of his 83rd birthday. *(E. B. Jeppesen collection)*

with ten members of the city council voting in favor, two against, and one abstaining. [21]

After it became certain that the main terminal would be named Jeppesen Terminal, Jeppesen Sanderson established a 501(c)(3) non-profit organization, the Jeppesen Aviation Foundation, to commission a sculptor and raise money for a statue of Jepp.

Finding the sculptor was the easy part. Raising the needed funds would prove to be much more difficult than any of them had imagined.

An entire year passed before the matter of what to name the terminal was officially resolved. On February 12, 1991, after Ralph Latimer
meet with Mayor Peña, the mayor declared his support for the idea and,
a week later, a formal resolution to that effect was passed. Members of
the city council were: Robert Crider, Hiawatha Davis, Mary DeGroot,
Dave Doering, Cathy Donahue, Stephanie Foote, Ted Hackworth,
Allegra "Happy" Haynes, Ramona Martinez, Debby Ortega, Cathy
Reynolds, William Scheitler, and Paul Swalm.

9: CAST IN BRONZE

In the early 1990s, when the Inverness headquarters building was undergoing expansion, Horst Bergmann gave Jepp a tour of the half-finished space. They came to an empty office with a nice view of the Rocky Mountains and Jepp asked who was going to be in that space. Horst told him, in a half-jesting manner, "That's going to be your office."

Wayne Rosenkrans said, "Jepp called me and all his friends and said, 'Horst wants me to come back to work but I just don't know if I can.' He was then eighty-five or eighty-six years old. Horst was in a little bit of a panic about what he would do if Jepp said, 'Okay, I'm ready.' He didn't do that, though." [1]

Jeppesen Sanderson made news in September 1992, an election year, when incumbent president George H. W. Bush came to Denver on his campaign tour and used the company headquarters in the Inverness Business Park as the backdrop for his rally.

A registered Republican, Jepp was pleased and proud that the president who, as a naval aviator during the Second World War had been shot down by the Japanese near the island of Chichi Jima, had chosen to hold a rally on the company's property. A reporter asked Jepp about his feelings on the occasion, to which he responded, "I'm delighted, thrilled to death. I think it's a great honor." [2]

Jepp got another thrill when he was invited to meet the president. As the two men shook hands, Jepp said to Bush, " 'What's an old fighter pilot like you doing in a job like this?' The president just broke up." [3]

As Horst Bergmann and Senior Vice President of Marketing and Sales Bob Hopkins look on, Jepp shakes hands with President George H. W. Bush during the incumbent's campaign stop at Jeppesen Sanderson in 1990. *(E. B. Jeppesen collection)*

Meanwhile the search for a sculptor swung into high gear. Don Sellars, along with Ralph Latimer (the latter now hired by the Jeppesen Aviation Foundation as a full-time consultant to coordinate the effort), headed a six-person sculptor selection board. In 1992, a "call for entries" announcement went out to about 150 sculptors across the country, requesting an indication of their interest in working on such a project, photographs of their work, and their estimated costs.

"We had all kinds of proposals," Sellars recalled, "statues, obelisks, all kinds of things. One proposal was a 120-foot set of wings, artistic wings, that would be suspended from the roof of the passenger terminal." [4]

"We got more than sixty responses," Latimer said. "We whittled the list down to fifteen, and then ten, and finally five. Then it was down to two—a fellow out in California who did the statue of John Wayne at the airport there in Orange County and George Lundeen in Loveland, Colorado." [5]

Sellars said that Lundeen was chosen "because of his demonstrated ability to actually put into a statue that was almost twice life size the real facial expressions of Jepp Jeppesen in the 1920s." [6]

Loveland, Colorado, about fifty miles north of Denver, has one of the largest and most vibrant communities of sculptors and bronze-casting foundries in the country. On the basis of the quality of Lundeen's work, and the proximity of Loveland to Denver, Lundeen was awarded the job.

Internationally known sculptor Lundeen admitted that, until he received a letter notifying him that he had won the commission, he had never even heard of Elrey B. Jeppesen. "Until that time," he said, "only my secretary had read anything about Jepp, and she had only read what a friend of mine had sent to me, which was a prospectus for the commission. She sent some slides of my work back to them and, the next thing you know, we had the commission!"

Lundeen had grown up in a small town in Nebraska and attended Hastings College before being admitted to graduate school in the University of Illinois College of Fine Art and then doing post-graduate study in Italy on a Fulbright scholarship. As it happened, Lundeen's father had also been an aviator in the 1930s and 1940s and was familiar with Jeppesen.

Intrigued by the subject matter, Lundeen called Ralph Latimer and set up a meeting to discuss the project in more depth. Ralph told him about Jepp and his great influence on the aviation industry, the first to start producing maps for pilots.

"Then I called Jepp himself," Lundeen said. "I hadn't met him yet, hadn't seen him or a photograph of him, so I asked him how tall he was. He said, 'Well, I'm about six feet tall.' So I figured, okay, the statue will be about nine feet high. For a statue like this, I usually make it about one-and-a-half times as tall as the actual person."

After the sculpture was complete, George Lundeen signed and presented Ralph Latimer with the orginal napkin sketch. *(Courtesy Ralph Latimer)*

Lundeen based his initial prices on this size. Then he met Jepp in person. "He was about five-feet-six. Maybe the tallest he was in his life was five-feet-eight. We could have saved about $20,000 worth of bronze by doing it to the right size!"

During a lunch meeting in October 1992 with Ralph, Jepp, Sellars, and Lundeen, concepts were discussed. The artist said, "They were telling me how they thought that the sculpture should show Jepp writing or drawing something in his notebook. I didn't like that idea; I couldn't imagine a figure of somebody looking down being heroic-looking. I sketched something out on a napkin in which Jepp was standing in front of his first old Jenny, just kind of looking up at the sky, with his little black book in his hand.

"The others said they didn't have enough money to cast an entire Jenny and put it behind Jepp. I had to explain to them that all we would do is just put a little vignette together of the prop, and maybe a little bit of the engine cowling. We actually worked out the design that day and Jepp approved it and thought it would be great. We had a year-and-a-half to do it."

The first step in sculpting is to make a detailed sketch to scale, followed by a miniature clay version. Once that is approved, a full-size clay sculpture is created. From this is made a hollow mold into which the molten bronze will be poured.

The clay stages went quickly and without major revisions (the idea of showing part of the engine was dropped to simplify the design). Lundeen depicted a young Jepp in leather jacket and flying helmet, goggles, bow tie, tall boots, and jodhpurs. "I wanted to give him a nice curve to his body, and I wanted to make him look strong," said the artist. He showed Jepp with his left arm resting on a vertical two-blade propeller meant to represent the Jenny. In his right hand was his little black book. He was looking at the sky—and toward the future.

Lundeen wanted to capture those youthful eyes. He said, "I've always felt you could look into Jepp's eyes and see the excitement when he's talking to you about flying. I wanted to convey that." [7]

Sculptor George Lundeen working on the full-size clay model of the Jeppesen statue.
(E. B. Jeppesen collection)

Don Sellars remembered that Lundeen made a clay prototype about two feet tall and presented it to the selection board. "We looked at it and suggested a couple or three changes and approved him to go to the full size," Sellars said. [8]

Despite the fact that the Denver City Council had initially given the statue project its blessing, the sculpture committee ran into a serious snag.

Denver has a requirement that calls for one percent of the construction budget for a public-works project to be ear-marked for art, and all proposed public art must be approved by a cultural review committee known as the "Mayor's Office of Art, Culture and Film." Ralph Latimer, George Lundeen, and others from the Silver Wings Fraternity and the Foundation met with the cultural review committee to show them the concept and get approval for Lundeen's sculpture—a meeting that nearly turned into a jousting tournament.

"They did not consider what we were doing to be 'art,'" Latimer said. "They didn't accept it."

According to the cultural committee, the art at the airport was going to be Indian pots and bronze dinosaur bones set into the floor and gargoyles coming out of suitcases and a collection of rusty farm implements and impressionistic murals. Latimer continued, "This guy on the cultural committee said, 'Have you considered—' what's the word for free-form something? Anyway, I said, 'No, it's going to be Jepp in flying boots and helmet, because that's Jepp,' and he said, 'Nobody pays any attention to statues anymore. You have to have free form.' I said, 'No, that's not what we're doing.'

"Later George Lundeen presented a model to them and some thought it was fine, but this one person went, 'Ugh.' Someone asked George, 'What kind of patina are you going to put on it?' and George said, 'Whatever patina I decide is appropriate.'" [9]

After much kicking and screaming on the part of the cultural review committee, Lundeen's concept was finally, if somewhat grudgingly, approved, and the money-raising aspect swung into high gear. Don Sellars noted, "We were kind of panicked because we realized we had to raise a tremendous amount of money pretty quickly [the cost for the statue was estimated at $189,000], so we sent out letters to all our prime customers and to every airline in the world." [10]

Ralph Latimer spent three days at the Denver Public Library looking up foundations that awarded grants to aviation-related projects. He also added to his list organizations such as the Airline Pilots Association, Aircraft Owners and Pilots Association, United Airline Pilots Association, Boeing—any other corporate entity he could think of that was related to flight. [11]

Jepp also gave Janet Conner, the Jeppesen corporation's communications manger, a list of names of people and companies he was sure would contribute and asked her to start contacting them, but raising the money was hard. The airlines were going through an especially challenging economic period and few had any extra cash lying around to support such a venture. [12]

Ralph Latimer said, "Initially, we didn't get anything from the U.S. airlines. Aeroflot, the Russian airline, gave us $2,000, so we went back to the airlines and said something like, 'You want Aeroflot's name on the plaque and not yours?' Eventually a few of them made contributions, but it was much more difficult than any of us had expected." [13]

Don Sellars recalled, "The Jeppesen employees themselves were very generous, contributing a total of nearly $50,000. Times Mirror matched every employee's donation, plus they gave a substantial additional amount. We had many $1,000 donations from Jepp's friends and other pilots." [14]

Through Horst Bergmann's personal efforts, he was able to convince Times Mirror to donate $150,000.

Ralph Latimer said that the city of Denver also made a contribution in the form of floor space in the Jeppesen Terminal. "But to be very frank, if it hadn't been for Times Mirror, I don't think we could have done this. We just didn't have the financial strength to do it." [15] In the end, a total of $338,000 was raised. [16]

In addition to the statue, the Foundation also wanted to have a large sign outside the terminal and a number of museum-quality display cases made that could be filled with Jeppesen memorabilia—eight cases made in Germany that cost $114,000. The city picked up the tab for the display cases—a gesture for which Latimer and the others were forever grateful.

"The city was absolutely unbelievably good to us," Latimer said. "They had already given us 970 square feet on the fifth level of the main terminal. And they paid for an ILS [instrument landing system] mosaic inlay in the marble floor leading up to the statue. Gosh, I was almost dancing!" [17]

Selecting the Jeppesen memorabilia to go into the display cases also proved to be a difficult endeavor. Ralph Latimer and Donna Chandler (now Donna Miller), a Jeppesen Sanderson employee and later a

Jeppesen Sanderson Company President Horst Bergmann (center) accepts a $5,000 donation from National Paper Company's General Manager Dave Stauhl while Sales Manager Mark Gravit looks on. *(E. B. Jeppesen collection)*

commercial airline pilot, were given the nearly Herculean task of going through the mountain of artifacts that Jepp had kept in his home and deciding which items to display; the job took four months.

At first Ralph and Donna had no idea of how to begin organizing everything. She said, "There were just mounds of stuff in his basement. Where do you start? What corner do you even start in? He didn't throw anything away. So we just started with one box in one corner. I created a database and thought if we could get a picture to correspond, we can change the information later if we have to. So that's where we started, and it took quite a long time. Months. We worked for four hours almost every afternoon, pretty much just Ralph and me in the basement. They had photographers from the company come out and photograph each of the items that we pulled out and set aside. I felt so honored to be actually cataloging his memorabilia and writing a short history of each thing or exactly what it was. If we couldn't identify an item, he'd tell us a story about it. It was absolutely fascinating."

Donna Chandler also felt she got to know Nadine during the months she spent at the Jeppesen home. "Nadine has been recognized through Women in Aviation Pioneer Hall of Fame," she said, "and the Katherine Wright Award from the National Aeronautical Association, but she was an integral part of that company that most people didn't see. She was the secretary/treasurer for a long, long time. But because she wasn't a pilot or the dashing young aviator, she didn't get the credit she deserved. She had a very quiet determination, though, of going about things and getting things done."

Donna recalled that Jepp was getting considerable pressure from his friends to donate his memorabilia to this place or that place and was struggling with the decision. "I think people were really trying to look out for his best interests, that maybe he would pass away without having made a decision. I think he knew that Tal Miller had his best interests at heart and Tal wasn't going to try to get him to do anything he really didn't want to do. So one day I told him, 'You just need to do what you want to do.'"

Among the sixty items finally selected for display were Jepp's original leather helmet; Varney Air Lines flying suit; the damaged goggles recovered from his 1932 crash in Iowa; a copy of his pilot's license signed by Orville Wright; scale models of the planes he flew as a young airmail pilot; and, of course, a copy of the little black book. Additional items included his 1930s United Airlines pilot's uniform, and a variety of photos and navigation charts. [18]

The exterior airport signage, however, was a problem. Long-time friend Ray Lee said, "Jepp was very upset that the city wanted him to pay to have a sign put up at the airport. It was a hell of a note after they named it the Jeppesen Terminal. Jepp was having apoplexy over it. I told him, 'Don't worry about that—they'll finally get a sign put up.'"

Glowing like beacons in the night are the Jeppesen Terminal sign and the translucent fabric of the terminal's roof. *(Courtesy Jeppesen)*

For several months Jepp and Nadine were frequent visitors to the artist's studio in Loveland. "He would come up every couple of weeks," Lundeen said, "to check on the piece and make sure we were doing it right. I put a tool in his hand and he'd be fooling around with the clay. He enjoyed it. He still had a lot of energy, even at his age. His eyes weren't very good and his hearing was poor, but he'd look at a photo of his old Jenny and he'd start telling me ten stories about that particular time. He told me about how Tex Rankin had taught him to fly. He had a lot of memories about Tex and all the people that he flew with. One story would go into another. He'd talk about his days in Mexico when the Mexicans would shoot at him because they had never seen an airplane before, and about the time he flew with Varney Airlines and how, when they hooked up with Boeing Airlines, they created United Airlines."

On occasion Lundeen would travel to Denver and root around with Jepp in his basement, looking for props. "He showed me his goggles that were half burned up from that airmail plane crash when he barely crawled away. I said, 'What did you do after that?' He said, 'Well, I just got another plane and started flying again.'

"One of the first times I was in his office, he was on the phone with a guy, just kind of joking around with him, saying, 'Well, I'll call you later, Jimmy. We'll talk about that.' He got off the phone and I said, 'Who was that, Jepp?' and he said, 'Oh, that was Jimmy Doolittle. He calls about once a month.'" ★

Sharing his father's World War II experiences with Jepp, the two men developed a deep bond, and the artist introduced Jepp to his father. "My father was a pilot back in the Thirties so anytime my dad met with Jepp, they always talked about the old days in the old airplanes they used to fly that were very similar to each other. Jepp thought it was pretty neat that my dad was a glider pilot and was one of the first guys into France on D-Day. He was shot down a number of times during the war."

Lundeen worked hard to capture the face of the youthful Jepp. "As a sculptor who does portraits," Lundeen said, "it's maddening to try and find good photographs of your subject. Most of the time they don't look the way you want them to. Thank goodness we had a couple of really good shots of Jepp as a young man and they worked out pretty well."

Lundeen was sensitive to the importance of eyesight to a pilot. "If you want to be a pilot," he said, "the first thing they check is your eyes. Every time Jepp was in the studio, he was always looking around. He was always aware of where he was and who was in the room with him, and he hated the fact that sometimes he couldn't see very well. But he was always aware of his surroundings, and I could tell that his vision was probably one of the things that made him such a great pilot."

Lundeen himself was something of an aviator. One day while Jepp was visiting the studio, an ultralight aircraft—a paraplane with a top speed of twenty-seven miles per hour and a ceiling of 14,000 feet—was delivered to Lundeen. He noted, "Jepp was here the day they delivered that little aircraft to my studio. We went out there and it was just like Jepp looking at his first airplane. He went over and checked out all the cables. You could see he was looking to make sure that this cable held

---

★ Doolittle, an Army Air Corps pilot, set many speed and endurance records during the 1930s. He is probably most famous for commanding sixteen B-25 bombers that took off from the deck of the aircraft carrier U.S.S. *Hornet* on April 18, 1942, to make the first bombing run over Tokyo. Doolittle was promoted to general and awarded the Medal of Honor. (www.arlingtoncemetary.net/jdoolitt.)

up that wheel and whatnot. He said, 'Now this is a big parachute. I've seen these. This parachute comes up when you go so many miles an hour.' He figured that was around thirty miles an hour."

Lundeen said that Jepp walked around the little craft for about ten minutes, checking out everything. He asked Jepp if he would want to fly an ultralight and the old pilot replied, "Yeah, this looks like a lot of fun. If my eyes were better, I'd fly this tomorrow."

Jepp asked about the horsepower rating of the engine. Lundeen told him about fifty. "Gosh," said Jepp, "I don't think my Jenny had much more than that."★

Each time he came to Loveland, Jepp had some new stories for Lundeen—stories about his World War II experiences, stories about famous celebrities, stories about golfing with Arnold Palmer and Jack Nicklaus, stories about Bob Hope. "He told me about the first time he met Bob Hope," Lundeen said. "It was when he first started flying for the commercial airlines. He said there was this crazy Englishman on board and he'd start telling jokes, and he said he'd laugh so hard he wanted to throw him off the airplane. It turned out to be Bob Hope. He later became good friends with Bob Hope. The two belonged to the same golf club at Palm Springs and would golf together."

Besides his sense of humor, Jepp brought his sharp, critical eye to Lundeen's studio. They got into a mild argument about the boots that the artist was modeling in clay. "We went round and round about the boots," Lundeen recalled. "I wanted to make the boots more interesting than just an ordinary pair of engineer-type boots. In one photograph, he had on a pair of what looked like lace-up riding boots. Jepp said, 'I don't think I ever had a pair of boots like that.' So I took this one photo and had it blown up and showed it to him. After that, he just kind of laughed and no more was ever said about it."

They had the same problem with the propeller. Jepp was such a stickler for detail that when Lundeen put the prop on the original model, Jepp was sure that the pitch was going in the wrong direction.

★ A few weeks later Lundeen crashed the ultralight and Jepp gave him hell about it. He asked, "What happened? Pilot error?" "One hundred percent," said the artist. (Lundeen interview)

Lundeen said, "Every time Jepp came up, he looked at that and said, 'I just don't know if that's right.' Finally I went to a hock shop here in town where there was an old propeller. It wasn't a Jenny propeller, but it was a World War II single-engine propeller. I bought it and brought it back to the studio and mounted it so it would stand upright and when Jepp came back I said, 'Now Jepp, look at this. This is the way the prop's going. I don't want to hear any more about it.' He looked at it and looked at an old photograph and said, 'That's great.' I never heard another word about it."

On occasion Jepp would bring Nadine up to Lundeen's studio to solicit her opinion. She was always very positive about the sculpture, Lundeen said. "She would look at it and say, 'I think you look real good there.' One time she may have said something under her breath like, 'He never looked so good.'" [20]

Once the full-scale clay sculpture was finished, it was time to cast the bronze.

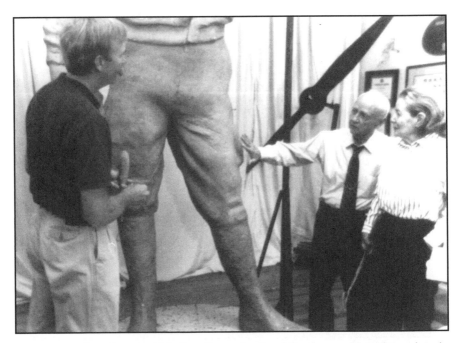

George Lundeen, Jepp, and Nadine discuss details of the clay model in the sculptor's Loveland, Colorado, studio. *(E. B. Jeppesen collection)*

Meanwhile, as the airport took shape and the statue was cast and the name "Jeppesen" became more well known around Denver, Jepp found himself in high demand as a public speaker.

"The *Denver Post* and *Rocky Mountain News* ran a lot of articles about Jepp," recalled Don Sellars. "Jepp couldn't handle all the interview requests he was getting. He was old and getting more feeble and he just wasn't able to do it.

"Every Kiwanis Club and Lions Club in Colorado wanted Jepp to be a speaker. We were just staggered by the number of invitations pouring in. We could not accept them all. But Ralph and I would pick a few and then drive Jepp to them—he couldn't drive at night. He would regale the audience for half an hour with his stories."

Sellars related one of Jepp's favorite tales. "He talked about the time he was a United Airlines captain and, before a flight, his co-pilot was telling him that on his previous flight one of the engines quit. Jepp said, 'I don't allow engines to quit on me.' So the co-pilot asked, 'Well, how

In 1992, Jepp posed in leathers with an Alexander Eaglerock at Centennial Airport near Denver. He inscribed the picture "To my good friend Ralph L. [Latimer] with best wishes and clear skies. Capt. E. B. Jeppesen, 'Jepp'" *(Courtesy Ralph Latimer)*

do you keep that from happening?' and Jepp said, 'I lay my hands on them and refuse to let them quit.' He tells that as a joke and the audiences always laugh, but it's sort of half serious. He evidently didn't lose many engines in his career. He was a very safe and responsible pilot." [21]

Ralph Latimer also has warm memories of Jepp's public-speaking idiosyncrasies. "I would introduce Jepp, but he had to have some type of written speech in front of him. He liked little index cards. I would write out ten or twelve cards for him. He'd take those up to the podium and the Parkinson's would get to him and he'd always begin, 'If I ever get over these shakes, I'm going back to wing-walking,' and everybody would laugh. He would fumble around a little bit and then shove the cards aside and start reminiscing, and that's what the audiences loved. He could tell stories and he did it very well." [22]

Despite all the attention being lavished on him, Jepp remained modest and humble. One reporter asked him if he thought he should be included among aviation's "greats," and Jepp replied simply, "I'm just another pilot, another throttle pusher who tried to help his fellow airmen." [23]

George Lundeen's bronze statue of Jepp was unveiled in a ceremony a year prior to the opening of the airport itself. The dedication preceded a reception and dinner honoring civic officials, contributors, the Silver Wings Fraternity group, Jeppesen Aviation Foundation board members, Jeppesen Sanderson employees, George Lundeen, and many others who had done so much to make the idea a reality. Also honored, of course, were Jepp and Nadine.

Tal Miller recalled that during the statue's dedication, Jepp said, "Hell, I didn't know I was that tall." When they pulled the black cloth off the bronze, Jepp said, "Hell, I didn't know I was that handsome, either." [24]

Jepp and George Lundeen pose with the finished bronze before it is delivered to Denver International. *(E. B. Jeppesen collection)*

The statue arrives at DIA. *(Courtesy Ralph Latimer)*

Jeppesen booster Carl Williams and Jepp pose in front of the statue during the dedication. Williams donated a restored 1930 Alexander Eaglerock for display at the new airport. *(Courtesy Jeppesen)*

During the year between the statue's dedication and the grand opening of the new airport, Denver International suffered the slings and arrows of outraged indignation. Allegations of graft and corruption flew back and forth as members of the local and national news media took sides. Charges and counter-charges flew, apoplectic politicians howled, late-night comics mocked, and lawsuits were filed, but the airport, like a 747 with its wheel chocks removed, rolled forward under its own power, unstoppable.

CBS's Dan Rather had tried to stir up indignation by calling attention to some questionable aspects of DIA's financing. On ABC's *World News Tonight,* Cokie Roberts had called DIA the "Rolls-Royce of Colorado," while local KTLK radio talk-show host Peter Boyles, who had been lambasting the project since its inception, hit a new high for scorn, labeling it a "boondoggle" for its serious cost overruns, its distance from Denver, its location in Colorado's notorious "tornado alley," and its extravagant marble and murals.

Viewers across the nation were treated to nightly news clips of United's million-dollar, high-tech automated baggage system devouring suitcases during operational tests. New York Senator Alphonse D'Amato asked his colleagues on the Senate floor, "Why was this Taj Mahal of the Rockies ever built?" and used the airport's sixteen-month delay and $3.2 billion cost overrun as an example of Congress's lack of fiscal restraint and the need for a balanced budget. [25]

Federico Peña, the Denver mayor under whose tenure the project had been launched, and now the U.S. Secretary of Transportation in the Clinton administration, was beaming under the television lights, deflecting with a cheery smile any criticism and the accusations that the airport was "Federico's Folly." He told CBS's Harry Smith that DIA, whatever earlier problems it had had, "was the most efficient, most cost-effective, most safety-minded, most technologically advanced, most environmentally friendly, most handicapped-accessible, most artistically inspired, heck—the most of anything good—airport ever built." [26]

An architect's rendering of Denver International Airport that was presented to Jepp by the mayor, Federico Peña. *(E. B. Jeppesen collection)*

February 28, 1995—the day for the grand opening of Denver International Airport and the Jeppesen Terminal—had arrived. No one could remember when any single event had ever stirred up such excitement, hype, hoopla, glitz, or glamour in the Mile High City. An avalanche of out-of-town newspeople prompted one local television journalist to remark that Denver looked "like a city under siege."

There was only one problem. It had begun to snow the day before, and it was still snowing. An Arctic cold front was plunging down from Canada with sub-zero temperatures in its wake. The city fathers and airport executives held their collective breaths; they had been touting DIA's ability to operate as an "all-weather" airport and it looked like DIA was going to have the opportunity to prove or disprove that thesis on its opening day.

United Airlines, as DIA's largest tenant, had requested the honor of making the last flight out of the old airport and the first flight into the new one—a request that was granted. A special plane was scheduled to take Jepp, Horst Bergmann, members of the Jeppesen Aviation Foundation, and various media types on the final flight from Stapleton on February 27 and fly them sixty miles south to Colorado Springs. There the group, along with friends, major Jeppesen vendors, and old pilot friends of Jepp, would spend the night and then become the first arrival at DIA the next day.

"We had to get up at 4:30 in the morning," recalled Don Sellars, "because we had to be the first scheduled flight into DIA. Jepp and Nadine were on that flight and everybody wanted Jepp's autograph. We had built all the new charts to DIA and made sort of a souvenir package with the first charts, and he was passing those around, signing them." [27]

United Flight 1474, a Boeing 737 piloted by Captain Joe Rozic, left Colorado Springs shortly before 6:00 a.m. Within the plane's fuselage, a festive mood reigned. People laughed and sang and the champagne flowed. One reporter said it reminded her of the giddy atmosphere on a "cheerleading bus in high school." [28]

Less than thirty minutes after take-off, Flight 1474 was descending through the dark, flake-filled skies above DIA. Visibility was near zero but the plane, with the help of on-board Jeppesen navigational aids, made a smooth and uneventful flight, approach, and landing.

On the snowy tarmac outside the gate, a line of people carrying dozens of international flags waited to greet the flight, but then a problem developed. It was so cold outside that the passenger jetway that formed a bridge from the plane to the terminal was frozen solid and wouldn't budge!

The plane was towed to a different gate, where Jepp was led down the jetway by the captain and into a sea of flashing strobe lights and helium-filled balloons and more media attention than usually accompanies a Denver Broncos football game. Waiting to greet the first-ever arrival was Colorado Governor Roy Romer, Denver Mayor Wellington Webb, his predecessor, Federico Peña, plus numerous members of the state legislature and Denver and Aurora city councils, and ordinary well-wishers, not to mention hundreds of persons waiting to take later flights. It was a circus. [29]

Don Sellars said, "When we got into the terminal, all the flashbulbs and strobes were going off, and Jepp was the hero of the day. He was

Jepp and Nadine greet well-wishers during the opening of the Jeppesen Terminal at
Denver International Airport, February 28, 1995. *(E. B. Jeppesen collection)*

eighty-eight then. It was just a fantastic time. People were trying to get
his autograph and reporters were trying to get a statement from him. It
was almost overwhelming for him." [30]

Once the passengers elbowed their way into United's Concourse B,
Jepp was invited to help cut the ribbon and officially open the airport.
He did so with gusto, his Parkinson's barely in evidence. "This is pretty
exciting for me," Jepp told a *Denver Post* reporter, "since I remember
landing on grass strips. It's pretty hard to believe."

The group then made its way via the underground train system to
the main terminal—Jeppesen Terminal—where Jepp and Nadine looked
up at his bronze likeness at the north end of the cavernous space.

"I guess that's one way to get some of your age back," Jepp remarked
with a smile. Everyone in the entourage laughed. [31]

Janet Conner was deeply involved in making Jepp's role in the DIA
terminal dedication a reality. "I think that the dedication, the naming

the terminal in his honor, was the highlight of his life. I think he was absolutely thrilled to death over it." [32]

One could look at the statue and almost see a young Elrey Jeppesen standing in front of one of Tex Rankin's flying machines, getting ready to twist the prop, hear the sputtering and then the roar of a primitive engine, and watch the prop spinning around and around like a silvery disk, the engine humming on all cylinders, watching a life come full circle.

The finished statue and display cases after the opening of DIA. (Due to a reconfiguration of the main terminal for security reasons after September 11, 2001, the display cases were moved to the level above the statue.) *(E. B. Jeppesen collection)*

10: GOING WEST

The opening of the Jeppesen Terminal at DIA was the apogee, the high point of Jepp's amazing, high-flying life. Nothing again would ever be so great, so grand. Yet, even as the afterglow of the celebration continued to warm him, it was clear that his beloved Neddy was slipping away, and he perhaps felt his own end approaching.

The Jeppesens had not been in good health for years. Nadine's emphysema had become worse and, to aggravate matters, she refused to give up smoking. Jepp had a bad hip and he continued to struggle with Parkinson's disease which caused his hands to shake and his legs to hurt. Tal Miller said, "Sometimes when he and Nadine and Yvette and I would go out to Cherry Hills Country Club for dinner, he'd get up from the table in the middle of dinner and go walking to lessen the pain in his legs—that would help him.

"One night we were there and he got up and didn't come back. Nadine said that I'd better go look for him. I looked everywhere—the bar, the pool, the lavatory, and the locker room. I saw a light on in the pro shop and went in and there he was. He had about a hundred golf clubs out and was doing a little practice putting in the pro shop. The manager had wanted to go home a couple of hours earlier, but if Jepp wanted to try out some putters, that was all right with him." [1]

Miller's wife, Yvette, said that Jepp could laugh at his illness. "He had a dry sense of humor," she related. "He would say, 'I'm shaking so badly with this Parkinson's, everybody thinks I'm waving at them.'" [2]

Tal added, "You'd ask him how he felt and he'd say, 'Well, the head's okay, but the body's not coming with it.'" [3]

It wasn't long after DIA's opening in 1995 that the people at the Museum of Flight in Seattle, a private entity which has a solid connection with the Boeing Company and helps Boeing preserve its history, began to show an interest in becoming the repository for Jepp's basement full of artifacts—but only on the condition that Jepp donate a substantial sum of money for the collection's display and upkeep. Ray Lee told the museum people that it just wasn't going to happen. "They finally agreed to take it without a monetary contribution on Jepp's part," Lee said. "Dennis Parks and Michael Friedline came to Denver and looked the collection over and catalogued everything. Jepp still wasn't sure he wanted to give anything away. He wanted to have it memorialized somewhere, but he didn't want to take the final step of actually seeing it go out the door." [4]

Donna Chandler Miller recalled, "The people from the Museum of Flight were very nice, very respectful. I think Captain Jepp was concerned that if his memorabilia didn't go to the right people, that it would just get sold off. I think he wanted it to go to someone who cared about it or that it would be in a museum where people could learn from it. He wanted to be able to inspire kids or young people to fly, and the Museum of Flight people assured him that his memorabilia would be well taken care of." [5]

The pieces of the Jeppesen collection which were not on display at DIA were boxed up and stored in the basement, awaiting shipment to their new home in Seattle. For his part, Ray Lee was glad to see that a substantial organization such as the Museum of Flight would be the caretakers of the Jeppesen collection. Lee recalled that Jepp looked at the sealed boxes and asked, "'Well, do you think this is a good idea?' I said, 'Jepp, I think it's an excellent idea and you should go along with it. These people are honest, decent, and it's the best deal we can find. We're very fortunate to have people like that who are interested.' He nodded his head, and that's about as much as you could get from Jepp—a nod of the head on something like that." [6]

For many years, Nadine worked as a volunteer at the local Veterans Administration hospital, but her own health continued on a slow, downward spiral and she had to give up the work. Annette Brott recalled that Nadine was having terrible coughing fits, once bad enough for her to be hospitalized; the doctor cut her off from her cigarettes. "She offered one of the nurses' aides thirty-five dollars for a cigarette," said Annette. "'Don't you do it,'" I told her, "'or you'll get fired.'"

After Nadine came home from the hospital, Annette spoke with the doctor, who said that he had told Nadine that her lungs were in bad shape and that he was going to stop her from smoking. Nadine reportedly put her hands on her hips and indignantly replied, "Better men than you have tried to get me to stop smoking. What makes you think you can?" Eventually, however, she gave up the habit but, by then, it was too late. [7]

Ernestine Boyd remembered that Nadine had some words of wisdom for her: "'If you don't have your health, Ernestine, then you don't have anything. Wealth isn't worth a dime if you're not well enough to do something with it and enjoy.' I used to think about that—would I want to be rich and sick?" [8]

Annette said that Jepp and Nadine were very much into a fixed routine. "You had to do everything in accordance with what you always did. For example, Friday was the day for washing and curling Nadine's hair; you didn't do it on Thursday or Saturday." [9]

Both Annette and Ernestine saw the great fondness and attachment Jepp and Nadine had for one another. Ernestine said, "I remember when Mrs. Jeppesen got sick. He just cried and cried and cried, worried that somethin' was goin' to happen to her. He was sitting on the edge of the bed, holding Mrs. Jeppesen. He had her hugged up, and they were both just cryin'. That was a relationship like you wouldn't believe. He was so devoted to her."

Ernestine also recalled that Jepp frequently told her he hoped he would die before his wife did. "He used to tell me, 'Ernestine, promise me you'll come out here and stay with Nadine when I'm gone.' I'd say, 'Mr. Jeppesen, you ain't goin' no place. Where you plannin' on goin'?' And he'd say, 'Oh, I don't know. Maybe back to Louisiana.' I'd say, 'Yeah, sure, right back down to them swamps where you said you came from.' We always'd laugh about that." [10]

Annette also remembered an emotional time. Jepp was in the hospital after having hip surgery, and Nadine, fearing that she would lose him, clutched Annette and began sobbing. The nurse recalled, "She said, 'Oh, I can't lose Jepp. I want to go before him.' It was the first time I had seen her cry or be emotional, but she just cried and cried and said, 'Don't let Jepp die. Don't let Jepp die.'" [11]

It was, however, Nadine who passed away first. Their son Jim recalled the days leading up to his mother's death: "Mom hadn't been feeling very well for several days. Then on Thursday, May 30, 1996, Annette called me early in the morning and asked if I would help her take Mom to the doctor's office. Mom was experiencing severe lower chest pains and breathing problems and the doctor wanted to see her right away. We literally carried her out of the house and into the car; Dad stayed home. After the doctor evaluated her condition, he immediately admitted her to St. Joseph's Hospital. After we got her settled in, Dad called, wanting to come down to the hospital. So Annette and I left to go get him. Mom was doing much better at this point.

"Later that afternoon, after she ate lunch and before Dad arrived, she experienced a severe convulsion that put her in the intensive-care unit. She remained there for about six days, conscious and fairly alert. But due to the breathing tube, she couldn't speak. The doctor met with the whole family a few days later, explained her condition, and recommended that she be taken off the breathing machine, as it was really causing her too much anxiety. But he warned she could then possibly go into cardiac arrest and die.

"We all decided it was best for Mom to make her comfortable and pray for a good outcome. She came through okay but her condition continued to deteriorate rapidly over the next few days. We had just completed making arrangements to have her moved to a hospice-care facility close to home either that afternoon or the next morning when, on June 10, 1996, she suddenly died." [12]

Nadine Liscomb Jeppesen was buried at Denver's Fairmont Cemetery. The pallbearers were Horst Bergmann, Ray Lee, Dan Lynch, Tal Miller, Virg Vaughn, and Jim Warren. Corky Douglas, Jess Egurrola, Eddie Mehlin, Don Provost, George Reeves, John Reynolds, and Hugh Shockly served as honorary pallbearers. [13]

Jepp was beside himself with grief. His wife's death was a blow from which he never recovered. His old friend Ted Boerstler saw him decline. "Shortly after Nadine died, Jepp said to me, 'Well, there's just nothing left now. There's nothing left, nothing left.' He was deeply committed to her. He was a man of character." [14]

The house at 37 Sedgwick Drive was now very quiet. Annette continued to live in the spare bedroom there, and Jim and Joyce and Corky and Ted still dropped by regularly, but it wasn't the same. The Jeppesen's other son Richard and his wife Nancy and their children were now living in Florida. Annette saw how lonely Jepp was.

"At night I would hear him mumbling and talking," she related, "so I would go into his room and ask him, 'Who are you talking to?' and he'd say, 'Nadine.' I'd say, 'Nadine's not here,' and he would say, 'I know, but she was here. She was here.'

"I'd say, 'No, Mr. Jeppesen, Nadine's gone. I told you, remember?' He'd say, 'I know, but she talks to me.' He would talk to her. He said he would talk to her a lot of times. I'd argue with him. I said, 'No, Mr. Jeppesen. You might have heard something else, but you didn't hear her,' and he'd say, 'I know, but she was laying right here. She was laying right here.'"

Annette added, "I told Jim this a lot of times—I think that God just let her go before him. I said that God just knew that Nadine couldn't have handled it with him gone; I know she would have had a nervous breakdown or something if he had gone first. He was strong. He coped with her death, but he missed her so much."

Jepp wasn't the only one who missed her. The Jeppesens had a Sheltie named Blazer that had belonged to son Richard and his wife Nancy; they gave them the dog when they moved to Australia for a few years. The Jeppesens had always had and loved dogs. While Nadine was alive, the dog would sleep on the floor at the foot of the Jeppesens' bed; after Nadine passed away, Annette said Blazer would not go into the room for about a week. "He'd sit outside the door to their room," she said. "Mr. Jeppesen would have to offer him treats to get him to go in. Finally, the dog was sleeping on the bed with Mr. Jeppesen."

Jepp began to depend on Annette more than ever. She said, "After Nadine died, Mr. Jeppesen really needed me, so I had to stay there all the time. He wouldn't let me go home. His son Jim and his wife Joyce would come visit and I could go home for a while then, but that was it. I finally told him that I was going to need a little help; I'm going to have to hire somebody. My oldest daughter, Tanya, was in college then, and she came to help. Mr. Jeppesen really liked Tanya and she really babied him—she shaved him, brushed his teeth for him, gave him haircuts, baked cookies for him. He really, really loved those cookies." [15]

Donna Chandler Miller, who continued to visit the Jeppesens regularly long after Jepp's memorabilia had been sent to DIA and the Museum of Flight, remembered that she could see a steady, day-to-day decline in Jepp's health and in his will to live. "The spark was gone," she said. "He missed Nadine so dearly. It was frightening for me to see that, because I knew he wasn't going to wait around very long. It broke my heart to see him so sad. I think he felt that such a large part of him was gone. The whole house changed. Even Blazer was different." [16]

In the months following Nadine's death, Ernestine Boyd also watched her employer slowly fading. "I'd come to work in the morning and he'd say, 'Oh, Ernestine, you know Neddy fell last night,' and I'd say, 'No, she didn't fall; Mrs. Jeppesen gone to heaven, don't you know that?' And he'd say, 'Yeah, I guess she has. I'll be so glad when I can join her.' And then he'd call Annette 'Neddy,' like he couldn't remember that Mrs. Jeppesen was gone." [17]

On occasion, when he felt his spirits needed a lift, Jepp would have Jim and Joyce or Ted Boerstler or Corky Douglas over for Friday night dinners, or accept the dinner invitations from friends, but would not go out unless Annette escorted him. He avoided Cherry Hills, however, because people there would always ask him how he was doing, and that bothered him.

He spent much of his time gazing at the framed photos of his wife, lost in melancholy. Annette recounted, "He would look at the pictures and say, 'Oh, my sweet Nadine. I miss her a lot.' And he did. He cried for her every day, every day. People would say, 'He's not going to last. After six months he'll be gone.' And I'd say, 'Oh, no, Mr. Jeppesen's going to be okay.' But he cried and cried for her all the time and would say, 'What am I going to do without my Nadine?' There wasn't one day since she died that he didn't cry for her. Her missed her so much." [18]

It was Monday, November 25. Thanksgiving was three days away. Jepp had had a good evening. Ted Boerstler had come over to dine with him and Annette and a home-care nurse named Kathy.

Boerstler remembered, "I called over there and Annette said, 'Jepp wants you to come over and have dinner with him,' so I did. I remember Annette had fixed a nice steak dinner, so we had steak and just talked." [19]

Jepp seemed to be in a good mood, even though he only picked at his food. After 10:00 p.m., Ted said goodnight and left, then Annette and Kathy got Jepp ready for bed. In the middle of the night he awoke, calling out his wife's name. Annette came into his room and said, "Mr. Jeppesen, Nadine's not here any longer."

"Oh, I know," said Jepp. "But I'd still like to see her."

"I understand," said Annette. She sat by his bedside for another ten minutes while he talked before dozing off.

The next morning, Jim Jeppesen, as was his custom, called to ask how his father had fared during the evening. "Annette said he had had a rough night but that he seemed to be better that morning," Jim said. "I was alone—Joyce was a United Airlines flight attendant and was gone to Hong Kong—but I said that I would stop by that afternoon with a turkey dinner that Dad and I would have on Thursday. I wanted Annette to take Thanksgiving off and have dinner with her family." [20]

After the telephone conversation, Annette was giving Jepp a sponge bath in bed when, without warning, he lost consciousness.

"Mr. Jeppesen? Mr. Jeppesen?" Annette said to him, with some alarm in her voice. "You're not going to do this to me, Mr. Jeppesen!" He opened his blue eyes and looked at her and then his head slumped. "I thought, 'Oh, my God.' I think that was the worst moment that I have ever encountered."

She tried giving CPR but he was unresponsive. She dialed 911 and got an emergency team dispatched, then continued performing CPR until the paramedics arrived. She called Jim but he wasn't home; he had already left to take Joyce to the airport. Then she dialed Tal Miller; he said he would be right over. [21]

Before Jim arrived, the police got there and helped the paramedics perform CPR. She said, "We couldn't get any response from him at all. He was just barely breathing. Then the paramedics said they didn't think he was going to make it. Then Jim and Tal Miller arrived." [22]

Jim saw the emergency vehicles in front of the house and he was suddenly filled with worry. Entering the home, he asked a policeman in the kitchen what had happened. "The cop told me to 'go on back through the house and ask the lady; she'll tell you,'" said Jim. "He was referring to Annette. She immediately told me that an ambulance had just taken my dad to Swedish Hospital. I asked Annette to call the other family members, Horst at the company, and a few others. Then Tal Miller drove me to the hospital." [23]

Annette stayed behind to make calls and answer the phone. Soon everyone was calling, wanting to know what had happened to Jepp, where he was, what his condition was, asking if Annette thought he was going to pull through. She didn't know what to say. [24]

On the afternoon of November 26, 1996, just two months short of his ninetieth birthday, Elrey Borge Jeppesen passed into history—"went West," as the pilots say, their euphemism for dying.

The obituary read, "Pilot and aviation charting pioneer Elrey Borge Jeppesen died at 2:40 p.m. on Tuesday, Nov. 26, 1996, in his Cherry Hills Village home. He was 89. Services will be held this week at First Church of the Nazarene, with interment in Fairmont Cemetery. His wife, Nadine, preceded him by five months." [25]

Monday, December 2, 1996, was a raw, cold, blustery day in Denver. Pallbearers at Jepp's funeral were Horst Bergmann, Ted Boerstler, Dan Guthrie, Charles Haskell II, Tal Miller, and Jim Warren, all close friends. Serving as honorary pallbearers were John Andrews, Paul Burke, Corky Douglas, Jess Egurrola, Dan Lynch, William Kelley, Don Provost, George Reeves, Wayne Rosenkrans, Ralph Stewart, Virg Vaughn, and Carl Williams.

The three pilots who flew the memorial salute over Jepp's funeral. Left to right: president of the Colorado Historical Aviation Society, Jack Wilhite (Eaglerock), Mike Baldwin (Stearman), and Eric Baldwin (Stearman).
(E. B. Jeppesen collection)

Howard W. Reid, a long-time friend, fellow aviator (he once flew with Tex Rankin's Flying Circus as well as for United), and early Jeppesen chart customer (since 1941), also attended the funeral. He recalled that, as Jepp was being laid to rest beside Neddy at Fairmont, he heard the buzz of antique aircraft engines overhead and looked up.

"Three of his buddies in little airplanes were flying over," Reid said. "I thought that was kind of nice." [26]

There in the gray sky, fighting the stiff wind, were Jack Wilhite flying an Eaglerock, and Mike Baldwin and Eric Baldwin flying Stearmans in a V-formation.

Jim Jeppesen recalled, "It was an impressive sight and a moving experience for all of us gathered at the gravesite."[27]

The day after Jepp died, a black arm band appeared on the statue of Capt. Jepp at DIA; the sculptor George Lundeen had placed it there. [28]

Elrey Borge "Jepp" Jeppesen, pilot, barnstormer, wing walker, instructor, air navigation pioneer, business innovator. January 28, 1907 – November 26, 1996.
(E. B. Jeppesen collection)

EPILOGUE

Elrey B. Jeppesen's contributions to aviation were, and are, immense and incalculable. Of the many awards he received in his lifetime and posthumously, the following stand out:
- Air Traffic Control Association – Glen A. Gilbert Memorial Award (1995)
- Airport Operators Council International – William C. Downes Award (1980)
- American Society of Travel Agents (ASTA) – Travel Hall of Fame (1983)
- Boeing Pathfinder Award (1996)
- Colorado Aviation Historical Society – Hall of Fame (1970)
- Colorado Business Hall of Fame (1994)
- Colorado Department of Transportation – Roderick L. Downing Award
- Coors American Ingenuity Award (1993)
- Federal Aviation Administration – Distinguished Service Award (1971)
- First Flight Centennial Foundation "100 Heroes of Aviation" (2003)
- Freedom Foundation Valley Forge – George Washington Honor Medal (1994)
- International Aerospace Hall of Fame (1995)
- International Civil Aviation Organization – Edward Warner Award (1995)
- Institute of Navigation – P.V. H. Weems Award (1996)
- Kitty Hawk Society – Hall of Fame (1994)
- National Aeronautic Association – Elder Statesman of Aviation Award (1983)
- National Business Aircraft Association – Meritorious Service to Aviation Award (1965)
- Northwest Aviation Council – Roll of Honor Award (1980)
- Oregon Aviation Hall of Honor (2006)
- Silver Wings Fraternity – Achievement Award (1963)
- U. S. National Aviation Hall of Fame (1990)

Jepp was also a member of numerous professional societies. Here are but a few:
- Airline Pilots' Association
- American Congress of Surveying and Mapping
- Flight Safety Foundation Board of Directors
- Honorary Member, Air Mail Pioneers
- Institute of Navigation
- Life Member, Air Force Academy Foundation
- National Aeronautic Association
- National Pilots' Association

The Jeppesen Aviation Foundation did not go out of existence after the mission of raising funds for the DIA statue, display cases, and signage was complete. (See "About the Jeppesen Aviation Foundation," page 286): Nor did the passing of Elrey Borge Jeppesen mean the death of the company he had started on a shoestring budget in his basement in 1934. To the contrary, the company continued to grow stronger and solidify its position as the world's foremost supplier of navigational aids. But big changes were in the wind.

In March 2000, the Chandler family sold the Times Mirror Corporation to the Tribune Company—owners of the *Chicago Tribune*, three other newspapers, twenty-two television stations, four radio stations, and the Chicago Cubs baseball team—for $8 billion. Jeppesen Sanderson was included in the deal. Perhaps not knowing what to do with the aviation-navigation company, the Tribune Company sold it five months later to a most-logical new parent: the Boeing Company. The sale price? $1.5 billion. [1]

The purchase was a smart one for Boeing. In 1999, Jeppesen Sanderson had posted revenues of $235 million (the "Sanderson" named was dropped soon after Boeing bought the company) and was continuing to show an upward growth curve.

When asked about Jeppesen's place in the Boeing corporate matrix, Boeing CEO James McNerney said in June 2006, "I think Jeppesen has been a home run [for us]. And we're adding to it a couple of rich acquisitions, so we're feeling very good about Jeppesen. It's profitable. It's well led. It's a nice market for us." [2]

Boeing also purchased Carmen Systems, a Sweden-based software company specializing in products that handle air crew scheduling, fleet dispatching, aircraft rotations, and even train routing, and placed it under Jeppesen's wing.

Current Jeppesen president and chief operating officer Mark Van Tine said in a news release, "Carmen's aviation business is a natural fit for Jeppesen and will enhance our existing portfolio of airline operations services by adding their crew, fleet, and logistics resource optimization solutions. In addition, its railroad business offers new opportunities, which are consistent with our growth strategy of applying our technology to new markets." [3]

In a 2005 article about the company in *Twin & Turbine* magazine, author

Jeppesen's state-of-the-art Global Support and Control Center monitors all flights around the world in real time. *(Courtesy Jeppesen)*

Mike Haenggi writes, "When there was a strategic fit, other companies were purchased. Nearly a dozen aviation firms were acquired and integrated into Jeppesen to help it expand its expertise and increase its global coverage. The company methodically grew into the world's largest provider of aviation information." [4]

Today the Jeppesen Company is a giant in its field, with over 700,000 subscribers and practically no competition. Jeppesen today provides highly

Mark Van Tine, current Jeppesen president. *(Courtesy Jeppesen)*

sophisticated aerial navigation aids for more than 300,000 pilots and 400 airlines worldwide from over eighty countries. It is estimated that eighty percent of all the world's private, commercial, and military pilots use Jeppesen navigation aids.

From the early days, when Jepp was hand-drawing approach routes to primitive airports, the company has expanded a thousand-fold to offer worldwide flight-information services, flight-operations service, international trip-planning services, aviation weather services, and aviation training programs.

Jeppesen has also recently added a marine division that provides navigational and maritime data services to pleasure-boat operators, cruise ships, commercial ships, and military vessels. The company has expanded its offices around the globe; in addition to the U.S. and Germany offices, Jeppesen now maintains offices in Australia, China, France, Russia, and the United Kingdom.

The company is not about to rest on its hard-won laurels. "Elrey Jeppesen was a pioneer, an innovator, a visionary," said Van Tine, "and we continue to move forward in that same spirit."

When one stands beneath the towering bronze figure of Jepp at Denver International Airport and looks up into his eyes, one can see him scanning the far horizon of the future. It's almost as though he is reflecting upon Mark Van Tine's words: "When space travel becomes commercially viable, you can bet that Jeppesen systems will be on board the space vehicles heading to the moon and Mars and the outer planets." [5]

It's a lovely vision, and one that Capt. Jepp, no doubt, would have heartily endorsed.

APPENDIX

How Pilots Use Jeppesen Navigation Charts

by Jim Terpstra
(Retired Jeppesen Senior Vice President)

Jepp had a passion. His passion was for knowing as much as he could about where he was, where he was going, the best route to get there, and all the other details from takeoff to landing.

For pilots today, what is especially appreciated about Jepp is that he recognized the importance of capturing the details on paper—and not only in text, but also with graphics. Looking back at Jepp's "little black book," most of the pages were filled with diagrams and illustrations, with supporting text where needed. It could probably be stated that most pilots are visual people—maybe more visual- than text-oriented. Jepp must have felt that—at least everything he did for himself was primarily visual.

The fundamentals that Jepp took from his creative mind and placed on paper are still the same now as they were in the 1930s. Paths for flight with courses and altitudes, airports with runway layouts, information on how to get the best weather—all these were on Jepp's original charts and remain there today.

When Jepp first started, his efforts went toward airport charts—not only the runway layouts, but also with additional information such as radio navigation frequencies, availability of fuel, weather station information, and surrounding terrain so he could be vigilant for hills and potential obstacles and obstructions as well as the impact the terrain had on winds near the airports. By drawing any gullies and hills around the various airports, he could know ahead of time what runways would be treacherous if the winds were from certain directions. Always thinking—that is one thing you could count on from Jepp.

After the airport charts, Jepp started his work on the enroute charts between the airports (airways). Some of the routes were prescribed, but most of his work was trying to determine the best routes between airports based on the existing few navigation radio aids and the very challenging terrain between Cheyenne, Wyoming, and Salt Lake City, Utah. Since Jepp and the other pilots didn't get paid unless they got the mail to the other end, his incentive was double—being able to safely find his destination, plus getting paid for all the flying. And knowing all the details of those prescribed routes was the key to what Jepp got started long ago.

VFR and IFR

These two abbreviations are used frequently in the aviation world and their meanings are a big differentiation for pilots. The letters VFR stand for "visual flight rules" and the letters IFR mean "instrument flight rules." When the clouds are more than 1,000 feet AGL, or above ground level, and the visibility is three miles or greater, the weather is considered VFR at the airport. Also when airborne, there is a general requirement to remain a specified distance from all clouds and have a visibility of three miles or more.

When the weather is less than VFR, then a whole lot of rules come into play. Some of the "big" rules are: first, the pilot must be instrument rated (having passed a rigorous test to be able to fly solely by observing his or her instruments); must file an IFR flight plan; and must have enough information on charts for the entire flight. Although most of those rules were not in existence when Jepp flew, he recognized the importance of the charts for IFR flight. For Jepp, the charts used for flying in instrument conditions were the most important, since the need for flying in all weather conditions really enabled him to complete his flights. In this section, most of the discussion will be on IFR charts.

In aviation, pilots use aeronautical charts in much the same way as the very familiar city and highway maps we frequently use when driving a car. Each type of aeronautical chart has a different scale, depending on the type of information needed for various portions of each flight.

Airport Charts

The aeronautical charts with the most detail are airport charts, sometimes called airport diagrams. On these charts, all the runways, taxiways, airport buildings, and other details are depicted at a scale of about 1,000 to 2,000 feet per inch. The airport charts are the approximate equivalents to city maps for driving.

At the former Stapleton Airport in Denver, Jepp included all the elements we see today. (Figure 1). The most important and most obvious part of the airport chart was the diagram of all the runways and the taxiways—when they were available. Each runway had the length in feet indicated adjacent to the runway—a technique still in use today. Jepp also included the runway number at the end of the runway so when the tower cleared you to land on Runway 26, you knew you had the right one. In the runway diagram for Stapleton, you can see the number "26" on the right side of the airport to show the end of Runway 26. This technique survives today. (All runway numbers are created by determining the magnetic heading of the runway and then rounding to the nearest 10 degrees. So Runway Number 26 means a runway with the direction of 260 degrees.)

Since all IFR flights end up with at least some visibility, Jepp included some visual features to ensure he could spot the airport and the surrounding area. There is a power line north of the airport (that looks like a line of Ts with dashes connecting them). Power lines are major visual landmarks and when you see them in relationship to the airport, it helps with the verification that you have found the right airport.

At the top of the airport chart, there is important information, such as the airport elevation (5,308 feet MSL, mean sea level, or above sea level). The airport is the municipal airport for Denver (before it was named for Denver Mayor Ben Stapleton), as well as the tower and ground control radio frequencies.

The large shaded symbol running north and south across the chart and under the runways is an old means of radio navigation. It was known as the four-course range and transmitted on a frequency about

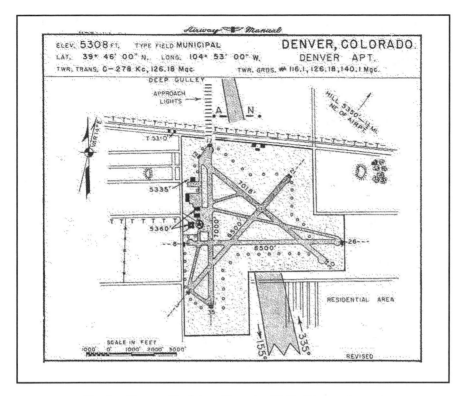

Fig. 1— Denver Stapleton Airport - 1945   *(Courtesy Jeppesen)*

in the same range as AM radio. It was full of static, but transmitted two signals—one was the Morse Code letter A (a dot followed by a dash) and the other signal was the Morse Code letter N (a dash followed by a dot). The signal was transmitted in such a way that if you were on the center-line of the two signals the dots and dashes merged with each to form a single solid tone you heard in your headset. If you went to the side of the A, then the dot-dash became slightly louder than the dash-dot and you had to make a slight turn to return to the centerline of the signal. It was crude compared to today's technology, but Jepp used the four-course range many times and showed it on his charts whenever it was available.

Figure 2 illustrates the airport chart published for Cheyenne, Wyoming, in a recent revision sent to Jeppesen chart subscribers. The similarities to the 1945 chart for Denver are very apparent. (Cheyenne airport is the one where Jepp was based when he was flying airmail to Salt Lake City, Utah.)

As with Denver, the length of the runway is shown in feet adjacent to the runway on the chart and the runway number is at the end of the runway. Small features, such as the exact runway heading, have been added at the bottom of the runway number, and the elevation at the end of the runway is shown at the end of each runway. Today, the pilot can tell if the runway has an upslope or downslope by comparing the elevations of the two ends of the runway.

At the top of the Cheyenne airport chart, the same information is included today, although the amount of information has expanded as new capabilities become available. As an example, the letters "KCYS" are shown at the top of the chart. The letters are the International Civil Aviation Organization (ICAO) letters assigned to Cheyenne and are the letters used by pilots when filing flight plans to Cheyenne either domestically or internationally. Following the ICAO identifier are the letters "CYS" that are printed on the baggage tags when flying to Cheyenne (just as "DEN" is the identifier for Denver).

In addition to the identifiers on the chart, the radio frequencies needed to talk to the tower and ground control are shown. New features, such at the Automatic Terminal Information Service (ATIS), which transmit all the current weather and landing conditions, are shown. When departing Cheyenne on an IFR flight plan, pilots use two frequencies: the departure control (124.55 MHz), followed by the Denver Air Route Traffic Control Center on 125.9 MHz.

Below the large area that shows the runway pattern, today's charts include details in a textual format such as the runway lighting, the runway widths, and other details such as runway grooving when available to enable shorter landing distances when the runway is wet.

When Capt. Jepp was flying, the concept of landing and takeoff minimums didn't really exist. On the bottom of the Cheyenne chart, there is a box that states the minimum visibility for various types of operations when departing Cheyenne.

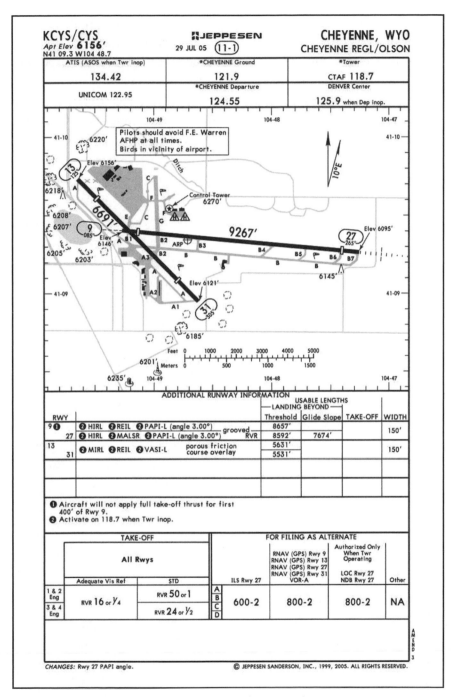

Fig. 2 — Current Cheyenne, Wyoming, Airport Chart *(Courtesy Jeppesen)*

During Capt. Jepp's flying days, he had a major advantage: there wasn't much air traffic—especially when compared to today. Back in the 1960s, after Jepp retired as a pilot, the departure controllers found they were saying the same words so often during the day to pilots that they decided to publish those clearances and call them Standard Instrument Departures. Pilots now refer to them as SIDs. Now when departing major airports, pilots use published SIDS for planning purposes and the actual paths they will use to get out of the local flying area. In the Salt Lake SID, the large gray circle surrounds the airport layout to help pilots spot the runway amidst all the other lines, text, and symbols.

At Salt Lake, pilots flying to the south will use the "SEVYR One Departure" procedure following the lines and maintaining the altitudes shown adjacent to the departure paths. At the end of the SEVYR Departure, there are radio navigation aids called VORs (Very High Frequency Omni-directional Radio) depicted with the circles with ticks adjacent to the circles. Inside the circles are additional circles with scallops that illustrate that the VOR also has Distance Measuring Equipment (DME). The VORs define the tracks and the DME provides signals that show the distance to the location. At the end of the SEVYR departure, one of the navaids is the Milford VOR that transmits on the VHF frequency of 112.1 MHz. The latitude and longitude of the VOR is included with the other information for pilots who have GPS (Global Positioning System) and want to fly to the VOR location using this new technology.

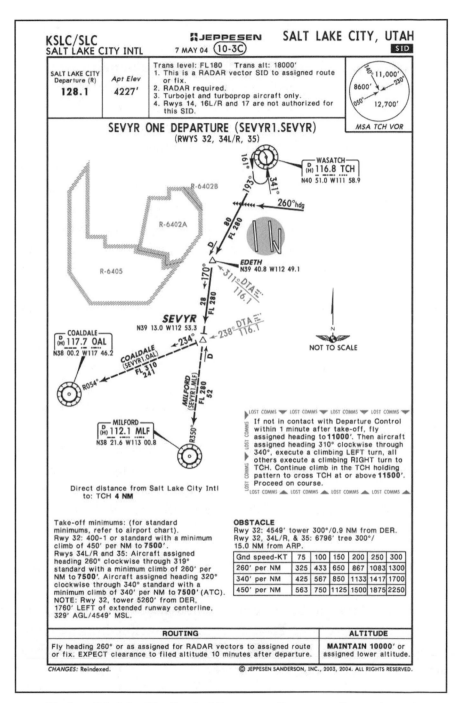

Fig. 3 — Salt Lake City Standard Instrument Departure *(Courtesy Jeppesen)*

Enroute Charts

When Capt. Jepp was flying between airports, there were some routes between the few radio navigation aids that existed then. The charts that are used between airports are called enroute charts. The enroute chart in Figure 4 shows the route between the Lewis navaid in Nevada and the Limestone navaid in Utah—a route that crosses the high mountains west of Salt Lake City. The top part of the chart shows the profile view of the routes. Back in Capt. Jepp's days, knowing the elevation of the terrain below your route of flight was extremely important when flying in the clouds, especially considering the lesser reliability of engines back in the 1930s. The terrain is graphically depicted so the pilots could see exactly their clearance between the altitude they were flying and what was beneath them. The graphic bird's eye view of the routes are in the lower left corner while the distances and bearings along the airways are shown in a separate table in the lower right.

When pilots are shown Capt. Jepp's early charts with the graphical depiction of the terrain on them, they keep asking why Jeppesen does not do that today. Actually, the terrain is shown in a profile view in Jeppesen's latest electronic enroute chart depiction but still not on the Jeppesen paper enroute charts.

In the boxes below the airways, Capt. Jepp included airports along the way, along with their elevations. The distances along the airway were shown in the box in the lower right with the magnetic bearings leading to and away from the airport along the route. Note that statute miles were used by Capt. Jepp, whereas nautical miles are used today. A nautical mile equals roughly a statute mile times 1.15.

Today, depending on the altitude a pilot will fly, the flight will either use a low-altitude enroute chart or a high-altitude enroute chart. The dividing line between the low charts and the high charts in the United States is 18,000 feet MSL. Pilots flying in the low altitude fly on airways called Victor airways and pilots flying in the high altitude structure fly on airways called Jet airways—or Jet routes.

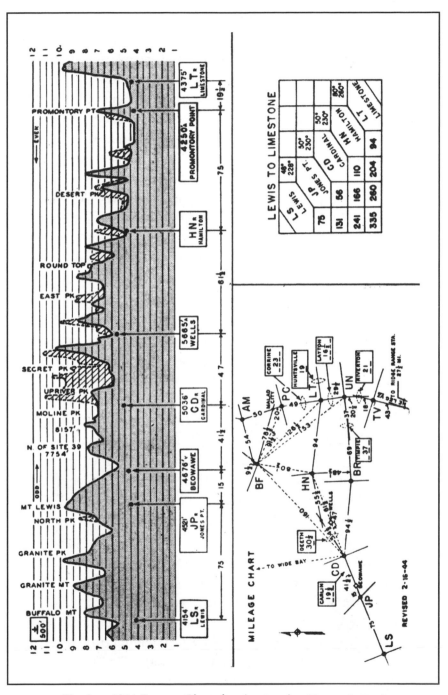

Fig. 4 — 1944 Enroute Chart showing terrain *(Courtesy Jeppesen)*

There are fifty-two low-altitude charts that cover the entire United States, while it takes only about six high-altitude charts to cover the U.S. The low-altitude charts depict all the airways for the low altitude plus all the airports that have instrument approaches. Most of the VFR airports are also shown on the low-altitude charts. Both the high and low charts show all the radio navigation aids and the airways that connect the navigation aids. The low altitude charts are usually about twenty miles to the inch and the high-altitude charts are about thirty or forty miles to the inch.

The low altitude enroute chart in Figure 5 looks quite a bit different today than when published by Capt. Jepp. The Drummond VOR is now near the Drummond airport, so navigation is much easier. Also, there are so many airways that publishing the profile views like the one produced by Capt. Jepp would consume so many pages, it would be difficult to carry all the paper. So much for progress—more paper and less terrain! The enroute charts today are generally seventeen inches high and many are fifty-five inches wide, so they cover a substantial amount of territory—very good for getting the "big picture" when flying.

Many of Jepp's other original ideas still exist today. Adjacent to the Drummond VOR, south of the Missoula VOR, the number "12" appears with a smaller "3" appear. These were created by Jepp and called Minimum Off Route Altitudes (MORAs). They still exist today and have been adopted by ICAO as standard information for when flying off the airways. The numbers mean that if you fly at an altitude of 12,300 feet MSL, you will clear all terrain and obstacles by at least 2,000 feet AGL, or above ground level, in the mountainous area near Drummond.

Capt. Jepp was such a stickler for detail that he even insisted on the company developing a special type font so that some numbers didn't get confused with other numbers. Instead of using the digit "3" with a rounded top, he devised a new font that showed the digit with a horizontal top ("**3**") so that it wouldn't be confused with the number "8."

Back in Jepp's days, before the advent of computerized typesetting, most of the lettering was done with what was called "strip film," and before that with the ink-drawn Leroy lettering system. The options back then gave the person doing the lettering the option of using a 3

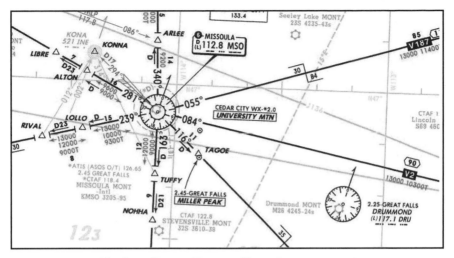

Fig. 5 — Current Enroute Chart *(Courtesy Jeppesen)*

with a flat top. Later, commercially available type fonts were used in which all the number 3s had rounded tops. Evidently, Jepp knew of the differences back then and used the flat-top 3, but later, the limitations of fonts didn't have a 3 with the flat tops. One Saturday night Jepp was looking at an old chart of his and comparing it to some of the new charts when he noticed the difference in the 3s. That's when he called me and asked about our capabilities with our type fonts at Jeppesen. When I told him that we made our own fonts for the charts, he then suggested the 3 with the flat top. All of the charts that the company produces today by human compilers have the 3 with the flat top. Unfortunately, Jeppesen is often limited to the commercially available fonts on PCs—and there are no really good fonts today on the PC that have a 3 with a flat top. (The enroute chart around Bozeman was produced using what is call data-driven technology and the charts are drawn by the computer on a PC, not at a Production Department workstation in the office.)

Approach Charts

When pilots get close to an airport for landing, an approach chart is used as the final chart before landing. The main difference between the different types of approach charts are the types of radio navigation aids used to guide the pilot. And with each type of radio navigation aid, there are different authorizations for how close to the airport a pilot may go while still flying in instrument conditions. The approach charts are mostly at a scale of about five miles to the inch.

The approach chart in Figure 6 is for the old Denver Municipal Airport that became Stapleton Field. Just like today, the approach chart is divided into major areas. The top is called the heading, the large area below is called the plan view, and below that is the profile view. Even today, Jeppesen includes the "conversion" tables that give the time, speed, and distance from the final navaid to the airport—just like Capt. Jepp's chart from 1944.

In the heading of the chart, the frequency, identifier, and Morse code of the four-course course range is given. Also in the heading is the minimum safe altitude created by Capt. Jepp—a concept in use today and officially known worldwide as the MSA, or "minimum safe altitude," within twenty-five miles from the primary navaid.

In the plan view, the dominant lines are the courses from the four-course low frequency range station. If flying in from the east, west, or south, it required a turn to the north after passing the navaid so the airplane could reduce altitude, reduce speed, and get turned around again heading south in a stabilized configuration when passing the navaid again southbound.

The profile view shows that the altitude for crossing the navaid the first time is 8,000 feet MSL, followed by a descent northbound to 6,300 feet MSL while turning around. After turned around and heading toward the navaid, an altitude of 6,100 feet MSL could be used. For efficiency, this approach was good for both the Denver airport and the Lowry Air Base field. If you were going to Denver Municipal, the minimum altitude was 5,708 feet MSL, or 400 feet AGL. If going to Lowry, the minimum altitude was 5,800 feet MSL, or 409 feet AGL above the airport.

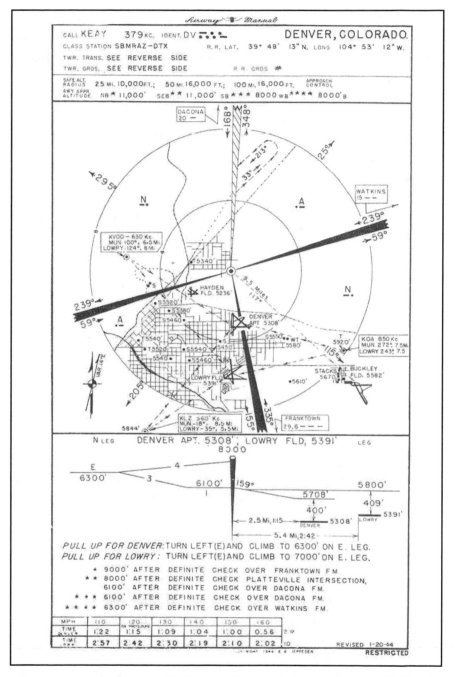

Fig. 6 — Combined Approach Chart for Denver Municipal at Stapleton Field and Lowry Field - 1944 *(Courtesy Jeppesen)*

Not all approaches while flying in the clouds end up with the pilot successfully finding the airport. So Jepp wisely included what were called "pull up" procedures of what to do at each airport. The pull up procedures gave both a direction to fly and the altitude to try the approach again (hopefully the weather might be a bit better the next time around.)

What is really interesting to see is the most current technology today—the Global Positioning System (GPS) as the guiding navigation system. Look closely at the approach chart for the new Denver International Airport in Figure 7. You can see Capt. Jepp's format from more than sixty years earlier still being used. Yes, many, many details are different, but the same basic structure with heading, plan view, profile view, and conversion table are there today. Pilots flying into Denver today have the luxury of radar from air traffic control that gives them specific headings and altitudes to fly. As their airplanes get near the final approach course into the airport, the controller will give a final heading and altitude to intercept the inbound course to the airport so the turning around to get aligned for the final approach is no longer needed at major airports.

In the plan view of the chart, the navigation fixes called Hoope and Joule define the path for the final approach course for Runway 17R, or right, at Denver International. After passing the Hoope and Joule navigation fixes, the pilot makes the final approach course of 170 degrees while descending to the final altitude of 5,920 feet MSL. If, when reaching 5,920 feet, the airport is in sight and the visibility is a half mile or better, then the pilot can continue to a landing.

If, however, when reaching 5,920 feet MSL and the airport is not in sight, then the missed approach (called the pull-up by Capt. Jepp) must be flown and the pilot will fly to the Jakur navigation fix, then make a slight turn to the right and continue climbing to the Hohum navigation fix to fly a holding pattern at 10,000 feet MSL.

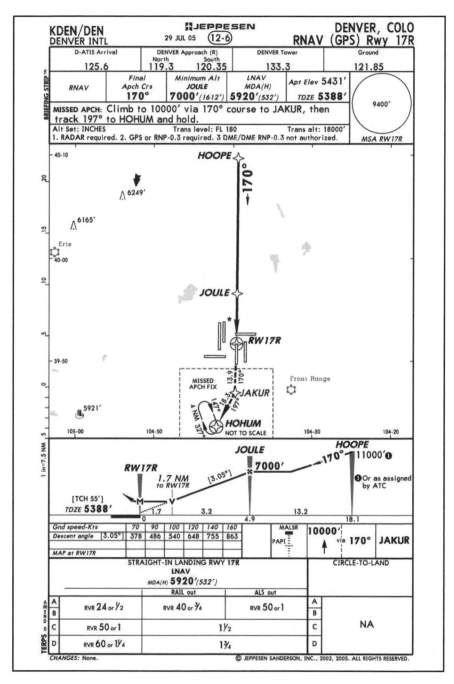

Fig. 7 — Current Approach Chart - the new Denver International Airport that opened in 1995 *(Courtesy Jeppesen)*

Summary

Technology has taken us very far today with all the automation in the cockpit and in air traffic control. There are many elements of sophistication that make flying easier and safer today, but the fundamentals haven't changed: Fly the airplane, stay above the minimum altitudes, and keep vigilant continuously from takeoff to landing. Capt. Jepp obviously did that—while at the same time creating the foundation of a whole series of aeronautical charts that continue to be the basis of charts used by the vast majority of pilots around the world today.

It is amazing to see what Capt. Jepp did back in the early days—and to see the similarities between his charts and what is in use today. Thank you for your creativity and foresight, Capt. Jepp.

ACKNOWLEDGMENTS

This book is the work of many people who were eager to have the life story of Elrey Borge Jeppesen told to a wider audience. In fact, so many are due heartfelt thanks for their contributions that it is almost impossible to decide where to begin.

But since we must begin somewhere, let us start with Jepp's eldest son Jim who, as director of the Jeppesen Aviation Foundation, was the ramrod behind the project and who worked tirelessly to make this book a reality.

Also deserving of the authors' deep gratitude are the more than thirty persons—relatives, friends, fellow aviators, and business associates—who knew Jepp at one point or another in his life and consented to be interviewed by Terry Barnhart. Each interviewee contributed a small (and oftentimes large) piece of the narrative and thus enabled the authors to construct a full portrait of the man honored in aviation circles as "the father of aerial navigation systems."

These interviewees include (in alphabetical order): Dick Bergesen, Horst Bergmann, Ted Boerstler, Ernestine Boyd, Annette Brott, Paul and Tally Burke, Lou Clinton, Harry Combs, Janet Conner, William Corbin "Corky" Douglas II, Jim Jeppesen, Richard Jeppesen, Ralph Latimer, Ray Lee, George Lundeen, Ed Mehlin, Donna Chandler Miller, Tal and Yvette Miller, Durham "Durrie" Monsma, Osgood Philpott, Harald Prommel, Howard Reid, Wayne Rosenkrans, John Schoonhoven, Don Sellars, Hal Shelton, Mark Van Tine, Virgil and Cookie Vaughn, and Carl Williams. Many of these interviewees, it should be sadly noted, have themselves "gone West" since telling their stories about Jepp and the early days of aviation.

Deserving of special mention and several gold stars beside her name is Mavis Neslen, who worked at Jeppesen for many years, became close friends with Jepp and, at Jepp's urging, conducted lengthy interviews with him with the intent of someday writing his biography. She gave him a tape recorder so that he could put down his life experiences, then spent hours transcribing his words. The authors have found these interviews with Jepp an invaluable primary source and we greatly appreciate her willingness to allow excerpts from the tapes to be used in this book.

The authors are also indebted to Ralph Latimer who gave several drafts of the manuscript a careful going-over, and especially to Janet Conner who served above and beyond the call of duty to transcribe all the interview tapes, helped provide many of the photos and printed documentation, provided personal insights, then performed the essential role of proof-reader for numerous copies of the drafts of the manuscript.

We also deeply appreciate the fine work of Nan Wisherd, our editor at Savage Press, our agent Jody Rein, and the book's graphic designer, Debbie Zime.

Also standing in the long line of people needing to be thanked are Dennis Parks of the Museum of Flight in Seattle, and Michael Lombardi, the Boeing corporate historian. Invaluable assistance in finding vintage aviation photographs was also provided by the staffs of the National Archives and Records Administration in College Park, Maryland, the Smithsonian Air and Space Museum in Washington, D.C., and Jim Culberson at Sea Bird Publishing.

We also cannot begin to fully express our gratitude to Mark Van Tine, president of Jeppesen, and his Manager of Corporate Communications Mike Pound, without whose support this book would never have rolled down the runway, let alone gotten off the ground. Rich Hahn and Gary Kennedy of Jeppesen also performed yeoman service in the hunt for photographs and data. Jim Terpstra, too, was extraordinarily helpful in providing, in clear and understandable terms, the Appendix on how to use Jeppesen aerial charts.

Last but not least is Elrey Borge Jeppesen himself, whose amazing life story has, for too long, gone untold. Even though he is no longer with us, his spirit continues to soar every time an airplane leaves the earth.

Terry L. Barnhart
Flint Whitlock

ABOUT THE AUTHORS

Flint Whitlock and Terry L. Barnhart have a friendship and working relationship that dates back to 1976 when Whitlock became the Creative Director for Barnhart and Company, then a fledgling Denver advertising agency.

While Whitlock left the agency after five years to pursue other opportunities (including that of a full-time author), Barnhart guided his agency to become one of the largest and most successful in Denver.

One of Barnhart's clients at the time was Jeppesen, the world's leading producer of aerial navigation systems. Barnhart, who is also a licensed private pilot and has contributed many articles to aviation magazines, became intrigued with the many stories he heard about "Capt. Jepp." Over a period of several years he interviewed more than thirty of Jepp's family members, long-time friends, and business associates to gather material for this biography.

In the fall of 2005 Barnhart brought Whitlock, a Pulitzer-nominated author with five books and two dozen magazine articles to his credit, into the project. The two began collaborating to turn the book idea into reality in time for 2007—the 100th anniversary of Capt. Jepp's birth.

Barnhart lives in Franktown, Colorado, with his wife, Carly, and Whitlock lives in Denver with his wife, Mary Ann Watson.

SOURCE NOTES

Chapter 1: The Early Days

1. Bilstein, Roger E. *Flight Patterns: Trends of Aeronautical Development in the United States, 1918-1929.* Athens: University of Georgia Press, 1983, pp. 29-30; www.early aviators.com/eovington; www.airmailpioneers.org/history/milestone3

2. Bilstein, 30-31; Jackson, Donald D. "Up, Up And Away (But Just Barely) With 'Aerial Mail,'" *Smithsonian,* (issue date unknown), pp. 83-85; Smith, Henry L. *Airways: The History of Commercial Aviation in the United States.* New York: Knopf, 1942, pp. 58-59.

3. www.postalmuseum.si.edu/airmail/pilot/Lamborn; Jackson, 83).

4. www.postal museum.si.edu/airmail/pilot/Ames.

5. www.postalmuseum.si.edu/airmail/pilot/Carlton.

6. www.postalmuseum.si.edu/airmail/pilot/Stoner.

7. www.postalmuseum.si.edu/airmail/pilot/Sherlock.

8. www.postalmuseum.si.edu/airmail/pilot/Woodward.

9. www.postalmuseum.si.edu/airmail/pilot/Robinson.

10. www.postalmuseum.si.edu/airmail/pilot/Gautier.

11. www.postalmuseum.si.edu/airmail/pilot/Moore.

12. www.postalmuseum.si.edu/airmail/pilot/Hyde-Pearson.

13. www.postalmuseum.si.edu/airmail/pilot/Smith.

14. www.postalmuseum.si.edu/airmail/pilot/Hopson.

Chapter 2: This Was Magic

1. Logan, William. "E. B. Jeppesen: Pioneer In Aviation," *Rocky Mountain News,* January 7, 1968.

2. Official records, Jeppesen family archives.

3. Elrey Jeppesen interview by Mavis Neslen, July 1993, Jeppesen family archives.

4. www.sprucegoose.org/aircraft ("Tex Rankin").

5. Elrey Jeppesen interview by Mavis Neslen, July 1993, Jeppesen family archives.

6. Jim Jeppesen interview by Terry Barnhart, August 24, 2000.

7. Berg, A. Scott. *Lindbergh.* New York: Berkley Publishing, 1999, pp. 60-61.

8. en.wikipedia.org/wiki ("Alcock and Brown").

9. en.wikipedia.org/wiki ("NC-4").

10. en.wikipedia.org/wiki ("R-34").

11. www.ciderpresspottery.com/ZLA/greatzeps ("Zeppelin").

12. Berg, pp. 90-129.

13. *Tampa Commerce*, May 1981.

14. Allen, Oliver E. *The Airline Builders*. (*The Epic of Flight* series.) Alexandria, VA: Time-Life Books, 1981, p. 53.

15. Allen, pp. 51-53.

16. Allen, p. 53.

17. www.centennialofflight/gov.essay ("The Evolution of Airway Lights and Electronic Navigation Aids").

18. Logan, William. "E. B. Jeppesen: Pioneer In Aviation," *Rocky Mountain News*, January 7, 1968.

19. Ibid.

20. Elrey Jeppesen interview by Mavis Neslen, July 1993, Jeppesen family archives.

Chapter 3: A Barnstormer's Life

1. O'Neil, Paul. *Barnstormers and Speed Kings*. (*The Epic of Flight* series). Alexandria, VA: Time-Life Books, 1981, pp. 48-67.

2. O'Neil, pp. 39, 67.

3. Richard Jeppesen interview by Terry Barnhart, September 6, 2000.

4. Elrey Jeppesen interview by Mavis Neslen, July 1993, Jeppesen family archives.

5. Logan, William. "E. B. Jeppesen: Pioneer In Aviation," *Rocky Mountain News*, January 7, 1968.

6. Crick, Rolla J. "Oregon Aviatrix Honored," *Oregon Journal*, October 28, 1980.

7. Jeppesen family archives.

8. avstop.com/Stories/inspection ("The History of Flight Inspection in the United States of America").

9. Jim Jeppesen interview by Terry Barnhart, August 24, 2000.

10. Elrey Jeppesen interview by Mavis Neslen, July 1993, Jeppesen family archives.

11. Letter, Tex Rankin "To whom it may concern," October 11, 1928, Jeppesen family archives.

12. Elrey Jeppesen interview by Mavis Neslen, July 1993, Jeppesen family archives.

13. www.bcwarbirds.com/sherman_fairchild_bio ("Sherman Fairchild").

14. Bilstein, p. 86.

15. Bilstein, pp. 88-89.

16. www.bcwarbirds.com/sherman_fairchild_bio ("Sherman Fairchild").

17. Elrey Jeppesen interview by Mavis Neslen, July 1993, Jeppesen family archives.

Chapter 4: Mexican Interlude

1. Allen, p. 66.
2. Elrey Jeppesen interview by Mavis Neslen, July 1993, Jeppesen family archives.
3. Elrey Jeppesen, speech to AOCI, Oct. 1, 1980, typescript in Jeppesen family archives.
4. Elrey Jeppesen interview by Mavis Neslen, July 1993, Jeppesen family archives.
5. Tal Miller interview by Terry Barnhart, Aug. 24, 2000.
6. www.century-of-flight.freeola.com ("Fairchild FC-2").
7. Elrey Jeppesen interview by Mavis Neslen, July 1993, Jeppesen family archives.
8. *Museum of Flight News*, May/June 1985 (Letter to the editor from Elrey B. Jeppesen).
9. Elrey Jeppesen interview by Mavis Neslen, July 1993, Jeppesen family archives.
10. www.united.com ("Flight Attendant History").
11. Allen, pp. 81-82.
12. Smith, pp. 156-157.
13. Smith, p. 157.
14. Smith, pp. 160-163.
15. Allen, pp. 81-86.
16. Elrey Jeppesen interview by Mavis Neslen, July 1993, Jeppesen family archives.
17. Smith, pp. 191-193.
18. Davies, R.E.G. *Airlines of the United States Since 1914.* Washington, D.C.: Smithsonian Institution Press, 1998, pp. 118-119.
19. Elrey Jeppesen interview by Mavis Neslen, July 1993, Jeppesen family archives.
20. Elrey Jeppesen, speech to AOCI, Oct. 1, 1980, typescript in Jeppesen family archives; Moll, Nigel. "Charting Jeppesen," Flying, January 1989, p. 32.
21. "Sixty Years of Jeppesen Flight Information: From Hand-Sketched Navigation Charts to Sophisticated Electronic Services." (Unpublished draft article for *Leading Edge* magazine, March 24, 1995, author unknown, Jeppesen family archives); Stevens, C. A. "Jepp's 'Little Black Book,' " *Frontier* (Frontier Airlines' in-flight magazine, date unknown; possibly 1973).
22. Richard Jeppesen interview by Terry Barnhart, September 6, 2000.
23. Bilstein, pp. 43, 45.
24. Jim Jeppesen interview by Terry Barnhart, August 24, 2000.
25. Elrey Jeppesen interview by Mavis Neslen, July 1993, Jeppesen family archives.
26. Dick Bergesen interview by Terry Barnhart, March 10, 2000.
27. Best, Sonia. "The Legend Of Captain Jepp," SAGA *International Aviator*, April/May/June 1993.
28. Logan, William. "E. B. Jeppesen: Pioneer In Aviation," *Rocky Mountain News*, January 7, 1968.
29. Elrey Jeppesen interview by Mavis Neslen, July 1993, Jeppesen family archives.

Chapter 5: The Little Black Book

1. Letter, Elrey Jeppesen to parents, Feb. 28, 1933, Jeppesen family archives.

2. "Sixty Years of Jeppesen Flight Information: From Hand-Sketched Navigation Charts to Sophisticated Electronic Services," (Unpublished draft article for *Leading Edge* magazine, March 24, 1995, author unknown, Jeppesen family archives).

3. Johnson, Richard. "Charting His Own Course: The Quiet Hero Of Aeronautical History," *Denver Post*, February 26, 1989.

4. "Elrey Jeppesen: That Little Old Mapmaker Who Charted The Airspace Of The World," *FAA Aviation News*, April 1972.

5. Elrey Jeppesen interview by Mavis Neslen, July 1993, Jeppesen family archives.

6. Moll, *Flying*, p. 31.

7. Elrey Jeppesen interview by Mavis Neslen, July 1993, Jeppesen family archives.

8. Harry B. Combs interviewed by Terry Barnhart, October 2, 2000.

9. Logan, William. "E. B. Jeppesen: Pioneer In Aviation," *Rocky Mountain News*, January 7, 1968.

10. Allen, pp. 88-91; Bilstein, p. 132; www.aviationexplorer.com/braniff_airlines ("Braniff history").

11. Elrey Jeppesen interview by Mavis Neslen, July 1993, Jeppesen family archives.

12. Elrey Jeppesen, notes for speech, undated, Jeppesen family archives.

13. Jim Jeppesen correspondence with authors, April 27, 2006.

14. Elrey Jeppesen interview by Mavis Neslen, July 1993, Jeppesen family archives.

15. www.boeing.com ("Jeppesen and Winchell").

16. "Elrey B. Jeppesen Honored With NAA Elder Statesman Award," Checklist, Vol. XXI, No. 2, Summer 1984, p. 3.

17. Elrey Jeppesen interview by Mavis Neslen, July 1993, Jeppesen family archives.

18. Elrey Jeppesen interview by Mavis Neslen, August 1993, Jeppesen family archives.

19. Jim Jeppesen interview by Terry Barnhart, Aug. 24, 2000.

20. Lou Clinton by Terry Barnhart, July 10, 2000.

Chapter 6: The War Years

1. De Seversky, Alexander P. *Victory Through Air Power*. New York: Simon and Schuster, 1942, pp. 21-47.

2. www.centennialofflight/gov.essay/DC-3.

3. Ted Boerstler interview by Terry Barnhart, December 1, 1999.

4. Official accident report, June 10, 1941, Jeppesen family archives.

5. Elrey Jeppesen interview by Mavis Neslen, August 1993, Jeppesen family archives.

6. O'Neill, William L. *A Democracy at War: America's Fight at Home and Abroad in World War II.* New York: Free Press, 1993, p. 218.

7. Elrey Jeppesen interview by Mavis Neslen, August 1993, Jeppesen family archives.

8. Wayne Rosenkrans interview by Terry Barnhart, August 11, 1999.

9. Elrey Jeppesen interview by Mavis Neslen, August 1993, Jeppesen family archives.

10. Letter, Elrey Jeppesen to parents, May 21, 1942, Jeppesen family archives.

11. Elrey Jeppesen interview by Mavis Neslen, August 1993, Jeppesen family archives.

12. home.att.net/~jbaugher2/b24_26 ("C-87").

13. Letter, Elrey Jeppesen to Jack Parshall, Aug. 9, 1943, Jeppesen family archives.

14. Letter, Elrey Jeppesen to George Tremble, Dec. 30, 1943, Jeppesen family archives.

15. Elrey Jeppesen interview by Mavis Neslen, August 1993, Jeppesen family archives.

16. Wayne Rosenkrans interview by Terry Barnhart, August 11, 1999.

17. Letter, G B. Bryan to Elrey Jeppesen, June 21, 1945, Jeppesen family archives.

18. *Checklist*, p. 3.

19. Letter, Bruce Painter to ?, January 8, 1992, Jeppesen family archives.

20. "Crash Blamed On Dense Fog," *Denver Post*, Sept. 6, 1946.

21. Letter, Bruce Painter to ?, January 8, 1992, Jeppesen family archives.

22. William C. "Corky" Douglas interview by Terry Barnhart, August 31, 1999.

23. *Checklist*, p. 3.

24. Haenggi, Mike. "Inside The Chart Factory," *Twin & Turbine*, January, 2005, p. 20.

25. Harald Prommel interview by Terry Barnhart, October 27, 1999.

26. Hal Shelton interview by Terry Barnhart, December 2, 1999.

27. "Aviation's Amazing Mr. Jeppesen: Chartmaker Extraordinary," *Airlift*, April 1960, p. 48.

28. McMorris, Robert. "She Was Gorgeous," *Omaha World-Herald*, June 25, 1969.

29. Jim Jeppesen interview by Terry Barnhart, Aug. 24, 2000.

30. Hal Shelton interview by Terry Barnhart, December 2, 1999.

31. Jim Jeppesen interview by Terry Barnhart, Aug. 24, 2000.

32. Elrey Jeppesen interview by Mavis Neslen, August 1993, Jeppesen family archives.

33. Wayne Rosenkrans interview by Terry Barnhart, August 11, 1999.

34. Harald Prommel interview by Terry Barnhart, October 27, 1999.

35. Ernestine Boyd interview by Terry Barnhart, January 25, 2000.

36. "Jeppesen & Co. To Expand Plant For Production Of Aviation Aids," *Denver Post*, December 17, 1958.

37. Wayne Rosenkrans interview by Terry Barnhart, August 11, 1999.

Chapter 7: A Changing of the Guard

1. Wayne Rosenkrans interview by Terry Barnhart, August 11, 1999.
2. Tal Miller interview by Terry Barnhart, Aug. 24, 2000.
3. Wayne Rosenkrans interview by Terry Barnhart, August 11, 1999.
4. Don Sellars interview by Terry Barnhart, November 9, 1999.
5. Harald Prommel interview by Terry Barnhart, October 27, 1999.
6. "Elrey Jeppesen: That Little Old Mapmaker Who Charted The Airspace Of The World," *FAA Aviation News*, April 1972, p. 11.
7. Elrey Jeppesen, speech to AOCI, Oct. 1, 1980, typescript in Jeppesen family archives.
8. "Elrey Jeppesen: That Little Old Mapmaker Who Charted The Airspace Of The World," *FAA Aviation News*, April 1972, p. 11.
9. Paul Burke interview by Terry Barnhart, February 26, 2000.
10. Wayne Rosenkrans interview by Terry Barnhart, August 11, 1999.
11. Best, *Saga*, p. 10.
12. Wayne Rosenkrans interview by Terry Barnhart, August 11, 1999.
13. Best, Saga, p. 10.
14. *Checklist*, p. 3.
15. Wayne Rosenkrans interview by Terry Barnhart, August 11, 1999.
16. Best, *Saga*, p. 10.
17. Ibid.
18. Wayne Rosenkrans interview by Terry Barnhart, August 11, 1999.
19. Don Sellars interview by Terry Barnhart, November 9, 1999.
20. Elrey Jeppesen interview by Mavis Neslen, August 1993, Jeppesen family archives.
21. www.airdisaster.com ("Aetna Casualty v. Jeppesen").
22. www.lawrencesavell.com ("Brocklesby v. Jeppesen").
23. "E. B. Jeppesen Wins Meritorious Service Award," *Denver Post*, September 12, 1965.
24. Wayne Rosenkrans interview by Terry Barnhart, August 11, 1999.
25. Ibid.
26. Tal Miller interview by Terry Barnhart, Aug. 24, 2000.
27. "Chairman Of Board: E. B. Jeppesen," *Denver Post*, Dec. 24, 1967.
28. Durham "Durrie" Monsma interview by Terry Barnhart, January 6, 2000.
29. Logan, William. "E. B. Jeppesen: Pioneer In Aviation," *Rocky Mountain News*, January 7, 1968.
30. Don Sellars interview by Terry Barnhart, November 9, 1999.
31. Jeppesen Sanderson News Release, Nov. 4, 1999.
32. Don Sellars interview by Terry Barnhart, November 9, 1999.

33. Wayne Rosenkrans interview by Terry Barnhart, August 11, 1999.

34. Don Sellars interview by Terry Barnhart, November 9, 1999.

35. Wayne Rosenkrans interview by Terry Barnhart, August 11, 1999.

36. Paul Burke interview by Terry Barnhart, February 26, 2000.

37. Wayne Rosenkrans interview by Terry Barnhart, August 11, 1999.

38. Logan, William. "E. B. Jeppesen: Pioneer In Aviation," *Rocky Mountain News*, January 7, 1968.

39. Don Sellars interview by Terry Barnhart, November 9, 1999.

40. Jim Jeppesen interview by Terry Barnhart, August 24, 2000.

41. Paul Burke interview by Terry Barnhart, February 26, 2000.

42. Ray Lee interview by Terry Barnhart, April 18, 2000.

43. Wayne Rosenkrans interview by Terry Barnhart, August 11, 1999.

Chapter 8: New Blood

1. Jim Jeppesen interview by Terry Barnhart, August 24, 2000.

2. Horst Bergmann interview by Terry Barnhart, January 18, 2000.

3. Durham "Durrie" Monsma interview by Terry Barnhart, January 6, 2000.

4. Janet Conner interview by Terry Barnhart, June 6, 2000.

5. Haselbush, *Denver Post*, April 2, 1978.

6. Horst Bergmann interview by Terry Barnhart, January 18, 2000.

7. Don Sellars interview by Terry Barnhart, November 9, 1999.

8. Annette Brott interview by Terry Barnhart, October 29, 1999.

9. Dumovitch, Eve. "The Early Adventures Of Captain Jepp." *Boeing Frontiers*, August 2005, p. 14.

10. Ted Boerstler interview by Terry Barnhart, December 1, 1999.

11. Ray Lee interview by Terry Barnhart, April 18, 2000.

12. Tal Miller interview by Terry Barnhart, August 24, 2000.

13. en.wikipedia.org/wiki/Denver_International_Airport.

14. Tom Hudgens, Letter to the Editor, *Denver Post*, July 23, 1988.

15. Don Sellars interview by Terry Barnhart, November 9, 1999.

16. Tal Miller interview by Terry Barnhart, August 24, 2000.

17. Ralph Latimer interview by Terry Barnhart, October 11, 1999.

18. Tal Miller interview by Terry Barnhart, Aug. 24, 2000.

19. William C. "Corky" Douglas interview by Terry Barnhart, August 31, 1999.

20. Certificate, Resolution 13, City and County of Denver, January 29, 1990, Jeppesen family archives.

21. Ralph Latimer interview by Terry Barnhart, October 11, 1999.

Chapter 9: Cast In Bronze

1. Wayne Rosenkrans interview by Terry Barnhart, August 11, 1999.

2. Colman, Price. "President Plans To Drop In On Flight Pioneer Jeppesen," *Rocky Mountain News*, September 13 and 16, 1992.

3. Janet Conner correspondence with authors, July 7, 2006.

4. Don Sellars interview by Terry Barnhart, November 9, 1999.

5. Ralph Latimer interview by Terry Barnhart, October 11, 1999.

6. Don Sellars interview by Terry Barnhart, November 9, 1999.

7. George Lundeen interview by Terry Barnhart, January 19, 2000.

8. Don Sellars interview by Terry Barnhart, November 9, 1999.

9. Ralph Latimer interview by Terry Barnhart, October 11, 1999.

10. Don Sellars interview by Terry Barnhart, November 9, 1999.

11. Ralph Latimer interview by Terry Barnhart, October 11, 1999.

12. Janet Conner interview by Terry Barnhart, June 6, 2000.

13. Ralph Latimer interview by Terry Barnhart, October 11, 1999.

14. Don Sellars interview by Terry Barnhart, November 9, 1999.

15. Ralph Latimer interview by Terry Barnhart, October 11, 1999.

16. Don Sellars interview by Terry Barnhart, November 9, 1999.

17. Ralph Latimer interview by Terry Barnhart, October 11, 1999.

18. Donna Chandler Miller interview by Terry Barnhart, March 15, 2001.

19. Ray Lee interview by Terry Barnhart, April 18, 2000.

20. George Lundeen interview by Terry Barnhart, January 19, 2000.

21. Don Sellars interview by Terry Barnhart, November 9, 1999.

22. Ralph Latimer interview by Terry Barnhart, October 11, 1999.

23. Murphy, Kevin D. "Capt. Elrey Jeppesen: Charting The Way," *Private Pilot*, May 1993.

24. Tal Miller interview by Terry Barnhart, August 24, 2000.

25. Broderick, Christopher, and Flynn, Kevin. "At Last — Denver Soars Into The Future;" Saunders, Dusty, "The Puns Fly As Media Flock To Opening," *Rocky Mountain News*, Feb. 28, 1995; "DIA Still Under Attack," *Denver Post*, Mar. 1, 1995.

26. Obmasic, Mark. "Airport's Proud Father Gets Up Early, Goes Nonstop," *Denver Post*, March 1, 1995.

27. Don Sellars interview by Terry Barnhart, November 9, 1999.

28. Ostrow, Joanne, "Local TV Swept Away By Extravagance Of Opening," *Denver Post*, March 1, 1995.

29. Booth, Michael, and Brown, Fred, "DIA Shows Its Stuff In Snow;" Huspeni, Dennis, "Early Birds Get To Make Historic trip;" Lopez, Christopher, "Webb Walking On Air;"

30. Don Sellars interview by Terry Barnhart, November 9, 1999.

31. Huspeni, Dennis. "Early Birds Get To Make Historic Trip," *Denver Post*, March 1, 1995.

32. Janet Conner interview by Terry Barnhart, June 6, 2000.

Chapter 10: Going West

1. Tal Miller interview by Terry Barnhart, August 24, 2000.

2. Yvette Miller interview by Terry Barnhart, August 24, 2000.

3. Tal Miller interview by Terry Barnhart, August 24, 2000.

4. Ray Lee interview by Terry Barnhart, April 18, 2000.

5. Donna Chandler Miller interview by Terry Barnhart, March 15, 2001.

6. Ray Lee interview by Terry Barnhart, April 18, 2000.

7. Annette Brott interview by Terry Barnhart, October 29, 1999.

8. Ernestine Boyd interview by Terry Barnhart, January 25, 2000.

9. Annette Brott interview by Terry Barnhart, October 29, 1999.

10. Ernestine Boyd interview by Terry Barnhart, January 25, 2000.

11. Annette Brott interview by Terry Barnhart, October 29, 1999.

12. Jim Jeppesen interview by Terry Barnhart, August 24, 2000.

13. Funeral card for Nadine L. Jeppesen, Jeppesen family archives.

14. Ted Boerstler interview by Terry Barnhart, December 1, 1999.

15. Annette Brott interview by Terry Barnhart, October 29, 1999.

16. Donna Chandler Miller interview by Terry Barnhart, March 15, 2001.

17. Ernestine Boyd interview by Terry Barnhart, January 25, 2000.

18. Annette Brott interview by Terry Barnhart, October 29, 1999.

19. Ted Boerstler interview by Terry Barnhart, December 1, 1999.

20. Jim Jeppesen interview by Terry Barnhart, August 24, 2000.

21. Annette Brott interview by Terry Barnhart, October 29, 1999; Jim Jeppesen interview by Terry Barnhart, August 24, 2000.

22. Annette Brott interview by Terry Barnhart, October 29, 1999.

23. Jim Jeppesen interview by Terry Barnhart, August 24, 2000.

24. Annette Brott interview by Terry Barnhart, October 29, 1999.

25. Snel, Alan. "Aviation Pioneer Is Dead At Age 89," *Denver Post*, November 27, 1996.

26. Howard W. Reid interview by Terry Barnhart, October 4, 2000.

27. Jim Jeppesen interview by Terry Barnhart, August 24, 2000.

28. Janet Conner interview by Terry Barnhart, June 6, 2000.

Epilogue:

1. "Boeing Agrees To Buy A Provider Of Flight Data," *New York Times*, August 16, 2000.
2. www.flightglobal.com ("Jeppesen Good for Boeing").
3. Jeppesen News Release, March 1, 2006.
4. Haenggi, Mike. "Inside The Chart Factory," *Twin & Turbine*, January, 2005, p. 20.
5. Mark Van Tine interview by Terry Barnhart, September 1, 2001.

BIBLIOGRAPHY

Oral Histories/Interviews:

Conducted by: Mavis Neslen

Elrey B. Jeppesen, July, August, September, 1993.

Conducted by: Terry Barnhart

Dick Bergesen, March 10, 2000.

Horst Bergmann, January 18, 2000.

Ted Boerstler, December 1, 1999.

Ernestine Boyd, January 25, 2000.

Annette Brott, October 29, 1999.

Paul and Tally Burke, February 26, 2000.

Lou Clinton, July 10, 2000.

Harry B. Combs, October 2, 2000.

Janet Conner, June 6, 2000.

William C. "Corky" Douglas II, August 31, 1999.

Jim Jeppesen, August 24, 2000.

Richard Jeppesen, September 6, 2000.

Ralph Latimer, October 11, 1999.

Ray Lee, April 18, 2000.

George Lundeen, January 19, 2000.

Ed Mehlin, October 25, 2000.

Donna Chandler Miller, March 15, 2001.

Tal and Yvette Miller, August 24, 2000.

Durham "Durrie" Monsma, January 6, 2000.

Mavis Neslen, May 25, 2000.

Osgood Philpott, May 1, 2000.

Harald Prommel, October 27, 1999.

Howard W. Reid, October 4, 2000.

Wayne Rosenkrans, August 11, 1999, September 16, 1999, and July 5, 2000.

John Schoonhoven, March 7, 2000.

Don Sellars, November 9, 1999.

Hal Shelton, December 2, 1999.

Mark Van Tine, September 1, 2001, July 25, 2006

Virgil and Cookie Vaughn, March 30, 2000.

Carl Williams, March 7, 2000.

Books:

Allen, Oliver E. *The Airline Builders.* (*The Epic of Flight* series.)
    Alexandria, VA: Time-Life Books, 1981.

Berg, A. Scott. *Lindbergh.* New York: Berkley Publishing, 1999.

Bilstein, Roger E. *Flight Patterns: Trends of Aeronautical Development in the
    United States, 1918-1929.* Athens: University of Georgia Press, 1983

Davies, R.E.G. *Airlines of the United States Since 1914.* Washington, D.C.:
    Smithsonian Institution Press, 1998.

De Seversky, Alexander P. *Victory Through Air Power.* New York: Simon and
    Schuster, 1942.

deVries, John A. *Alexander Eaglerock: A History of Alexander Aircraft Company.*
    Colorado Springs, CO: Century One Press, 1985.

Heppenheimer, T.A. *Turbulent Skies: The History of Commercial Aviation.*
    New York: Wiley, 1995.

van der Linden, F. Robert. *Airlines and Air Mail: The Post Office and the Birth
    of the Commercial Aviation* Industry. Lexington, KY: University Press of
    Kentucky, 2001.

Morrison, Steven A. and Winston, Clifford. *The Evolution of the Airline
    Industry.* Washington, D.C.: The Brookings Institution, 1995.

Nielson, Dale, ed. *Saga of the U.S. Air Mail Service 1918-1927.*
    Air Mail Pioneers, 1962 (Place published unknown)

O'Neil, Paul. *Barnstormers and Speed Kings.* (*The Epic of Flight* series.)
    Alexandria, VA: Time-Life Books, 1981.

O'Neill, William L. *A Democracy at War: America's Fight at Home and Abroad in World War II.* New York: Free Press, 1993.

Smith, Henry L. *Airways: The History of Commercial Aviation in the United States.* New York: Knopf, 1942.

Walker, Jon. *A Century Airborne: Air Trails of Pearson Airpark.* Vancouver, WA: Rose Wind Publishing, 1994.

Newspapers and Periodicals:

"Aviation 'Oscar' Won By Denver Air Leader," *Denver Post*, September 12, 1965.

"Aviation's Amazing Mr. Jeppesen: Chartmaker Extraordinary," *Airlift*, April 1960.

Best, Sonia. "The Legend of Captain Jepp," *SAGA International Aviator*, April/May/June 1993.

"Boeing Agrees to Buy a Provider of Flight Data," *New York Times*, Aug. 16, 2000.

"Broderick, Christopher; Flynn, Kevin. "At Last — Denver Soars Into The Future," *Rocky Mountain News*, February 28, 1995.

"Capt. E. B. Jeppesen: An Aviation Pioneer's Contribution To Air Safety," *Journal of ATC,* September 1964.

Carnahan, Ann; and Foster, Dick. "First Landing Overshadows First Snafu," *Rocky Mountain News*, March 1, 1995.

"Chairman Of Board: E. B. Jeppesen," *Denver Post*, December 24, 1967.

Chotzinoff, Robin. "The Sky's the Limit; Jepp's Story—Plane and Simple," *Westword*, September 11, 1991.

Churches, James E. "Air Jeppesen," *Colorado Business*, January 1996.

Cleave, Al. "The Jeppesen Story," *Ag-Pilot International*, January, 1994.

Colman, Price. "President Plans to Drop In on Flight Pioneer Jeppesen," *Rocky Mountain News*, September 13 and 16, 1992.

"Colorado Aviation Groups Wants 'Jeppesen International' as Name for New Denver Airport," *General Aviation News,* February 13, 1989.

Crick, Rolla J. "Oregon Aviatrix Honored," *Oregon Journal,* October 28, 1980.

Deutsch, Linda. "First Stewardesses Often Carried Fried Chicken For 12, Had Only One Passenger," *Oregonian*, October 18, 1970.

Dumovitch, Eve. "The Early Adventures of Captain Jepp." *Boeing Frontiers,* August 2005.

"E. B. Jeppesen Wins Meritorious Service Award," *Denver Post,* September 12, 1965.

"Elrey Jeppesen" (Obituary), *The Economist,* December 14, 1996.

"Elrey Jeppesen: That Little Old Mapmaker Who Charted the Airspace of the World," *FAA Aviation News,* April 1972.

"Elrey B. Jeppesen Honored with NAA Elder Statesman Award," *Checklist,* Vol. XXI, No. 2, Summer 1984.

"FAA Honors Man Memorialized At DIA," *Denver Post,* February 19, 1995.

Flynn, Kevin. "E. B. Jeppesen, Pioneer Flier, Dies at Home," *Rocky Mountain News,* November 27, 1996.

Freeze, Di. "Jepp Climbs Every Mountain to Make Flying Safe," *Centennial Journal,* September 2000.

Fuchs, Alice S. "Pilot's Bible: All Over America, Pilots Swear By These Well-Known Aeronautical Manuals," *Flying,* October, 1958.

Haenggi, Mike. "Inside the Chart Factory," *Twin & Turbine,* January, 2005.

Haselbush, Willard. "Flight Information Firm Plans Inverness Complex," *Denver Post,* April 2, 1978.

_____. "Firm Prospers By Supplying Pilots Flight Data, *Denver Post,* January 12, 1958.

_____. "Publisher of 'Airway Manual' Plans Big Denver Expansion," *Denver Post,* January 28, 1962.

Hodges, Arthur. "Aviator's Life Was History of Flight," *Denver Post,* December 3, 1996.

"Honored For Putting Airports On The Map," *Air Travel Journal,* October 3, 1980.

Huspeni, Dennis. "Early Birds Get To Make Historic Trip," *Denver Post,* March 1, 1995.

"It Started With a Notebook," *The Westerner,* May 1962.
Jackson, Donald D. "Up, Up and Away (But Just Barely) with 'Aerial Mail,'" *Smithsonian,* (issue date unknown)

"Jeppesen & Co. to Expand Plant for Production of Aviation Aids," *Denver Post,* December 17, 1958.

"Jeppesen Finishing $500,000 Expansion," *Denver Post,* November 1, 1959.

Johnson, Richard. "Charting His Own Course," *Denver Post,* Feb. 26, 1989.

Kaplan, Howard. "The Man Who Mapped the Skyways," *Denver Post* "Empire" Section, October 30, 1977.

Krodel, Beth. "Behind The Statue in the Terminal is the Story of a Flight Pioneer," *Boulder Daily Camera*, February 23, 1995.

Larson, George C. "Fifty Years of Jeppesen Sanderson," *Business and Commercial Aviation*, October 1984.

_____."Navigation Databases: The Coming Power in Cockpit Management," *Business and Commercial Aviation*, October 1984.

Logan, William. "E. B. Jeppesen: Pioneer in Aviation," *Rocky Mountain News,* January 7, 1968.

Lopez, Christopher. "Webb Walking On Air," *Denver Post,* March 1, 1995.

Lopez, Greg. "Pioneer 'Took Fun Out Of' Flying," *Rocky Mountain News*, February 17, 1991.

_____. "Pioneer Pilot Will Get His Day At DIA," *Rocky Mountain News,* February 17, 1991.

Lindberg, Gene. "Denver Pilot Maps the World's Airlanes," *Denver Post,* March 16, 1947.

Marsh, Alton K. "Just A Little Bit Lower," *AOPA Pilot*, March 2001.

McMorris, Robert. "She Was Gorgeous," *Omaha World-Herald,* June 25, 1969.

"Meet Your Corporate Members: Jeppesen & Co.," *Flight Service Journal,* July-August 1965.

Miles, Marvin. "Air Safety Owes Much to Early-Day Pilot," *Los Angeles Times,* November 13, 1960.

Moll, Nigel. "Charting Jeppesen," *Flying,* January 1989.

_____. "Elrey Jeppesen, Grandfather of Air Navigation, Dies at 89," *Aviation International News,* January 1, 1997.

Murphy, Kevin D. "Capt. Elrey Jeppesen: Charting the Way," *Private Pilot,* May 1993.

Museum of Flight News, May/June 1985 (Letter to the editor from Elrey B. Jeppesen).

Obmasic, Mark. "Airport's Proud Father Gets Up Early, Goes Nonstop," *Denver Post,* March 1, 1995.

O'Driscoll, Patrick. "Aviator 'Jepp' Assumes His New Role As Celebrity," *Denver Post,* February 24, 1995.

Partner, Dan. " 'Jepp's' Charts Fly Worldwide," *Denver Post,* December 24, 1967.

"Personality of the Month: E. B. Jeppesen," *Pre-Flight Air News,* January 1962.

Prommel, Harald. "An Afternoon with 'Jepp' and the OX5," *Air Line Pilot,* March 1997.

"Round The World With Jeppesen," *National Aeronautics,* September 1965.

"Sculpture for New Denver Airport," *Colorado Country Life,* September 1993.

Searles, Denis M. "Aviation Pioneer From Oregon Turns up Nose at Jet Age," *The Oregonian,* June 3, 1990.

_____. "The Bygone Biplane Era: Aviation Pioneer Is Still Flying By The Seat Of His Pants," *Miami Herald,* June 3, 1990.

Snel, Alan. "Aviation Pioneer is Dead At Age 89," *Denver Post,* November 27, 1996.

Stevens, C. A. "Jepp's 'Little Black Book,'" *Frontier,* (Frontier Airlines' in-flight magazine, date unknown; possibly 1973).

Stokes, Jeanie. "Boeing Will Buy Jeppesen," *Rocky Mountain News,* August 16, 2000.

"21 Die When Chartered Plane Crashes on Low Nevada Hill," *Denver Post,* September 6, 1946.

Webb, Walter. "The $200,000 Hobby," *Air Transport,* September 1944.

Weeghman, Richard B. "Charting the Future with Jeppesen," *Flying,* January 1964.

"Who Was Tony Jannus?" *Tampa Commerce,* May 1981.

Woolley, Brian. "Where I Come From: Ed Seay, Sr.," *Dallas Morning News,* October 29, 2000.

Web Sites:

avstop.com/Stories/inspection ("The History of Flight Inspection in the United States of America")
en.wikipedia.org/wiki ("Alcock and Brown," "Denver International Airport," "NC-4," "R-34," "Varney Airlines")
home.att.net/~jbaugher2/b24_26 ("C-87")
maverick.rootsweb.com ("Basil Russell death")
members.aol.com/jaydeebee1/crash30s ("Basil Russell death")
www.airdisaster.com ("Aetna Casualty v. Jeppesen")
www.airmailpioneers.org/history/milestone3 ("Earl Ovington")
www.aviationexplorer.com/braniff_airlines ("Braniff history")
www.arlingtoncemetery.net/jdoolitt ("Jimmy Doolittle")
www.arlingtoncemetery.net/usgs ("Coast and Geodetic Survey")
www.bcwarbirds.com/sherman_fairchild_bio ("Sherman Fairchild")
www.billysunday.org ("Billy Sunday)
www.boeing.com ("Jeppesen and Winchell")
www.braniffpages.com ("Braniff")
www.centennialofflight/gov.essay ("The Evolution of Airway Lights and Electronic Navigation Aids," "Aerospace/Fairchild/Aero25," "DC-3")
www.century-of-flight.freeola.com ("Fairchild FC-2")
www.ciderpresspottery.com/ZLA/greatzeps ("Zeppelin")
www.denver-den.com ("Deniver International Airport")
www.earlyaviators.com/eovington ("Earl Ovington")
www.flightglobal.com ("Jeppesen Good For Boeing")
www.historyofaircargo.com ("Varney Airlines")
www.lawrencesavell.com ("Brocklesby v. Jeppesen")
www.michiganaviation.org ("William Boeing")
www.museumofflight.org/news/jeppesen ("Elrey Jeppesen")
www.nasm.si.edu/research/aero/aircraft/loening ("Pan-American Goodwill Flight")
www.postalmuseum.si.edu/airmail/pilot ("Charles Ames," "John Carlton," "Robert Gautier," "William Hopson," "Leonard Hyde-Pearson," "Charlie Lamborn," "James Moore," "Frederick Robinson," "Harry Sherlock," "Arthur Smith," "Clayton Stoner," "John Woodward")
www.shadedrelief.com/shelton ("Hal Shelton")
www.spatial.maine.edu ("Brocklesby v. Jeppesen")
www.sprucegoose.org/aircraft ("Tex Rankin")
www.timetableimages.com/ttimages/varney/historytogo.utah.gov ("Varney Airlines")
www.understandingparkinsons.com ("Parkinson's Disease")
www.united.com ("Flight Attendant History")
www.wyomingfirstflight.org ("Aviation in Wyoming")
www2.newpaltz.edu ("Aetna Casualty v. Jeppesen")

Miscellaneous:

Booklet: *History of the Jeppesen Aviation Foundation* Denver:
    Jeppesen Aviation Foundation, 1995.

Booklet: *Jeppesen Sanderson — A Golden Anniversary*, 1984.

Congressional Record, March 10, 1993; Nov. 16, 2005.

E-mail correspondence, Jim Jeppesen to authors, April 27, 2006.

Jeppesen New Release, March 1, 2006.

Jeppesen Sanderson News Release, Nov. 4, 1999.

Letter, Tex Rankin "To whom it may concern," October 11, 1928
    (Jeppesen archives).

Letters of agreement to sell, Jeppesen-Goushá, January, February, 1961.

Report of DC-3 Accident, June 10, 1941 (Jeppesen archives).

"Sixty Years of Jeppesen Flight Information: From Hand-Sketched Navigation
    Charts to Sophisticated Electronic Services." Unpublished draft article for
    Leading Edge magazine, 3/24/95, author unknown (Jeppesen archives).

Speech, E.B. Jeppesen, Airport Operators Council International, October 1, 1980
    (Jeppesen archives).

About The Jeppesen
Aviation Foundation

In 1992, the Jeppesen Aviation Foundation (JAF), a 501(c)3 non-profit corporation, was organized to commission a sculptor and raise funds for the Capt. Jepp statue presently residing inside the Denver International Airport terminal. JAF also maintains the unique collection of Capt. Jepp's personal artifacts and some of the Jeppesen Corporation's historic aeronautical memorabilia on exhibit within the terminal.

JAF has now expanded its mission, bringing the love of flying to students in the form of scholarships to various colleges nationwide and providing grants to special aviation-related programs. Most, if not all, of the scholarships will assist aviation students who might otherwise not be able to begin, continue, or finish their aviation programs. Just as a kindly benefactor enabled young Elrey Jeppesen to learn to fly so many decades ago, the JAF hopes to continue Capt. Jepp's legacy far into the future.

If you would like more information about the Jeppesen Aviation Foundation or would like to make a tax-deductible contribution, please contact:

JEPPESEN AVIATION FOUNDATION
55 Inverness Drive East
Englewood, CO 80112-5498
(303) 799-9090

A portion of the sale of this book goes to the Jeppesen Aviation Foundation.

OTHER SAVAGE PRESS BOOKS

OUTDOORS, SPORTS & RECREATION

Curling Superiority! by John Gidley

Packers "verses" Vikings
by Carl W. Nelson

ESSAY

Awakening of the Heart, Second Printing
by Jill Downs

Battlenotes: Music of the Vietnam War
by Lee Andresen

Color on the Land by Irene I. Luethge

*Following in the Footsteps of Ernest
Hemingway* by Jay Ford Thurston

Potpourri From Kettle Land
by Irene I. Luethge

FICTION

Burn Baby Burn by Mike Savage

Enigmas by Fernando Arrojo

Lake Effect by Mike Savage

Lord of the Rinks by Mike Savage

Marks of the Forbidden by Olaf Danielson

No Peace in Exile by Olaf Danielson

Northern Lights Magic by Lori J. Glad

Off Season by Marshall J.Cook

Sailing Home by Lori J. Glad

Something in the Water by Mike Savage

Spirit of The Shadows by Rebel Sinclair

Summer Storm by Lori J. Glad

The Devil of Charleston by Rebel Sinclair

HISTORY & MEMOIR

DakotaLand by Howard Jones

Echoes from the Past by Nan Wisherd

Memories of Iron River by Bev Thivierge

Superior Catholics
by Cheney and Meronek

Pathways, Early History of Brule Wisconsin
by Nan Wisherd

BUSINESS

SoundBites
Second Edition by Kathy Kerchner

POETRY

A Woman for All Time
by Evelyn Gathman Haines

Portrait of the Mississippi
by Howard Jones

HUMOR

With Malice Toward Some
by Georgia Z. Post

CHILDREN'S BOOKS

Kat's Magic Bubble by Jeff Lower

Luella by Mindy Braun

Out of the Rainbow by Jay Ford Thurston

TO ORDER ADDITIONAL COPIES OF

CAPT. JEPP AND THE
LITTLE BLACK BOOK

OR OTHER SAVAGE PRESS BOOKS

Call

1-800-732-3867

or

E-mail:

mail@savpress.com

Purchase copies online at
www.savpress.com

Visa/MC/Discover/American Express/
ECheck are accepted via PayPal.

All Savage Press books are available through all chain
and independent bookstores nationwide.
Just ask them to special order if the title is not in stock.